Applied Economics and Policy Studies

The Applied Economics and Policy Studies present latest theoretical and methodological discussions to bear on the scholarly works covering economic theories, econometric analyses, as well as multifaceted issues arising out of emerging concerns from different industries and debates surrounding latest policies. Situated at the forefront of the interdisciplinary fields of applied economics and policy studies, this book series seeks to bring together the scholarly insights centering on economic development, infrastructure development, macroeconomic policy, governance of welfare policy, policies and governance of emerging markets, and relevant subfields that trace to the discipline of applied economics, public policy, policy studies, and combined fields of the aforementioned. The book series of Applied Economics and Policy Studies is dedicated to the gathering of intellectual views by scholars and policymakers. The publications included are relevant for scholars, policymakers, and students of economics, policy studies, and otherwise interdisciplinary programs.

Xiaolong Li · Lewei Liao · Pengfei Sun · Zhengyu Wu

Data as a New Factor of Production

Reshaping Growth, Innovation, and Labor in the Digital Economy

Springer

Xiaolong Li
Department of Economics and Management
Beijing University of Posts
and Telecommunications
Beijing, China

Lewei Liao
Guanghua School of Management
Peking University
Beijing, China

Pengfei Sun
School of Police Administration, People's
Public Security
University of China
Beijing, China

Zhengyu Wu
Faculty of Business and Economics
The University of Hong Kong
Hong Kong, China

ISSN 2731-4006 ISSN 2731-4014 (electronic)
Applied Economics and Policy Studies
ISBN 978-981-95-9984-4 ISBN 978-981-95-9985-1 (eBook)
https://doi.org/10.1007/978-981-95-9985-1

This Springer imprint is published by the registered company Springer Nature Singapore Pte Ltd.
The registered company address is: 152 Beach Road, #21-01/04 Gateway East, Singapore 189721, Singapore

Competing Interests The authors have no competing interests to declare that are relevant to the content of this manuscript.

Contents

List of Figures

List of Tables

Chapter 1
Introduction: The Reality of Data as a New Factor and Theoretical Challenges

1.1 Introduction

Globally, the rise of the digital economy is profoundly altering the logic and pathways of economic growth, reshaping the functions and boundaries of traditional production factors, and driving nations to seek new comparative advantages in the global competitive landscape. As digital technologies increasingly permeate all aspects of the economy and society, data is no longer merely a "byproduct" of information systems but has evolved into a fundamental production factor on par with land, labor, and capital. Its value is continuously unleashed and amplified through intelligent algorithms, platform economies, and industrial collaboration. In this context, artificial intelligence (AI), as a key data-driven technology, is becoming the core engine for advancing economic transformation and upgrading, reshaping innovation paradigms, corporate operational logic, and social governance models. The integration of data and artificial intelligence not only expands the spatial boundaries of production activities but also fundamentally challenges the core propositions of classical economics regarding the allocation of scarce resources.

Traditional economic theory emphasizes the finiteness of resources and the law of diminishing marginal returns, positing that land, capital, and labor—tangible and exclusive factors—serve as the fundamental drivers of economic growth. However, in the digital economy, data's non-rivalrous nature, its capacity for infinite replication, and its characteristic of increasing returns to scale in usage enable it to transcend the physical constraints of traditional factors, evolving into a novel element that "gains value with use.“ Data can be reused by multiple entities without diminishing its marginal value; in application, it exhibits exponential value increments as its dimensions diversify and semantic contexts expand. This nature provides a new paradigmatic foundation for technological innovation, business model evolution, and governance system upgrades.

The rapid advancement of artificial intelligence, particularly groundbreaking progress in generative AI (such as GPT and Stable Diffusion) in recent years, has

X. Li et al., *Data as a New Factor of Production*, Applied Economics and Policy Studies, https://doi.org/10.1007/978-981-95-9985-1_1

created a powerful technological pathway for unlocking data value. Through learning, training, and inference from data, AI not only enhances information processing capabilities but also achieves leaps in "machine intelligence" across multiple dimensions—perception, comprehension, generation, and decision-making—transforming data from "raw materials" into "decision-making capital." AI systems can accurately identify consumption trends, optimize supply chain management, and automatically generate content (such as copy or images), while also finding wide application in critical fields like medical-assisted diagnosis, autonomous driving, smart manufacturing, and public governance. It can be said that AI serves as a critical bridge for realizing the "assetization" and "productive transformation" of data elements, functioning as one of the dual driving forces propelling high-quality growth in the digital economy.

Precisely for this reason, data and AI, as the "twin engines" of the new era, are regarded by major global powers as core strategic resources for seizing the initiative in future development. Major economies such as the United States, Europe, and China have positioned the digital economy at the heart of their national development agendas, implementing systematic deployments in data circulation, AI R&D, platform governance, talent cultivation, and standard-setting. This has resulted in a competitive landscape characterized by clear strategic direction, diverse policy tools, and well-developed infrastructure. For instance, the United States leverages its technological leadership to strengthen foundational AI research and cloud computing ecosystem development, aiming to maintain global dominance in an integrated system spanning "algorithms—computing power—platforms—application scenarios." The European Union, under the banner of "data sovereignty" and "digital ethics," is constructing an institutional framework encompassing privacy protection, data sharing, and AI compliance, striving to secure the "moral high ground" in global digital rule-making. Meanwhile, China capitalizes on its advantages in data scale and scenario complexity, accelerating the cultivation of data factor markets and the industrial application of AI, gradually establishing a tiered advancement system from policy pilots to industrial implementation.

At the domestic level, data as a factor of production—a crucial pillar of the digital economy—has been explicitly incorporated into China's national system of production factors in recent years, becoming a key variable driving high-quality development. The state has introduced a series of significant policies to promote the establishment of mechanisms for defining rights, circulation, and trading of data resources. Initiatives such as the establishment of the National Data Administration, the setup of data exchanges, and piloting institutional innovations like the "separation of three data rights" (ownership, usage rights, and rights to proceeds aim to address core issues long plaguing data factor circulation—such as ambiguous ownership, unclear value, and transaction barriers—through institutional supply. Meanwhile, the deployment of data infrastructure, represented by the "East Data West Computing" project, is accelerating. Computing resources are gradually being extended to central and western regions, forming a new factor allocation system that synergistically optimizes "computing power-algorithms-data."

In the field of artificial intelligence, China has become one of the world's most active countries in AI applications. From urban transportation to smart healthcare, from government services to industrial manufacturing, AI systems are being deployed and scaled up on a massive level, empowering the upgrading and transformation of traditional industries. The rapid expansion of the AI industry has not only driven the practical application of core technologies such as computer vision, speech recognition, and natural language processing but also given rise to a large number of new job roles and novel business models. However, at the foundational level, China's AI development still faces "bottleneck" challenges in key core areas. There remains significant external dependence on high-end chips, fundamental algorithms, and core frameworks, while algorithmic originality and computing power security continue to be prominent bottlenecks constraining development. Therefore, national-level efforts are continuously increasing investment in basic research and independent control capabilities in key fields, while gradually establishing a comprehensive governance system encompassing technology R&D, ethical oversight, and security assessment.

From a global perspective, the development of the digital economy driven by data and artificial intelligence is not a natural evolution of technological processes but rather the outcome of interactive games among national strategies, institutional arrangements, and market mechanisms. On one hand, digital infrastructure (such as data centers, 5G networks, and edge computing) constitutes the physical support system for data flow, serving as a necessary condition for efficient data transmission and AI training; on the other hand, institutional arrangements such as data ownership confirmation, data compliance, and algorithm auditing directly determine whether data can circulate smoothly and be utilized fairly across industries, regions, and even national borders. Technological innovation, particularly the accumulation of AI capabilities, is constrained by both the scale and quality of data and is reliant on the institutional environment's ability to stimulate and protect innovative vitality. Therefore, a nation's performance in digital economy competition hinges on its ability to achieve the trinity of "technological pathway—institutional pathway—market pathway," thereby constructing a "new development system" conducive to the co-evolution of data and AI.

However, this process is fraught with profound challenges and contradictions. For instance, platform enterprises' monopolization of data resources may exacerbate market inequality and stifle innovation; structural tensions exist between data privacy protection and personalized services; and regional digital divides may widen further due to disparities in infrastructure and varying rates of technological penetration. Furthermore, the rapid expansion of emerging technologies such as generative AI has introduced novel risks including algorithmic bias, deepfakes, and data security concerns, necessitating parallel advancements in technology ethics and regulatory frameworks to build a more robust, transparent, and equitable digital governance system.

In this context, this chapter will systematically analyze how data as a production factor and artificial intelligence serve as new drivers of growth from both domestic and international perspectives. It will examine their mechanisms for reshaping traditional production factor structures and assess the institutional bottlenecks and governance challenges they face in practice. Specifically, we will first outline the strategic pathways and institutional logic of major economies in developing data elements and AI, comparing how different nations localize technological dividends through policy design and industrial deployment. Second, we will delve into China's institutional innovations and practical experiences in data ownership confirmation, circulation, and trading, and AI industrial applications, evaluating their concrete outcomes in enhancing factor allocation efficiency and cultivating new growth drivers. Finally, we will systematically analyze the systemic impacts of data-AI integration on production efficiency, industrial structure, employment patterns, and social governance, proposing forward-looking policy recommendations and research prospects.

Through the above discussion, this chapter aims to provide macro perspectives and micro-mechanism support for understanding how current digital technologies, via data factors and AI mechanisms, intervene in and reshape production processes, innovation models, and factor structures. It also seeks to establish a logical foundation and theoretical framework for subsequent chapters to further analyze the role of data factors at the enterprise, regional, and household levels.

1.1.1 The Chinese Context

1.1.1.1 The Scale Leap of the Digital Economy: From a New Growth Engine to the Main Form of Development

Since 2012, China's digital economy has undergone a transition from "quantitative change" to "qualitative change," with its scale expected to surpass 55 trillion yuan by 2023, accounting for 42.8% of GDP and contributing over 60% to economic growth for three consecutive years. This evolution is driven by a dual force of technological penetration and industrial integration. In the manufacturing sector, the number of industrial internet platforms has surpassed 200, with over 120 million connected devices. SANY Heavy Industry's "Lighthouse Factory," for example, optimizes stamping die loss prediction through AI algorithms, reducing equipment failure rates by 40% and energy consumption by 18%. In the services sector, e-commerce platforms have reached an annual transaction volume of 48 trillion yuan, while Meituan's smart dispatch system has compressed the average delivery time for food delivery riders to 27 min, supported by the computational power required to handle over one billion orders daily. In agriculture, digital technologies such as drone pest control and soil moisture monitoring have helped reduce production costs by 12% per mu and increase yields by 15% in Shouguang, Shandong Province. This entire industry-wide digital transformation has created a dual-driven structure of "digital industrialization" and "industrial digitalization." In 2023, the value added by digital industrialization reached 10.5 trillion yuan, with companies such as Huawei and Alibaba Cloud establishing competitiveness in 5G base stations (a total of 2.93

million) and cloud computing (with a global market share of 15%). Meanwhile, the scale of industrial digitalization reached 44.5 trillion yuan, with traditional industries such as steel and textiles achieving a 30% reduction in R&D cycles and a 25% improvement in inventory turnover rates through the construction of data platforms.

The leap in digital infrastructure development has provided foundational support for the integration of production factors. The nationwide integrated big data centers have formed a "East Data, West Computing" framework, with total computational power reaching 200 EFLOPS in 2023, and hubs in Guizhou and Inner Mongolia supporting 30% of the national computational demand. The 5G network covers 98% of urban areas in counties, supporting data transmission capabilities of 120 million GB per second, enabling low-latency applications such as remote surgeries and autonomous driving. Notably, the regional differentiation of the digital economy presents a "gradual progress" characteristic: the digital economy in coastal eastern regions exceeds 50% of GDP, with Zhejiang and Guangdong achieving full coverage of digital transformation for large-scale enterprises through "industrial brains." Central and western regions, on the other hand, rely on energy advantages to develop data center clusters. For example, the Qinyang "East Data, West Computing" hub in Gansu has attracted 20 leading companies, forming a distinctive model of "computing power export + data processing."

1.1.1.2 The Chinese Path to Artificial Intelligence Development: Coexisting Application Leadership and Technological Struggles

China's artificial intelligence (AI) industry presents a unique pattern of "breakthroughs in application, with the foundational layer catching up." In terms of application, technologies like computer vision and natural language processing have deeply penetrated various fields of society and the economy. SenseTime's AI vision solutions are used in over 1,000 hospitals nationwide, achieving an accuracy rate of 98.6% in detecting lung CT nodules, surpassing the average level of senior radiologists. iFlytek's intelligent speech system supports 70% of national government service hotlines, enabling automated answers to 85% of consultation inquiries. In urban governance, Shanghai's "City Brain" integrates over 2,000 data indicators from 16 departments, reducing traffic congestion by 18% and shortening emergency response times from 40 to 15 min. This application advantage stems from China's unique "scenario dividend"—its massive population and complex governance needs provide abundant training data and room for trial and error. By 2023, the scale of China's core AI industry reached 580 billion yuan, with more than 4,500 AI companies, 62% of which are application-layer enterprises.

However, there are still significant "bottlenecks" in foundational technologies. In high-end AI chips, domestic companies hold less than 15% of the market share, with 70% of GPUs imported. The 2023 export restrictions on NVIDIA's A100 chips directly affected domestic large model training progress. In deep learning frameworks, PyTorch and TensorFlow together dominate over 90% of the global market share, while domestic frameworks like Baidu's PaddlePaddle and Huawei's MindSpore are still developing. Moreover, the core AI architectures, such as Transformer and Diffusion, are all from overseas, with domestic research largely focused on optimizing applications. The talent imbalance exacerbates the technological gap—according to the "2024 China AI Talent Development Report," there is a shortage of 5.5 million AI professionals nationwide, with over 35% of this shortage in high-end roles like algorithm engineers and chip design experts. The number of relevant graduates from universities annually meets only 20% of the demand.

At the policy level, a three-dimensional promotion system has been formed, comprising national strategies, regional pilot programs, and industry applications. In 2023, the State Council issued the "Interim Measures for the Management of Generative AI Services," becoming the world's first regulatory framework for generative AI. Fifteen cities, including Beijing and Shanghai, have established national AI innovation application pilot zones, creating industry clusters such as "AI + finance" and "AI + healthcare." In Haidian District, Beijing, AI companies have exceeded 1,800, with 2023 revenues reaching 230 billion yuan. At the industry level, the "Financial Technology Development Plan (2023–2025)" requires that 90% of banks' AI risk controls be covered, while the "14th Five-Year Plan for the Development of Health Information Technology" sets a goal for the widespread use of AI-assisted diagnostic systems in tertiary hospitals. This policy combination not only promotes technological landing but also provides institutional guarantees for foundational research, with the National Natural Science Foundation's AI-related funding reaching 8.6 billion yuan in 2023, a 300% increase from 2018.

1.1.1.3 Marketization Reform of Data Factors: From Theoretical Exploration to Practical Breakthroughs

After data factors were officially included in the production factor system, China began its institutional innovation from "data resourceization" to "data assetization." In 2020, the "Opinions of the Central Committee of the Communist Party of China and the State Council on Building a More Perfect Market-Oriented Allocation Mechanism for Factors" first clearly defined the production factor attribute of data. In 2023, the National Data Bureau was established to comprehensively promote major reforms in data ownership, circulation, and revenue distribution. In local practices, Guizhou's Big Data Comprehensive Experimental Zone explored a "three rights separation" model (ownership belongs to the state, usage rights to enterprises, and revenue rights to individuals). The Guiyang Big Data Exchange saw its transaction volume exceed 60 billion yuan in 2023, covering more than 20 industries, including finance and healthcare, with the electricity data product "Load Forecasting Model" reaching a yearly transaction volume of 120 million yuan. Shenzhen's pilot program for "marketized allocation of data factors" launched the nation's first data property rights registration and management platform, allowing companies like Huawei and Tencent to assess and pledge the value of R&D data through registration, with a data financing scale of 8.5 billion yuan in 2023.

Simultaneously, the infrastructure for data factor circulation has been advancing. There are now 48 national-level data trading platforms, forming a layout of "national hubs + regional exchanges." Shanghai Data Exchange introduced the "data asset certificates" to enable cross-platform data product transactions. In terms of public data openness, the National Data Open Platform has aggregated over 8,000 data sets from 31 provinces, with high-frequency data such as transportation and weather being downloaded more than one billion times, supporting applications like Gaode Maps' real-time traffic and Moji Weather. However, the issue of data ownership remains unresolved—corporate, personal, and public data boundaries are blurred, leading to unclear rights and responsibilities during transactions. In 2023, data disputes increased by 42%, with ownership disputes accounting for 65%. To address this, Zhejiang and Fujian have piloted "data lineage tracking" technology, using blockchain to record the entire data collection, processing, and usage process, improving data ownership confirmation efficiency by 30%.

The integration of data factors with the real economy has spawned new business models. In manufacturing, the Haier COSMOPlat platform, which collects equipment data from over 3,000 companies, provides process optimization solutions that improve production efficiency by 22% on average for SMEs. In agriculture, Pinduoduo's "Farm Cloud Pool" system analyzes data from 800 million consumers' preferences to guide farmers on planting structure adjustments. The flower bases in Yunnan, for example, have reduced waste rates from 25 to 8% through data integration. In the service sector, Douyin e-commerce's "interest recommendation algorithm" uses user behavior data to reduce small and medium-sized businesses' customer acquisition costs by 40%, with agricultural product transactions reaching 240 billion yuan in 2023. This integration not only improves resource allocation efficiency but also reshapes industrial organizational forms—data-driven "platform enterprises" have become the core of resource integration. Among industrial enterprises above a designated size, 67% are now connected to industrial internet platforms, forming an ecosystem of "large enterprises building platforms and small and medium-sized enterprises using platforms."

1.1.1.4 Practical Demand and Strategic Depth: The Transformation Logic Driven by Data Factors

The intrinsic demand for economic transformation and upgrading has compelled a deep integration between data factors and artificial intelligence (AI). In traditional industries, the steel sector faces pressure under the "dual carbon" goals. For instance, Baowu Group has achieved a 12% reduction in coke oven energy consumption and cut annual carbon emissions by 2.8 million tons through its AI-based furnace temperature prediction system. In the textile sector, responding to the surge in personalized demand, Luthai Textile has used 3D virtual fitting data to shorten the delivery cycle for customized shirts from 15 days to just 3. Behind these transformations lies data's ability to transcend the law of diminishing marginal returns—while the marginal output of traditional capital and labor inputs has been declining by an average of

3.2% annually, the marginal benefit of data factors expands exponentially with scale. Empirical estimates suggest that a 10% improvement in corporate data utilization can raise total factor productivity (TFP) by 1.8–2.5 percentage points.

The modernization of social governance has created an urgent demand for data intelligence. During the pandemic in 2022, the “Health Code” system integrated transportation, consumption, and medical data to enhance contact tracing efficiency by 80%, achieving a testing accuracy rate of 99.9%. During the Beijing Winter Olympics, an AI-powered meteorological forecasting system reduced short-term precipitation prediction errors to within one millimeter, ensuring precise event scheduling. In grassroots governance, Zhejiang’s “Zheliban” platform incorporated over 12,000 government services, with AI-based customer service handling 75% of interactions and achieving a 96% public satisfaction rate. These applications highlight the unique value of data factors in improving governance efficiency—while the information transmission efficiency of traditional bureaucratic systems has declined by an average of 5.8% annually, data-driven flat governance models have shortened decision-making chains by 3–4 levels and improved response speed by more than 40%.

Amid intensifying global competition, data sovereignty has become a strategic battleground. China’s data output has reached 8.1 ZB, ranking second globally, yet cross-border data flows face regulatory frictions. The EU’s GDPR requires “adequacy determinations” for data exports, while the U.S. CLOUD Act compels companies to provide overseas data. In 2023, Chinese firms incurred compliance costs of approximately RMB 120 billion due to cross-border data issues. To safeguard data sovereignty, China introduced the Measures for Security Assessment of Cross-Border Data Transfers, establishing a “whitelist + security assessment” framework. ByteDance’s TikTok, for example, passed EU compliance reviews by localizing data storage. Simultaneously, China has actively participated in international rule-making, adopting a “negative list” approach to cross-border data flows under the RCEP, offering new governance models for developing economies.

The concurrent challenges of digital technological iteration and demographic transformation are becoming increasingly salient. With 19.8% of China’s population aged 60 or above and the labor force shrinking by three million annually, the integration of data and AI has become vital to addressing the “aging before affluence” dilemma. In elderly care, smart monitoring mattresses in Shanghai nursing homes have increased fall-warning accuracy to 95%, reducing caregiver demand by 30%. In education, the National Smart Education Platform for Primary and Secondary Schools uses AI-based homework analysis to boost grading efficiency in rural areas by 50%. This coexisting effect of substitution and creation renders AI’s net impact on employment complex: it is projected to create a net 15 million jobs in China, but eliminate 18% of low-skill positions. Consequently, vocational education systems are being reshaped toward digital skills, with 870 new training bases established nationwide in 2023, providing annual training capacity for 8 million individuals.

1.1.1.5 Intertwined Theoretical and Practical Dilemmas

Despite China's strong momentum in developing its digital economy—now a consistent engine of economic growth and a global leader in digital infrastructure, platform ecosystems, and data resource accumulation—a series of structural contradictions and institutional bottlenecks remain. These issues constrain the efficient allocation of data factors and affect the quality and evolution of downstream AI technologies, revealing a persistent tension between theoretical construction and practical operation. This section examines three pressing challenges—data monopoly, privacy protection, and regional disparity—through representative cases to illuminate the current dilemmas of China's digital economy and explore potential institutional and technological breakthroughs.

As platform enterprises gain dominance within industrial value chains, data resources have become increasingly concentrated among a few leading firms. According to data from the China Academy of Information and Communications Technology (CAICT, 2023)@@, top platforms control over 80% of consumer data, much of which remains in a "closed-use, exclusive-benefit" monopolistic state. This excessive concentration hinders new entrants and SMEs from accessing essential data, dampening innovation and entrenching industrial hierarchies. A notable case occurred in 2023, when a major e-commerce platform was fined RMB 5 million for refusing to share user behavior data with third-party service providers—an act deemed to obstruct fair competition. The incident not only drew public scrutiny over data abuse by dominant platforms but also signaled a shift from technical to policy-oriented challenges in competition governance. Fundamentally, under the current framework, data is not clearly defined as a social resource; platforms often treat it as private property, erecting barriers through encryption, user agreements, and internal rules. While this approach enhances platform efficiency, it suppresses the "positive externalities" of data, lowering aggregate social efficiency—a phenomenon consistent with the "underinvestment in data factors under market mechanisms" identified in Chapter 1's theoretical model.

To overcome this dilemma, institutional design must promote data openness and sharing. The "data trust" mechanism piloted in Shenzhen offers a promising pathway. Under this model, neutral third-party institutions manage and authorize the use of individual or corporate data, while platforms access data in accordance with trust agreements. Surveys show that data-sharing willingness increased by over 35% after the pilot, suggesting that institutional innovation can effectively balance monopoly reduction and rights protection.

With the implementation of the Personal Information Protection Law and the Data Security Law, China's data governance has entered an institutionalized, rule-based phase. Since 2022, the average number of permissions requested by major mobile apps has dropped by 40%, indicating progress in corporate compliance enforcement. However, stricter privacy regulation has also led to reduced service quality. A large internet company reported that, due to the lack of behavioral data, the accuracy of its AI recommendation algorithms fell by 22%, user retention dropped by 25%, and advertising conversion efficiency declined accordingly. This underscores the duality of data governance goals: the public seeks privacy protection and safeguards against "algorithmic harm," while enterprises rely on data to optimize services and enhance user experience. The resulting "efficiency–security paradox" forms the core dilemma of current digital governance. Without systemic technological support and institutional buffers, overregulation may stifle the productive transformation of data factors, creating unintended negative externalities.

Emerging technical solutions such as "data available but invisible" approaches provide a middle ground between privacy and utility. For example, Guizhou Province has employed Multi-Party Computation (MPC) and Trusted Execution Environment (TEE) technologies to enable collaborative AI modeling among hospitals without requiring raw data transfers. In a lung cancer AI diagnosis project, this approach improved prediction accuracy by 11 percentage points without any compliance incidents, becoming a national benchmark for "compliant data sharing."

Looking forward, privacy compliance should be guided by a differentiated authorization framework. Depending on data sensitivity and usage context, users should have greater autonomy across authorization, revocation, tracking, and compensation. This "user-centered" approach to data rights protection mirrors the "privacy utility cost function" in the theoretical model, providing a foundation for future algorithmic ethics and graded data governance.

Simultaneously, widening regional disparities in digital infrastructure, data accessibility, and technological capacity have produced a "Matthew effect" in digital development. The 2023 CNNIC Report shows that the digital economy accounts for over 45% of GDP in coastal provinces but less than 25% in some central and western regions. The east also enjoys pronounced advantages in data centers, algorithm R&D, and platform clustering, reinforcing a cumulative "platform–talent–data capital" agglomeration effect and amplifying spatial inequality.

Urban–rural divides are equally pronounced. In 2023, rural internet penetration stood at 43.2%, compared to 81.3% in cities. The number of fiber nodes per 10,000 people in eastern provinces is 3.2 times that of the west. In digital public services such as online education and telemedicine, rural user participation remains below 15%, further widening the information and welfare gap.

The economic consequences of these disparities extend beyond aggregate output to the structural absence of transformative momentum. Many central and western cities, deprived of high-quality data, are unable to participate in AI model training or platform-based economies, falling into a "low-quality factors–low efficiency–weak growth" trap—a typical manifestation of the "data misallocation and insufficient technological spillover" mechanism proposed in Chapter 1. The national "Eastern Data, Western Computing" initiative offers an institutional response by outsourcing data computation tasks from megacities in the east to data centers in the west, optimizing the allocation of energy, computing power, and land resources. This not only enhances data utilization efficiency but also stimulates digital infrastructure investment and industry growth in the western regions. In Guian New Area, for example, the establishment of national-level data center clusters has attracted major platforms such as Baidu and Huawei to deploy AI computing nodes, driving local digital economy growth at an annual rate exceeding 15% and gradually breaking industrial path dependence.

However, bridging the regional digital divide fundamentally requires an institutionalized mechanism for cross-regional data circulation. Establishing a unified national data exchange system—with standardized pricing, quality certification, and traceability—alongside fiscal and tax incentives to encourage leading platforms to set up R&D hubs in the central and western regions, can enhance the spatial efficiency of data factor allocation. This would operationalize the "planning-based regulatory mechanism driving lagging regions' technological leap" predicted in the theoretical model.

In the long term, the deep integration of data factors and AI will not only reshape China's production function, growth dynamics, and industrial organization but also trigger profound transformations in economic philosophy and institutional paradigms. By 2030, data factors are projected to contribute roughly 35% of China's GDP growth—surpassing capital to become the primary driver of economic expansion. AI technologies will further replace low-value-added labor and, through data-driven intelligent production and optimized decision-making, propel a systemic leap in total factor productivity.

This evolution signifies a structural shift from the traditional triad of "land–capital–labor" to a new trinity of "data–algorithm–knowledge." Such transformation transcends technological upgrading; it demands fundamental adjustments in property rights, income distribution, national governance, and global digital rule-making. First, property rights must evolve from static ownership to dynamic usage rights to accommodate the iterative, recombinatory nature of data utilization. Second, distribution mechanisms must transition from "platform monopoly" to "data co-governance," leveraging data dividends, algorithmic taxation, and data-sharing arrangements to mitigate inequality. Third, at the international level, China should actively shape global governance norms in digital trade, cross-border data flows, and AI ethics—asserting its institutional voice and contributing a uniquely Chinese "data development solution."

In summary, while China's digital economy has achieved remarkable progress in practice, it continues to face structural contradictions between theory and reality, platforms and markets, and growth and equity. By analyzing data monopolies, privacy dilemmas, regional divides, and institutional evolution—linked to the theoretical logic developed in Chapter 1—this section argues that future digital economic growth must rely on the dual engines of institutional reform and technological innovation to break through existing bottlenecks and establish a distinctive Chinese model of digital development.

1.1.2 International Context

1.1.2.1 Global Evolution of Artificial Intelligence and Industrial Transformation

The deep integration of artificial intelligence (AI) and data as production factors is reshaping the global economic landscape. As the most revolutionary combination of productive forces in the twenty-first century, their reconfiguration effect on traditional factors of production has transcended the realm of technology, becoming a core arena of national strategic competition. This section systematically reviews the evolutionary trajectory of AI technologies, analyzes the economic attributes and global allocation mechanisms of data as a production factor, explicates the digital economy strategies of major countries and regions, and examines how data reshapes traditional factors such as labor, capital, and land. It ultimately explores the current challenges and future trajectories of digital economic development, providing an analytical framework for understanding the logic of economic growth in the data era.

The development of AI has proceeded through several critical stages, from theoretical exploration to practical breakthroughs. Each iteration of its technological paradigm reflects the evolution of human cognition regarding the nature of intelligence. From the 1950s to the 1980s, three major schools—symbolism, connectionism, and behaviorism—laid the theoretical foundations of AI. Symbolism, represented by Newell and Simon's "Physical Symbol System Hypothesis," sought to realize intelligence through logical reasoning, as exemplified by the General Problem Solver (GPS). Connectionism, inspired by neural networks, produced early models such as the perceptron. Although criticized by Minsky and others, it sowed the seeds for modern deep learning. Behaviorism, represented by Brooks' "subsumption architecture," emphasized intelligence as an emergent property of agent–environment interaction, spurring early developments in robotics.

The limitations of this stage stemmed largely from insufficient computational power—mainstream computers in the 1980s possessed processing capacity barely one ten-thousandth that of a modern smartphone—and the scarcity of data. Consequently, AI applications remained largely confined to laboratory experiments.

Since the early twenty-first century, the maturation of big data technologies and breakthroughs in GPU parallel computing have propelled AI into a "data-driven" era of explosive growth. According to IDC, the global volume of data expanded from 1.2 zettabytes in 2000 to a projected 175 zettabytes in 2025, with unstructured data accounting for more than 80%, providing abundant "fuel" for AI model training. The innovation of deep learning algorithms marked a watershed: in 2012, AlexNet achieved a 15.3% error rate in the ImageNet competition, outperforming traditional methods (26.2%) and demonstrating the representational power of deep neural networks. The introduction of the Transformer architecture in 2017 further revolutionized natural language processing, elevating machine translation to near-human accuracy. By 2023, the global AI core industry exceeded USD 500 billion, with an annual average growth rate of 28.3%, forming a complete industrial chain from foundational layers (chips, algorithmic frameworks) to technology layers (computer vision, natural language processing) and application layers (intelligent manufacturing, smart healthcare).

Contemporary AI exhibits a dual-track developmental pattern. Reactive AI, the foundational type, focuses on immediate responses without learning capacity—such as industrial sensor systems that trigger robotic arms upon detecting material placement, without historical data storage or model optimization. In contrast, data-driven AI has become the mainstream. Its essence lies in improving model performance through massive-scale data training. Generative AI represents its cutting-edge manifestation, covering full-spectrum content creation from text (e.g., GPT-4) and image generation (e.g., Stable Diffusion) to video synthesis. OpenAI's research shows that when model parameters exceed the 100-billion scale (e.g., GPT-3 with 175 billion parameters), "emergent abilities" arise—such as logical reasoning and cross-domain generalization—marking a qualitative leap from tool-based intelligence to an innovation partner.

The commercialization of AI applications is reshaping industrial structures. In manufacturing, BMW optimizes its global supply chain through AI, reducing inventory costs across 2,000 suppliers by 25% and shortening order delivery cycles from 45 to 30 days. In healthcare, IBM Watson Health analyzes 30 million medical papers and 1 million cancer cases, achieving 92% accuracy in breast cancer treatment recommendations—surpassing the average performance of oncologists. In transportation, Waymo's Level-4 autonomous vehicle fleet operates commercially in 12 U.S. cities, having accumulated over 20 million miles of driving with an accident rate one-tenth that of human drivers. According to McKinsey Global Institute, widespread AI adoption could raise global labor productivity by 1.2 percentage points annually and add USD 13 trillion to the world economy by 2030—equivalent to creating another Japanese economy.

As the core production factor of the digital economy, data exhibits distinctive attributes and allocation mechanisms compared to traditional factors such as land and labor, forming the material foundation of a new production relationship. Take consumer data as an example: the same set of user behavior data can simultaneously support personalized recommendations on e-commerce platforms (increasing conversion rates by 15–20%), trend analysis for market research firms (raising accuracy by 30%), and risk assessment for financial institutions (reducing default rates by 25%), while its marginal cost of use approaches zero. Research at the Massachusetts Institute of Technology shows that the non-rivalry of data leads to exponentially increasing marginal returns with broader usage. When data-sharing participants exceed 100 entities, the total value generated can be more than ten times that of exclusive use.

However, privacy sensitivity imposes a fundamental constraint on data allocation. It encompasses three dimensions: personal information protection (e.g., GDPR's strict limits on biometric data), corporate trade secrets (e.g., proprietary industrial process data), and national security (e.g., restrictions on cross-border transfers of geospatial data). The EU's General Data Protection Regulation (GDPR) requires explicit consent before personal data collection, with violations punishable by up to 4% of global turnover. In 2023, Meta was fined EUR 1.2 billion for transferring EU user data across borders—the largest data compliance penalty in history. Conversely, the U.S. CLOUD Act mandates that technology companies provide data stored abroad to the U.S. government, creating regulatory conflict with GDPR. This fragmented data governance landscape has raised global cross-border data flow costs by 21%. The World Trade Organization estimates that data barriers result in approximately USD 1.2 trillion in annual global trade losses.

The increasing returns to scale inherent in data utilization generate a self-reinforcing "the strong get stronger" accumulation effect. As data volume and dimensionality grow, the value derived from integrated analysis expands exponentially. Empirical studies in medical imaging show that when the volume of training data increases from 100,000 to 1 million cases, AI diagnostic accuracy rises from 75 to 90%, and further to 98% at 10 million cases—illustrating the "data flywheel" effect that drives firms worldwide to accelerate data asset accumulation. Google invests over USD 20 billion annually in data centers and analytics; its distributed file system (GFS) can process exabyte-scale data, supporting synergistic optimization across search, advertising, and cloud services. Amazon, through AWS, holds about 32% of global enterprise data. Its AI service, Amazon SageMaker, has enabled over 100,000 firms to build customized models, forming a closed-loop ecosystem of "data accumulation – algorithm optimization – value-added services."

The global configuration of data factors reveals a pronounced "core–periphery" structure. Developed economies, leveraging technological advantages and industrial ecosystems, occupy the upper tiers of the value chain. The United States, as the principal rule-maker in global data governance, controls Internet root servers, key AI frameworks (TensorFlow holds 58% of the global AI framework market), and top talent (62% of the world's top 1,000 AI scholars are affiliated with U.S. institutions), capturing 38% of global data-related value. The European Union, through GDPR, has constructed data protection barriers aimed at balancing privacy with development. Its European Data Space initiative, launched in 2021, seeks to enable cross-sectoral data circulation in health, transport, and other fields by 2025, with the EU data factor market projected to grow from EUR 750 billion in 2023 to EUR 1.5 trillion by 2030. Asian economies exhibit distinctive patterns in data application and scale. China generated 8.1 zettabytes of data in 2022—second globally—while India has leveraged its Aadhaar system, the world's largest digital identity infrastructure covering 1.2 billion citizens, to support financial inclusion and public health services.

The mechanism through which data releases economic value is fundamentally transforming the logic of industrial competition—from a "land–capital-driven" model to a "data–algorithm-driven" one. In traditional manufacturing, competitiveness hinges on production capacity and cost efficiency. Tesla's Shanghai Gigafactory, by collecting real-time data from over 2,000 production nodes and employing AI to predict mold wear, reduced component scrap rates by 40% and per-unit energy consumption by 25%. The transformation in services is even more profound: Netflix, by analyzing behavioral data from 75 million users—including pauses, fast-forwards, and ratings—accurately predicted content preferences. The success of Squid Game added 15 million global subscribers, validating the new business logic that "data-driven decisions outperform experiential judgment." According to the World Economic Forum's Future of Jobs Report 2023, the deep application of data is expected to raise average productivity by 18% across 15 major industries worldwide, with finance, healthcare, and manufacturing leading at 24%, 22%, and 20%, respectively.

1.1.2.2 Comparative Digital Economy Strategies of Major Economies

In the global race toward a data-driven economy, major economies have formulated distinct digital economy strategies reflecting their institutional systems, industrial foundations, and technological capabilities. While the United States emphasizes technological hegemony and global ecosystem leadership, the European Union pursues ethical governance and data sovereignty, Japan follows a societal problem-solving model anchored in "Society 5.0", and South Korea advances a Digital New Deal aimed at industrial empowerment. Together, these models represent the evolving paradigms of global digital transformation and provide crucial insights into how nations reconcile innovation with governance, competitiveness, and inclusiveness in the era of artificial intelligence.

(1) United States: Technological Hegemony and Ecosystem Dominance

The U.S. digital economy strategy centers on preserving technological supremacy through a tripartite architecture of fundamental research, industrial ecosystems, and international rule-making. As the birthplace of modern AI theory, the United States retains a commanding lead in foundational research. According to Stanford's AI Index Report (2023), the U.S. accounts for 38% of global top-tier AI publications, with more than half of the breakthroughs in deep learning and reinforcement learning. It also holds 29% of global AI patents, particularly in chip architecture and algorithm optimization. NVIDIA's A100 chip, which dominates 82% of the global AI computing market, exemplifies this technological monopoly through its proprietary CUDA framework. Sustained public investment underpins this advantage—most notably the National AI Initiative Act (2021), which allocates USD 100 billion for AI R&D (2021–2025). The Defense Advanced Research Projects Agency (DARPA) alone spends USD 2.5 billion annually on its "Next-Generation AI" program, achieving 91% autonomous decision accuracy under complex battlefield conditions by 2023.

Industrial ecosystem construction follows a complete "chip–algorithm–platform–application" value chain. U.S. firms occupy 85% of the global AI chip market, led by NVIDIA, AMD, and Intel. Algorithm frameworks such as TensorFlow and PyTorch command 92% of global usage, while cloud service giants—AWS, Azure, and Google Cloud—collectively control 65% of the public cloud market. Their platforms enable rapid AI diffusion across sectors: IBM Watson Health processes over 30 million medical papers and 1 million cancer cases, achieving 92% accuracy in treatment recommendations; GE's Predix platform reduces turbine failure rates by 25% and maintenance costs by 30% through real-time analytics.

On the international front, the United States exports technological standards as instruments of rule-based power. The Partnership on AI (2016), co-founded with the U.K. and Canada, now includes 40 jurisdictions and has established globally adopted AI ethics standards. Trade agreements such as the USMCA enforce strict cross-border data provisions, effectively constructing a "digital alliance" excluding China. The 2023 G7 Hiroshima Principles on AI Governance further advanced the notion of "trustworthy AI," serving as a de facto access threshold for global markets.

Nevertheless, the U.S. faces growing criticism for a "technology-over-governance" bias. Major firms—Meta, Google, Amazon, and Apple—control 80% of consumer data, prompting antitrust investigations. In 2023, the FTC filed a landmark case against Amazon for unfair data-driven competition. Despite these governance challenges, the U.S. is expected to maintain leadership in the digital economy over the next decade, leveraging its unrivaled talent base (62% of the world's top 1,000 AI scholars) and dynamic innovation ecosystem (42% of global AI unicorns). Its strategic imperative remains clear: sustaining a generational technological gap through innovation leadership and regulatory influence.

(2) European Union: Ethical Governance and Data Sovereignty

The EU's digital economy strategy is built upon two institutional pillars—ethical governance and data sovereignty—reflecting its effort to reconcile technological progress with social values. The Artificial Intelligence Act (2021) established the world's first comprehensive AI regulatory framework, categorizing AI applications into four risk levels: unacceptable, high, limited, and minimal risk. Unacceptable applications (e.g., social scoring, real-time facial recognition) are prohibited, while high-risk systems—such as medical AI or autonomous vehicles—require pre-market documentation, risk assessments, and third-party certification. For instance, a German AI medical firm's product launch was suspended for failing to meet dataset diversity requirements. Limited-risk applications must disclose AI use, and minimal-risk systems are subject to self-regulation. This risk-tiered model reduced high-risk AI incidents in the EU by 40% within two years of implementation.

In data governance, the EU advances the European Data Space initiative to facilitate cross-border data sharing across healthcare, transportation, energy, and agriculture by 2025. Complementary measures include the Data Governance Act (DGA)—mandating public sector data sharing, and the Digital Markets Act (DMA)—requiring large platforms to open APIs to third parties. Apple, for instance, was compelled to allow third-party app stores, projected to generate EUR 20 billion in value for European developers. The EU's open data portal now provides over 5,000 datasets, driving entrepreneurship and efficiency. With full implementation, the European data market is expected to double from EUR 750 billion in 2023 to EUR 1.5 trillion by 2030.

The EU's approach prioritizes SMEs' digital transformation, compensating for its lack of global tech giants. The Digital Europe Programme (2021–2027) allocates EUR 20 billion to AI and cloud technologies, offering SMEs subsidies up to EUR 500,000. The AI Public–Private Partnership further pools EUR 15 billion to develop solutions in healthcare and green energy. The EU's Ethics Guidelines for Trustworthy AI (2023), emphasizing algorithmic transparency and human oversight, have been adopted by over 40 countries.

However, the EU's "strong governance but weak technology" model faces structural constraints—90% of AI chips are imported from NVIDIA, and only two EU firms rank among the world's top 20 tech companies. Initiatives such as the EU Chips Act (EUR 43 billion) and the European Cloud Project aim to build indigenous capacity and reduce dependence on AWS and Azure. Whether this model can sustain competitiveness depends on its ability to balance innovation and regulation while nurturing globally competitive technology enterprises.

(3) Japan: Societal Problem-Solving and Trustworthy AI

Japan's digital economy strategy is anchored in the Society 5.0 vision, which positions AI as a solution to pressing demographic challenges such as aging and labor shortages. With citizens aged 65 and above comprising 29% of the population and the labor force projected to shrink by 15% by 2030, Japan focuses on AI applications in healthcare, eldercare, and smart agriculture. SoftBank's Pepper robot, deployed in over 2,000 nursing homes, enhances care efficiency by 25% and patient satisfaction by 40%. Panasonic's AI diagnostic system for chest CT scans increases early-stage lung cancer detection by 15% and cuts diagnosis time from 30 to 5 min. In agriculture, Yamaha's AI-powered drone reduces pesticide use by 40% while boosting yields by 12%, serving 100,000 farmers.

Japan's hallmark is its emphasis on Trustworthy AI. The AI Trust Research Center (2023), funded with JPY 5 billion, developed "causal reasoning AI" technologies that ensure explainability in high-stakes contexts. A Japanese automaker's autonomous driving system, powered by such algorithms, achieves 98% prediction accuracy and provides full decision traceability. Fujitsu's Explainable AI Platform reduced financial complaint rates by 35% by clarifying credit decision logic.

Government–industry collaboration defines Japan's implementation pathway. The Ministry of Economy, Trade and Industry (METI) set a 2030 vision to make Japan "the world's most advanced AI application nation," funding pilot projects, talent training (100,000 AI professionals annually), and ethical review mechanisms. Industry leaders—Toyota, Sony, Hitachi—integrate AI into core operations, enhancing energy efficiency, production yield, and creative output.

Japan also exports AI solutions to ASEAN, combining technological diffusion with social impact diplomacy. It has established smart eldercare centers in Vietnam, trained AI medical professionals in the Philippines, and co-founded the East Asia AI Research Alliance with Korea and Taiwan. Yet, challenges persist: limited data openness (less than 30% data-sharing in healthcare and education) and weak startup vitality (AI startups are one-tenth of the U.S.). The Data Utilization Promotion Act and AI innovation zones in Tokyo and Osaka aim to overcome these constraints by enabling experimental data use and stimulating innovation. Japan's future competitiveness will hinge on balancing data privacy with openness and cultivating globally minded innovators.

(4) South Korea: The Digital New Deal and Manufacturing Empowerment

South Korea's Digital New Deal epitomizes a technology-driven industrial strategy, integrating AI into its manufacturing heartlands to enhance productivity and global competitiveness. The Basic Plan for the Digital New Deal (2020) commits ₩150 trillion (USD 110 billion) over six years, with ₩30 trillion dedicated to frontier technologies such as AI, 6G, and quantum computing. Samsung's Exynos chips and SK Hynix's AI-specific DRAM exemplify Korea's push for semiconductor sovereignty.

Manufacturing transformation is the cornerstone of Korea's model. Hyundai, LG, and POSCO have embedded AI in their production systems, achieving substantial efficiency gains—defect detection accuracy up to 99.7%, production throughput increases of 30%, and defect rates reduced by 60%. The government's Smart Factory Support Program subsidizes AI adoption among SMEs, reducing energy use by 25% in pilot cases.

Korea's tripartite innovation ecosystem—linking government, corporations, and research institutions—has been instrumental. MSIT's AI Innovation Centers support over 500 firms; Samsung's developer community involves one million members; KAIST trains 500 AI specialists annually. These synergies have produced globally recognized firms such as Coupang and Naver.

On the global stage, Korea builds digital alliances to amplify its influence. Partnerships with the U.S. on semiconductor AI supply chains, with Japan on NLP technologies, and with ASEAN on AI infrastructure all strengthen Korea's regional leadership.

However, Korea faces risks of data breaches and innovation homogenization. A 2023 production data leak cost one automaker USD 500 million, highlighting vulnerabilities. The Industrial Data Security Act and AI Innovation Fund seek to mitigate these issues and foster AI-driven product innovation. Korea's long-term competitiveness will depend on its ability to ascend the value chain—from manufacturing intelligence to innovation intelligence—and to strike a balance between data protection and data utilization.

In summary, the digital economy strategies of major economies illustrate four distinct paradigms: technological hegemony (United States), regulatory sovereignty (European Union), societal problem-solving (Japan), and industrial empowerment (South Korea). Each model reflects unique institutional logics and governance capacities. The comparative analysis underscores that while technological capability remains the foundation of digital competitiveness, institutional adaptability—manifested through governance frameworks, ethical norms, and ecosystem coordination—will determine leadership in the global digital order.

1.1.2.3 The Reconstructive Effects of Data Factors on Traditional Production Inputs

As an emerging production factor, data interacts dynamically with traditional inputs—labor, capital, and land—fundamentally reshaping the logic of economic growth. This reconstructive effect manifests not merely as substitution among factors but as synergistic enhancement, driving a transformation of the economic system from factor-input-driven to data-efficiency-driven growth. Under the influence of data, the allocation, value-creation mechanisms, and growth boundaries of traditional inputs are being redefined, giving rise to a new production paradigm centered on data.

In the labor market, data-driven artificial intelligence (AI) technologies exhibit distinct characteristics of creative destruction. On one hand, AI substitutes repetitive and standardized tasks—such as customer service, data entry, and assembly-line quality inspection—where automation has rapidly increased. According to the World Economic Forum's Future of Jobs Report, around 85 million jobs worldwide may be replaced by AI by 2025. On the other hand, data has catalyzed the emergence of new occupations—AI trainers, machine learning engineers, and data ethicists among them—creating an estimated 97 million new jobs within the same period, resulting in a net gain of approximately 12 million positions, particularly in green energy, digital technology, and creative services. Data from the U.S. Bureau of Labor Statistics show that in 2023, the average annual salary for AI-related jobs reached USD 125,000—2.3 times the median of traditional occupations—with an annual demand growth rate of 34%, revealing a "high-wage, high-growth" trajectory.

The transformation of labor skills is profound, shifting from "physical strength + experience" toward "data + algorithmic literacy." In traditional manufacturing, core competencies lay in operational expertise and mechanical proficiency. By contrast, next-generation intelligent manufacturing systems—such as Tesla's Shanghai Gigafactory—require workers capable of interpreting digital dashboards and responding to AI-based quality alerts, with digital literacy now the top hiring criterion. In the healthcare sector, the adoption of AI-assisted diagnostic systems is driving physicians from experience-based diagnosis toward data-validated decision-making. Empirical data from the Mayo Clinic indicate that doctors trained in AI collaboration improved diagnostic accuracy by an average of 18%, though such progress demands new proficiencies in algorithmic reasoning and data interpretation. This transformation has also generated structural skill mismatches: low-skilled workers face displacement risks, while high-skilled talent remains scarce. OECD research in 2023 found that only 28% of individuals aged 15–64 in member states possessed basic digital skills, and fewer than 10% met advanced AI-related skill thresholds. In response, governments are increasing investment in vocational education and digital skill development. For example, Germany's "Industry 4.0 Skill Enhancement Program" invests EUR 5 billion annually to train over one million workers in AI applications, mitigating structural imbalances in labor markets.

The influence of data extends deeply into capital allocation efficiency. At the micro level, AI-based credit assessment models incorporate non-financial data—such as transaction records, logistics flows, and online sentiment—to improve lending decisions. In the U.S., LendingClub's AI-driven risk-control system increased SME loan approval efficiency by 70%, reduced small-loan interest rates by 1.2 percentage points, and maintained default rates below 3%. At the macro level, data-driven industrial forecasting enables more precise capital flows. Empirical studies indicate that investment institutions employing AI for industry trend analysis achieved returns 2.3 percentage points higher than those using traditional models. Capital markets have also been restructured by data: high-frequency trading algorithms analyze massive datasets to execute millisecond-level trades, now accounting for over 60% of global stock trading volume. AI-based stock selection models, drawing from unstructured data—such as corporate report sentiment or satellite imagery—offer novel dimensions for value investing. Bridgewater Associates' AI strategy, for instance, has outperformed the S&P 500 index for five consecutive years.

The integration of data and land factors is reshaping spatial economic structures, shifting from location-driven to data-flow-driven activity. In commercial applications, Starbucks employs AI to analyze mobile signaling and social media check-in data, improving site-selection accuracy from 65 to 82%, with new stores in China achieving profitability rates above 90%. In industrial applications, the Suzhou Industrial Park utilizes enterprise-level data on energy use, patents, and output to construct a "land efficiency evaluation model," increasing output per square kilometer from RMB 5 billion in 2015 to RMB 12 billion in 2023. The rise of smart cities further underscores the fusion of data and land: Singapore's "Digital Twin City" integrates multisource data across transport, energy, and environment systems, enhancing land-use efficiency by 15% and reducing public service costs by 20%. This model of "data-empowered land" is being globally replicated, with the smart city market expected to reach USD 1.5 trillion by 2030.

The deep convergence of data and technology factors has accelerated innovation cycles, marking a shift from linear R&D to data-driven innovation. Traditional R&D follows a decade-long sequence from basic research to product development, whereas DeepMind's AI-powered pharmaceutical research—analyzing over 200 million protein structures—has reduced drug development cycles from ten years to eighteen months while cutting costs by 70%. Similarly, AI simulation in materials science has accelerated the discovery of new battery materials tenfold. The emergence of open innovation ecosystems amplifies the power of data sharing. Kaggle, hosting over ten million data scientists worldwide, has collaboratively solved more than 3,000 corporate problems through shared datasets and algorithms. NASA's Mars landing site project, leveraging crowdsourced data modeling, improved landing success rates by 35%. This "data–algorithm–application" innovation paradigm has elevated global R&D returns from 4.5% in 2010 to 6.8% in 2023.

The non-rivalrous and shareable nature of data has fostered new forms of factor collaboration, transforming usage patterns from exclusive appropriation to collaborative creation. The open-source ecosystem exemplified by Linux thrives on global cooperation in code and data sharing, capturing 78% of the global server market. In scientific research, open-access databases such as PubMed Central—hosting over 50 million papers and 10 petabytes of biomedical data—have accelerated cancer research breakthroughs by 40%. The EU's "Data Space Initiative" aims to establish cross-sectoral and transnational data-sharing mechanisms, projected to generate EUR 1.8 trillion in economic value by 2030. In this context, data factors are transcending traditional input boundaries, forming a new economic ethic centered on data sharing and co-created value.

1.1.2.4 Practical Challenges and Future Trends in Digital Economy Development

Despite its transformative potential, the broad application of data factors faces multiple structural and ethical challenges. The tension between privacy protection and data utilization is particularly acute. As AI's dependence on personal and enterprise data intensifies, risks of data leakage and misuse have surged. In 2023, 3,800 major data breaches compromised 42 billion records globally—over 60% in healthcare and finance. Conflicts between the EU's GDPR and the U.S. CLOUD Act have raised compliance costs for multinational firms by 15–20%; Microsoft alone reportedly incurs USD 800 million annually in dual compliance costs. While privacy-preserving computation methods—such as differential privacy and federated learning—enable partial protection through "usable yet invisible" data, they still reduce utility efficiency by 10–15%. Achieving equilibrium between privacy preservation and value realization has thus become a core issue in global data governance.

Data security threats have evolved toward specialization and industrialization, challenging economic resilience. State-level cyberattacks on critical infrastructure have become frequent. The 2023 ransomware attack on Colonial Pipeline in the U.S. forced shutdowns across 18 states, disrupting energy supply. The dark web data trade has grown into a USD 20 billion industry, trafficking in credit card and medical data. Technical vulnerabilities add further risks—mainstream AI models contain an average of 27 exploitable flaws, with adversarial attacks being particularly severe. Tesla and Waymo report over 100,000 targeted attacks on their AI systems annually. Consequently, establishing a comprehensive security framework—from algorithmic integrity to data protection and rapid response—has become a prerequisite for the digital economy's sustainability.

At the same time, data monopolies and digital divides exacerbate social and economic inequality. Major technology firms control over 80% of global consumer data, creating "data barriers" that constrain SME innovation. In 2023, the European Commission fined Amazon EUR 250 million for abusing merchant data to distort competition. Approximately 2.9 billion people—37% of the global population—remain offline; digital literacy rates stand at 68% in developed countries but only 12% in developing ones. Within China, regional disparities persist: eastern provinces host 72% of national data center capacity, compared to 18% in the west. According to UNDP estimates, a 10% rise in data inequality increases the global Gini coefficient by roughly 0.5 percentage points, deepening social polarization.

Technological ethics and algorithmic bias further challenge fairness and collective values. The opacity of AI decision-making has sparked "black box" controversies in areas such as sentencing and loan approval. U.S. studies reveal that certain AI risk assessment systems classify African Americans as "high risk" 45% more frequently than white defendants. Generative AI has introduced complex issues around copyright and liability; Stable Diffusion faces lawsuits for using copyrighted materials in its training datasets. The rise of autonomous weapon systems has raised ethical alarm, prompting the United Nations to initiate deliberations on AI arms restrictions.

More than 40 countries have issued AI ethics guidelines, while the EU's Artificial Intelligence Act and the OECD's AI Principles represent key steps toward a global ethical governance framework.

Looking forward, the convergence of data and AI will follow three major trends.

First, multimodal large models will dominate future development. Systems such as GPT-4 and Gemini already integrate understanding and generation across text, image, audio, and video. By 2025, model parameters are expected to surpass 10 trillion, signaling the emergence of Artificial General Intelligence (AGI) capable of cross-domain reasoning and continual learning.

Second, quantum computing–AI integration will overcome computational constraints. IBM's 53-qubit quantum processors have been successfully applied to AI model training; by 2030, quantum AI is expected to achieve processing power 100 million times greater than current supercomputers, accelerating breakthroughs in drug discovery, materials science, and climate modeling.

Third, embodied intelligence will extend AI from virtual to physical realms. Boston Dynamics' Atlas robot already demonstrates complex locomotion and manipulation; by 2030, embodied AI systems will be widely applied across manufacturing and services, transforming human–machine collaboration.

Simultaneously, data allocation mechanisms will evolve toward distributed and intelligent architectures. Blockchain technology enables a shift from centralized registration to distributed verification of data ownership. Ant Group's Quzhao platform has registered over one billion data ownership certificates with a 98% judicial acceptance rate. Smart contracts enable conditional data transactions, allowing, for example, medical data to be used solely for cancer research. Federated learning has made "data stays, models move" a reality: in China, a financial-sector federated learning consortium of over 100 banks has improved credit risk accuracy by 12% with zero data leakage. By 2030, China's data factor market is projected to grow from RMB 800 billion in 2023 to RMB 5 trillion.

The evolution of the digital economy will redefine global competitiveness, with data sovereignty becoming an extension of national sovereignty. The U.S. Data Act and China's Security Assessment Measures for Cross-Border Data Transfer have reinforced regulatory oversight and localization, though these trends conflict with the openness required for global digital trade. Divergent rule systems—such as the USMCA, which strengthens data sovereignty, and the CPTPP, which promotes free data flow—risk fragmenting the global digital landscape. The United Nations' proposed Global Data Convention seeks to reconcile privacy, security, and cross-border governance, providing a structural blueprint for inclusive, secure, and open global data governance.

Future data-driven economic growth will increasingly emphasize sustainability, with green data centers and low-carbon AI emerging as new priorities. Global data centers now consume 200 billion kilowatt-hours annually—the equivalent of 20 Three Gorges Dams. Google and Microsoft have pledged to achieve 24/7 carbon-free energy by 2030, while DeepMind's AI cooling system has reduced data center energy use by 30%. In industrial production, AI-optimized supply chains are lowering emissions; BMW, for instance, has reduced per-vehicle carbon output by 15%. This paradigm of data-enabled green transformation is becoming a hallmark of high-quality digital growth.

In sum, the deep integration of data and traditional production factors is redefining the foundations of economic growth. According to McKinsey, efficient data allocation could raise global labor productivity by 1.2 percentage points annually, contributing an additional USD 13 trillion to global GDP by 2030. To harness this historic transformation, nations must advance in technological innovation, institutional design, and international cooperation—unlocking the growth potential of data while safeguarding against technological and ethical risks—to promote an inclusive and sustainable digital economy. As Klaus Schwab, Chairman of the World Economic Forum, observed: "In the era of data, competition is not a zero-sum game; it depends on who can better integrate technological innovation with social value to create shared prosperity." The realization of this vision requires collective action among governments, enterprises, and civil society to build a data-driven, intelligent, and sustainable global economic order.

1.2 The Integration of Data as a Production Factor and Artificial Intelligence

The rise of data as a production factor signifies a paradigmatic shift in the composition of productive inputs—from the traditional triad of land, labor, and capital to the centrality of information in the digital era. Unlike traditional factors characterized by exclusivity and rivalry, data is inherently non-rivalrous, allowing multiple agents to access and utilize it simultaneously without diminishing its intrinsic value. This feature stands in sharp contrast to the scarcity-bound nature of tangible assets. At the same time, the privacy sensitivity of data necessitates the deployment of technological safeguards to protect personal information while harnessing its economic and social value. Furthermore, data exhibits increasing returns to scale: as the volume and dimensionality of data expand, the potential for value creation through integration and analysis grows exponentially. These characteristics collectively render data an indispensable driver in economic growth, technological innovation, enterprise operations, and social governance.

Concurrently, artificial intelligence (AI), as a data-driven technological innovation, is profoundly transforming the structure and dynamics of the global economy and society. Generative AI systems, trained on massive datasets, demonstrate strong capabilities in autonomous learning and task complementarity, thereby enhancing labor productivity when integrated into production processes. Within the digital economy, the co-evolution of data and AI constitutes a positive feedback loop: data fuels AI model training and performance optimization, while AI, in turn, extracts deeper insights from data through its advanced analytical capabilities. This mutual reinforcement accelerates technological progress and drives sustained economic expansion.

1.3 Data as a Production Factor and Economic Growth

In the era of the flourishing digital economy, data has emerged as a pivotal driver of economic growth, intricately and profoundly intertwined with macroeconomic dynamics. This relationship is reshaping the global economic landscape, redefining traditional growth paradigms, and injecting new dynamism and possibilities into national economies. A rigorous examination of the intrinsic linkage between data and economic growth is thus essential not only for understanding current economic transformations but also for anticipating future trends and formulating informed, evidence-based economic policies.

As a novel production factor, data differs fundamentally from traditional inputs and possesses distinctive attributes that underpin its impact on economic growth. Its non-rivalrous nature allows simultaneous use by multiple entities without depletion. For instance, consumer behavior data collected by an e-commerce platform can simultaneously serve multiple purposes: enhancing user experience through personalized product recommendations while enabling merchants to optimize product strategies via market analytics. This non-exclusivity mitigates the constraints of limited factor supply, creating broader room for sustained economic expansion. Moreover, data is infinitely replicable at near-zero marginal cost. An online education platform, for example, can distribute a recorded course to millions of learners without incurring additional reproduction expenses, thereby facilitating the low-cost diffusion of knowledge and the enhancement of human capital quality—both crucial to long-term growth.

Data also displays increasing marginal returns. As data accumulates and its applications diversify, the potential for value creation expands exponentially. Search engine companies, for instance, benefit from greater data volume: the more search queries they process, the more accurately they can model user intent, refine algorithms, attract additional users, and boost advertising revenue—creating a self-reinforcing cycle of value generation.

From the perspective of productive efficiency, data significantly enhances economic growth. In business operations, firms can collect, analyze, and mine production data to optimize workflows. Manufacturing firms, for instance, use sensor-generated machine data to monitor performance, energy consumption, and component wear, allowing predictive maintenance and reducing downtime. A leading automotive manufacturer, after adopting big data analytics, reduced production line downtime by 30% and increased capacity by 20%. Similarly, in supply chain management, data enables visibility and intelligence across suppliers, producers, and retailers. By integrating cross-stage data, firms can forecast demand more precisely, optimize inventory levels, and improve coordination efficiency. For example, a global apparel brand employing real-time big data analytics increased its inventory turnover by 40% and reduced stockout rates by 25%, markedly boosting operational efficiency and profitability—thus fueling economic growth.

At the technological innovation frontier, data is an irreplaceable catalyst. Innovation—an essential engine of sustained growth—relies on abundant, high-quality data as both a resource and a driver. In the AI domain, large-scale datasets are indispensable for training high-performance models. Image recognition technologies, for example, depend on billions of labeled images to accurately identify objects, scenes, and individuals, with applications spanning security, autonomous driving, and medical diagnostics. Empirical evidence shows that AI models trained on large medical imaging datasets can improve early disease detection accuracy by 15%–20%, marking a revolutionary advance in healthcare innovation. Furthermore, data accelerates the innovation process by reducing trial-and-error cycles. Traditional R&D is time- and cost-intensive, but big data simulations enable rapid virtual testing and validation. A case in point is an aerospace engine manufacturer that leveraged big data simulation to optimize engine designs, shortening its development cycle from eight to five years and substantially improving innovation efficiency—injecting new momentum into growth.

Data also drives economic growth by fostering new industries, business forms, and models. The rapid advancement of big data, cloud computing, and the Internet of Things (IoT) has given rise to data-intensive sectors. The data storage and processing industry, for instance, has expanded rapidly in response to the exponential surge in data generation, encompassing data center construction, hardware manufacturing, and software development. Market forecasts indicate a global annual growth rate of 15–20% in this sector over the next five years. The sharing economy epitomizes the emergence of new business forms, utilizing big data to enable efficient resource allocation in models such as bike-sharing and car-sharing, which redefine mobility and asset utilization. The global sharing economy market has already surpassed USD 300 billion and continues to grow at a robust pace. In terms of new business models, data-driven precision marketing on e-commerce platforms exemplifies the monetization of user information. By analyzing browsing histories and purchase preferences, platforms deliver personalized recommendations that improve conversion rates and sales performance. One leading e-commerce platform reported a 25% increase in conversion rates and a 30% rise in sales through precision marketing, underscoring data's tangible contribution to economic expansion.

At the macroeconomic level, the broad application of data enhances resource allocation, promotes structural transformation, and fosters sustainable and balanced growth. Through big data analytics, governments and enterprises can more accurately assess market demand, resource distribution, and industrial trends, thereby guiding resources toward sectors with higher efficiency and potential. In the energy sector, for example, consumption data analytics inform evidence-based policymaking, enabling enterprises to optimize energy use and accelerating the transition toward cleaner and more efficient energy systems. Data also facilitates the digital and intelligent transformation of traditional industries, catalyzing the rise of emerging sectors and optimizing the economic structure. Traditional manufacturing, by adopting the industrial internet, big data, and AI technologies, achieves intelligent production control and quality enhancement, moving toward high-end manufacturing. Meanwhile, emerging industries—such as digital finance, digital logistics, and creative digital services—leverage data as a core asset, steadily increasing their share in the economy and becoming new engines of growth.

In essence, the relationship between data and economic growth is multidimensional, profound, and dynamically evolving. Through its distinctive attributes, data influences the speed, quality, and structure of economic growth by enhancing productivity, fostering innovation, spawning new industries, and optimizing macro-level resource allocation. As digital technologies mature and data markets become more sophisticated, data will play an even more decisive role in shaping national and regional competitiveness. Therefore, governments worldwide should prioritize the development, use, and protection of data resources, promote the deep integration of data with the real economy, and fully unleash the immense potential of data-driven growth—paving the way for high-quality, sustainable economic development.

1.4 Practical and Theoretical Significance

1.4.1 Theoretical Significance

Traditional theories of economic growth have long conceptualized production factors as quantifiable and exclusive resources—land, labor, and capital. However, with the rise of the digital economy and the pervasive use of data across domains, data has emerged as a new and foundational factor of production, challenging and expanding the classical understanding of the production function. One of the principal theoretical contributions of this book is the formal integration of data into the analytical paradigm of modern economic growth theory. Building upon this, the book develops an endogenous growth model that incorporates both vertical and horizontal innovation mechanisms to systematically reveal how data drives innovation, optimizes resource allocation, and enhances productivity. By formally modeling the economic properties of data—its non-rivalry, increasing returns to scale, and privacy sensitivity—the book establishes a new dynamic growth logic distinct from traditional models, offering a robust explanation for the characteristics of high-quality growth in the digital economy. This theoretical framework not only fills the explanatory gap in existing models regarding contemporary structural transformation but also provides a structural rationale for data- and technology-driven growth pathways.

Moreover, this work extends the analytical scope of Schumpeterian creative destruction. Previous studies have largely treated innovation as a process of technological breakthrough or capital substitution, overlooking the dual role of data in the innovation mechanism. By examining firms' R&D activities, the book elucidates how data—through improving innovation success rates, reducing trial-and-error costs, and enhancing research efficiency—strengthens the competitive advantage of new entrants over incumbents via both vertical innovation (technological improvement) and horizontal innovation (product diversification). This data-driven innovation process represents a new production paradigm centered on algorithms and data accumulation rather than capital intensity or traditional R&D experience, marking a conceptual departure from the capital–labor-centered innovation theories. The model's exploration of the dynamic equilibrium between data and labor substitution theoretically supports the view that data, under specific conditions, can overcome the diminishing marginal returns of both capital and labor, thus forming a new endogenous engine of growth.

In the field of institutional economics, this book develops a theoretical framework for the property rights structure of data factors, proposing a "tripartite separation of rights"—ownership, usage rights, and income rights. This framework reflects the multi-agent participation typical of platform economies, contrasting with the exclusivity and singularity of traditional property rights. Combining theoretical modeling with empirical cases, the book highlights that the fundamental challenge of data ownership lies in its boundary ambiguity and dynamic value. Accordingly, it argues for the integration of technological solutions (e.g., blockchain-based tracing), institutional mechanisms (e.g., data lineage systems), and innovative governance structures to achieve alignment between ownership definition, data trading, and regulatory oversight. This novel property rights architecture transcends the limits of the Coasian framework and offers a viable reform path toward market-based allocation of production factors, thereby extending the applicability of institutional economics in the digital era.

The book also advances theory concerning the reconfiguration of government–market relations. Under classical economic theory, the government's role is primarily corrective—intervening in cases of market failure. Yet, when dealing with data, which embodies both public and private attributes, neither market forces nor unilateral government intervention alone can achieve both efficiency and equity. This book therefore advocates for institutional innovations such as policy sandboxes, data governance performance evaluation, and data exchange pilots to realize a dual mechanism of governmental guidance and market adjustment. Through a systematic analysis of how data can be embedded within macroeconomic regulation, the author proposes incorporating "data allocation capacity" into the framework of government performance evaluation. Furthermore, the book establishes a data governance performance index system grounded in the quality of data flows, efficiency of utilization, and transparency of transactions, thereby opening a new explanatory paradigm for macroeconomic regulation in the digital age.

In exploring the interplay between data and technological innovation, the book makes another major theoretical contribution by breaking away from the static conception of data as mere growth input. Instead, it formulates a dynamic feedback loop of "data–AI–innovation–growth." Through both theoretical derivation and empirical validation, it demonstrates how data enhances AI capabilities via model training, and how AI, in turn, strengthens firms' innovation performance and productivity, collectively transforming growth trajectories. In this process, data becomes not an auxiliary input but a strategic resource embedded in the firm's core decision-making chain—a vital link between technological breakthroughs and value realization. This theoretical loop challenges traditional innovation models such as Solow and Romer, while providing a foundational logic for understanding AI-led technological transformation.

At the microeconomic level, the book enriches the theory of firm heterogeneity by introducing a structural variable—the Big Data Capability Index (BDA Index)—which quantifies firms' capacity in data acquisition, management, analysis, and application. Empirical analysis demonstrates that higher digital capability significantly influences corporate behavior: firms with stronger data competencies exhibit higher R&D motivation, greater merger success rates, and lower operational volatility. These findings expand the explanatory scope of firm heterogeneity and lay the groundwork for developing firm-level theoretical systems attuned to the digital economy.

The book also provides a mechanistic explanation of employment structure transformation under digital conditions, constructing a data redistribution model within a labor economics framework. It argues that AI and data are increasingly substituting low-skilled labor, while traditional policies such as wage subsidies or minimum wage adjustments fail to alleviate inequality effectively. Consequently, the author proposes institutional mechanisms such as data dividend taxation and platform data revenue reinvestment. Quantitative estimates indicate that reallocating just 10% of platform firms' data-derived profits toward training and reskilling low-skilled workers could mitigate structural imbalances in the labor market by approximately 20%, offering theoretical support for a more inclusive and adaptive social protection system in the digital era.

A particularly innovative theoretical contribution lies in the exploration of data ethics and digital equity. The book introduces the Data Wellbeing Index, a multidimensional framework for assessing fairness in data distribution, encompassing individuals' control, participation, informed use, and technological neutrality. This metric transforms discussions of "data inequality" from descriptive assessments into quantifiable analysis, rendering fairness measurable. Additionally, the book systematically addresses the rights of "data laborers"—gig workers such as couriers or livestreamers who contribute significantly to platform operations through the data they generate. It argues that these workers deserve institutionalized compensation proportional to their data's contribution to algorithmic improvement and service enhancement. This digital reinterpretation of labor value extends the theoretical discourse on the interplay between equity, efficiency, and rights in labor economics.

Finally, from a global perspective, the book articulates a "Chinese approach" that combines theoretical coherence with policy feasibility in response to the fragmentation of global data governance. Through comparative analysis of the EU's GDPR, the U.S. CLOUD Act, and China's data outbound compliance framework, it proposes a "whitelist–risk assessment–data localization" tripartite mechanism balancing data sovereignty with secure cross-border flows. This framework not only safeguards national data security but also supports the internationalization of digital platforms, offering developing economies a theoretically grounded and policy-relevant strategy for engaging in global rule-making.

In sum, the book systematically elucidates the central role of data in the evolution of modern economic structures from multiple theoretical perspectives. It enriches theories of production factors, endogenous growth, and innovation dynamics, while extending inquiry into institutional design, labor transformation, and digital ethics.

Its core contribution lies in breaking away from binary oppositions—between data and growth, platform and governance, efficiency and equity—by integrating theoretical modeling with empirical evidence to establish a multi-level analytical framework spanning the macro, meso, and micro dimensions of the digital economy. This represents not only a digital-era reinterpretation of classical economic theory but also a foundational step in constructing the next-generation knowledge architecture of economics.

1.4.2 Practical Significance

Against the backdrop of rapid global digitalization, data is evolving into a foundational production factor with transformative implications for economic systems. By constructing an endogenous growth model centered on data, this chapter reveals the intrinsic mechanisms through which data drives technological progress, optimizes resource allocation, enhances innovation efficiency, and sustains long-term growth. Beyond its theoretical contributions, the model offers critical insights with substantial policy relevance and practical significance across several dimensions.

First, the model provides a robust theoretical foundation for China's ongoing reform toward market-based allocation of data factors and the construction of a "Digital China." In the national strategy of high-quality development driven by data, China is accelerating the establishment of systems for data property rights, circulation, trading, and regulation. Yet, the unique characteristics of data—particularly its non-rivalry and increasing returns—pose new challenges for efficiency, pricing, and transaction mechanisms. The model highlights that without appropriate institutional coordination, data markets may experience both undersupply and misallocation, inhibiting innovation diffusion and dampening growth potential. By incorporating consumers' disutility from privacy loss in data transactions, the model further formalizes the trade-off between privacy protection and economic efficiency, providing theoretical support for regulatory frameworks such as the Personal Information Protection Law and the Data Security Law.

From a policy standpoint, the model suggests that governments should establish a closed-loop institutional system encompassing data ownership confirmation, authorized usage, lawful trading, and benefit distribution, while promoting cross-regional and cross-sectoral interoperability of data infrastructure to strengthen the nationwide circulation of data resources.

In an era of heightened internal and external uncertainty, where traditional growth drivers—capital accumulation and external demand—face structural limitations, data offers a self-reinforcing and endogenous growth engine. Its strategic characteristics—irreversibility and path dependency—mean that once data advantages are established, they are difficult to replicate. Consequently, local governments have been accelerating data infrastructure investments, market cultivation, and rights system reforms in line with the model's mechanism of "marginal returns amplification through non-rival inputs."

The transformation of data from resource to asset hinges on its tradability and priceability. This transformation requires a comprehensive institutional infrastructure encompassing property definition, transaction platforms, valuation systems, and compliance oversight. The chapter's theoretical framework demonstrates that overcoming the "price mechanism failure" and "data underinvestment" problems in decentralized markets demands institutional coordination akin to a social planner's optimization.

Empirical evidence from pilot programs in Guizhou, Shanghai, and Shenzhen supports this theoretical insight. The Guizhou Big Data Exchange, for instance, has successfully implemented the "three-rights separation" mechanism—ownership, usage, and income rights—effectively addressing long-standing challenges of ownership ambiguity, valuation difficulty, and data sharing. Through blockchain-based data lineage tracking and data value certification, data now circulates securely among industrial participants, improving social data utilization efficiency and validating the model's prediction that coordinated governance yields higher welfare than decentralized equilibrium.

The book also confronts the issue of data monopolization in platform economies, urging the redefinition of data's public and proprietary attributes. Balancing innovation incentives with competitive fairness requires "co-opetition-oriented" governance, where competition and cooperation coexist. The institutional design model proposed herein provides a dynamic policy framework for optimizing the relationship between data concentration and innovation efficiency.

In the realm of social governance, the fusion of data and AI is reshaping administrative paradigms. The model's "data–AI feedback mechanism" is already evident in domains such as urban management, public safety, healthcare, and environmental monitoring. Cities like Beijing and Hangzhou have implemented urban brain systems integrating thousands of data sources to enable real-time monitoring and predictive governance, significantly enhancing administrative efficiency.

This shift underscores data's potential as a public resource facilitating intergovernmental information sharing, breaking data silos, and improving policy intelligence. The model's emphasis on data's non-rival and shareable nature provides theoretical grounding for integrated government data platforms, cross-departmental coordination, and improved public service quality. Furthermore, the marketization of public data assets has diversified fiscal resources. Some provinces, for example, have piloted the controlled licensing of government data to technology firms and research institutions for algorithm training and public service innovation—realizing both economic and social value. The chapter's data pricing framework, which balances social marginal cost constraints with privacy compensation mechanisms, offers practical guidance for achieving equilibrium between protection and utilization.

Within technology-empowered industrial systems, data exerts transformative effects on firm strategies, industrial chains, and platform ecosystems. Model analysis indicates that data enhances innovation success rates, expands product development boundaries, and reduces R&D failure costs—findings reflected in the practices of digital platforms and intelligent manufacturers. Firms like TikTok (Douyin), Pinduoduo, and Alibaba have established complete data-driven chains—from data collection and algorithm training to precision matching and monetization—creating multi-sided data feedback loops that dramatically increase transaction efficiency and reshape industry structures, empirically validating the model's "data-optimized horizontal innovation" mechanism.

Similarly, vertical innovation mechanisms manifest in industrial digitalization. Companies such as Haier and Foxconn employ industrial data platforms to collect and analyze equipment performance data, enabling predictive maintenance that reduces downtime and energy waste while boosting total factor productivity. These micro-level practices confirm the model's conceptualization of data-driven production functions.

The integration of AI and data has also redefined labor market dynamics. While AI increasingly substitutes for routine, low-skilled jobs—echoing the model's "labor–data substitution" hypothesis—it simultaneously generates new "data labor" roles, such as data labeling, algorithm training, and content moderation. In China, flexible employment now exceeds 200 million workers, nearly 20% of whom engage in data-related tasks. This dual phenomenon—substitution and regeneration—underscores the urgency of reskilling systems and validates the model's prediction that data can serve as an alternative income source for displaced labor.

Institutional innovations such as data trusts—piloted in Zhejiang and Shanghai—allow individuals to entrust their data to third-party custodians for collective monetization, partially mitigating income inequality. These mechanisms operationalize the model's "social planner" scenario, demonstrating welfare-enhancing potential through redistributive data governance.

Given China's pronounced regional disparities, the model's insight into data misallocation and growth inefficiency offers a theoretical framework for addressing the digital divide. Initiatives such as "Eastern Data, Western Computing" exemplify the model's principle of optimizing spatial factor allocation by relocating computational tasks from resource-intensive eastern regions to less-developed western areas. This strategy aligns computing capacity with energy resources, fostering regional industrial upgrading and balanced development.

At the global level, the model's components—data ownership mechanisms and privacy compensation structures—offer analytical tools for international data governance. In multilateral settings such as the RCEP and WTO e-commerce negotiations, China's proposal for "security-based and development-oriented" cross-border data flow mechanisms provides an alternative governance model for the Global South. The theoretical result that coordinated data allocation under a social planner yields greater welfare supports the broader logic that data governance is not merely a question of security, but also of equitable global growth and innovation opportunity distribution.

1.5 Overview of the Book

This book is structured around four interrelated themes—theoretical modeling, corporate risk, regional entrepreneurship, and household employment—reflecting the inherently multidimensional nature of research on data as a production factor and artificial intelligence (AI). The analytical design follows a macro–meso–micro logic, aligning with mainstream economic research paradigms while systematically revealing the transformation of production factors in the digital economy era.

1.5.1 From Theoretical Modeling to Empirical Validation

Chapter 1 develops an endogenous growth model that incorporates data as a production factor and generative AI within a unified analytical framework. By contrasting a decentralized economy with a social planner's economy, the model demonstrates how the non-rivalry and privacy sensitivity of data influence innovation efficiency and long-term growth trajectories.

This theoretical foundation provides the analytical basis for subsequent chapters. For instance, Chapter 2 derives a data-driven innovation mechanism from the model, which is empirically verified in Chapter 3 using a Big Data Analytics (BDA) capability index at the firm level—thus forming a closed loop between theoretical hypothesis and empirical test. The application of a difference-in-differences (DID) approach further confirms that the establishment of National Big Data Comprehensive Pilot Zones has increased entrepreneurial activity by 13.6%, offering quantitative support for the Chapter 1 hypothesis that data reduces entrepreneurial costs.

1.5.2 From Corporate Behavior to Regional Ecosystems

Chapter 3 focuses on corporate risk behavior, identifying the mechanisms through which big data analytics influence firms' risk-taking via investment, R&D, and M&A channels. Chapter 4 extends the analysis to regional entrepreneurship, exploring how data factors stimulate entrepreneurial vitality through technological innovation and cost-reduction effects.

This progression from firm-level behavior to regional-level dynamics illustrates the layered diffusion of production factor impacts. For example, digital transformation at the firm level enhances internal efficiency—raising R&D intensity by 22%—which translates into improved regional entrepreneurial ecosystems, as evidenced by an 18% reduction in start-up costs in the Guizhou pilot zone. Together, these results map the transmission chain from firms to regions.

1.5.3 From Economic Growth to Employment Dynamics

Chapter 5 broadens the analysis to the labor market, examining how data and generative AI jointly shape substitution and creation effects in employment. This serves as a logical extension of the preceding chapters: shifts in the growth model ultimately manifest as structural changes in employment. Model simulations show that, under sufficient data supply, per capita consumption growth rises by 2.74%, while labor supply declines by 1.18%, indicating an "efficiency-enhancement–labor-reallocation" mechanism. These findings echo the empirical evidence from Chapter 4, where entrepreneurial expansion increased local employment by 4.77%, together depicting a comprehensive chain of production factor effects in the digital economy.

1.5.4 Implicit Integration Across Disciplines

Each chapter draws on intersecting perspectives from economics, management, and sociology:

·The economic dimension analyzes the efficiency of data allocation, highlighting resource misallocation between decentralized and planned economies.

- The management perspective interprets firms' strategic decision-making, such as the link between BDA capabilities and risk-taking strategies.
- The sociological view captures labor market restructuring, including a 23% increase in demand for high-skilled workers.

This interdisciplinary synthesis allows the study to simultaneously uncover macro-level mechanisms of GDP growth (e.g., an estimated 0.5–1 percentage point increase in growth rate) and micro-level behavioral logics (e.g., heterogeneity in risk-taking under financing constraints).

1.5.5 From Phenomenon to Mechanism

The chapter sequence follows a clear cognitive progression from abstract theory to empirical application and real-world impact. The first two chapters formalize the theoretical interactions between data and AI; the middle chapters empirically test these mechanisms using firm- and region-level data; and the final chapter turns to welfare and employment, linking digital transformation to livelihood outcomes.

From the theoretical proposition of increasing returns to data scale in Chapter 1, to the empirical finding of enhanced entrepreneurial opportunities in Big Data pilot zones in Chapter 4, and finally to the counterfactual analysis in Chapter 5 showing employment deceleration under data constraints, the book presents a rigorous, layered reasoning framework connecting theory → evidence → policy.

1.6 Structure and Research Framework of the Book

The central theme of this book is the impact of data on other production factors in driving economic growth. It constructs an integrated analytical system that combines theoretical modeling, empirical testing, and policy evaluation, aiming to elucidate the multidimensional mechanisms through which data promotes innovation, optimizes resource allocation, reshapes firm behavior, and enhances employment.

The book comprises eight chapters, arranged along a macro–meso–micro analytical gradient and enriched by institutional case studies and model-based simulations, thereby combining theoretical rigor with practical relevance.

Chapter 1 establishes the theoretical foundation, embedding data factors within an endogenous growth framework. It introduces both vertical and horizontal innovation processes, generative AI training mechanisms, and privacy constraints to examine how data influences long-term growth and welfare. A comparative analysis between decentralized and planner economies highlights efficiency differentials in resource allocation.

Chapter 2 investigates the mechanisms through which data promotes technological innovation, using a quasi-natural experiment based on China's National Big Data Comprehensive Pilot Zones. A DID analysis reveals that the policy significantly increases patent outputs and R&D intensity, particularly among SMEs and non-monopolistic industries—empirically confirming the Chapter 1 hypothesis that data enhances innovation success rates.

Chapter 3 shifts to the firm level, constructing a Big Data Analytics (BDA) Capability Index to examine how data capabilities affect investment sensitivity, financing constraints, M&A strategies, and earnings volatility. The findings show that data-driven firms exhibit more stable capital allocation, higher merger success rates, and lower exposure to risk—demonstrating that data has become a core source of competitive advantage.

Chapter 4 centers on regional entrepreneurial dynamics, analyzing how data reduces entry barriers, enhances resource allocation, and strengthens institutional support for new ventures. Structural equation modeling (SEM) identifies a policy–platform–entrepreneurship transmission mechanism, providing empirical insights for digital-economy policy design.

Chapter 5 turns to household employment, employing a dynamic general equilibrium (DGE) model to capture how data and AI jointly reshape the labor market. The findings suggest that while AI substitutes for low-skilled labor, it simultaneously generates new forms of data-related labor (e.g., data labeling, algorithm training), and that data income-sharing mechanisms enhance household welfare.

Chapter 6 synthesizes the preceding theoretical and empirical results to propose a comprehensive framework of "digitally driven economic growth." It integrates four interlinked layers—technological innovation, firm upgrading, regional vitality, and employment restructuring—and advances policy recommendations on data governance, benefit distribution, and platform regulation, emphasizing the balance between growth, regulation, and equity.

Chapter 2
How Data Reshapes Technological Progress: Structural Impacts on Total Factor Productivity

2.1 Mechanisms of Data-Driven Technological Innovation

As an emerging factor of production, data has become a critical driver of innovation and economic growth. The United States leverages the platform economy to establish global data barriers, the European Union emphasizes regulatory governance and privacy protection, and China has achieved rapid advancement through a large user base and diverse application scenarios. Existing studies, however, largely focus on the direct benefits of data and remain insufficient to capture its systemic role in R&D output, knowledge accumulation, and innovation processes within an endogenous growth framework. Given data's unique capabilities in facilitating technology diffusion, shortening product cycles, and reducing innovation costs, this chapter incorporates it into an endogenous growth model to expand theoretical insights and inform policy design.

Building on Howitt's (1999) vertical innovation model, we introduce data as a key input and examine its role in both horizontal and vertical innovation. The model demonstrates that data can reduce innovation failure rates, release labor resources, and improve their allocation, thereby enhancing overall economic efficiency. These effects are particularly pronounced in environments characterized by rising labor costs and declining data costs. Furthermore, we integrate data usage with privacy costs to model the utility trade-offs consumers face when selling their data, and we compare data allocation efficiency and growth outcomes under decentralized versus socially planned economies. Our results indicate that, despite market failures in decentralized economies, rational allocation of data—facilitated through policy intervention or institutional design—can significantly enhance innovation performance and support long-term growth.

By contrast, a socially planned economy exhibits higher growth along the balanced growth path (BGP), driven by three factors: (1) monopoly markups in intermediate goods production that crowd out labor; (2) neglect of intertemporal spillovers in R&D activities; and (3) the requirement to purchase data at market prices in a decentralized

X. Li et al., *Data as a New Factor of Production*, Applied Economics and Policy Studies, https://doi.org/10.1007/978-981-95-9985-1_2

economy, whereas in a planned economy, data can be freely allocated. As a result, decentralized economies adopt more conservative strategies in data and labor utilization, leading to weaker innovation momentum. Moreover, in transitional dynamics, horizontal innovation influences the speed and volatility of convergence to the BGP, while vertical innovation determines the pre-BGP growth rate and social welfare outcomes.

This chapter contributes to the literature by extending the analysis of data's nonrivalrous nature (Cong et al., 2021; Farboodi & Veldkamp, 2021; Jones & Tonetti, 2020) and embedding it within classical endogenous growth frameworks (Aghion & Howitt, 1992; Howitt, 1999). It thus extends the growth logic beyond labor, physical capital, and human capital. The chapter also engages with research on information and privacy, tracing a line from Hirshleifer (1971) and Murphy (1996) to Choi et al. (2019) and Ichihashi (2020, 2021), by examining how voluntary consumer data sharing can mitigate privacy concerns and how human capital accumulation can further relax privacy constraints.

Methodologically, the chapter employs a combined approach of theoretical modeling, numerical simulation, and empirical analysis. We first construct an endogenous growth model, then test its predictions numerically, and finally validate the relationship between data as a production factor and economic growth using empirical data. The chapter is organized as follows: Sect. 2.2 develops the model for a decentralized economy; Sect. 2.3 analyzes its balanced growth path; Sect. 2.4 considers the socially planned economy; Sect. 2.5 examines data sovereignty scenarios; Sect. 2.6 investigates the role of human capital in the digital economy; Sect. 2.7 presents numerical simulations; and Sect. 2.8 concludes with policy implications and future research directions.

2.2 The Baseline Model

This paper incorporates key elements such as vertical innovation (creative destruction), horizontal innovation (digital knowledge accumulation), data production, and privacy concerns into a macroeconomic model within the framework of a decentralized economy. The aim is to capture the essential characteristics of economic growth in a dynamic digital economy. The dynamic digital economy model consists of various representative agents who fulfill multiple roles, acting as both consumers and workers, as well as horizontal and vertical innovators. Additionally, there are intermediate producers and a final goods producer within the model's structure. It is important to note that the model assumes a continuous and infinite time framework, providing a suitable context to examine the dynamics of the digital economy and its implications for economic growth.

2.2.1 Representative Consumers

The numerical value of homogeneous representative consumer groups within the model exhibits a constant growth rate denoted by n and reaches a population size of L(t) at time t. In addition to their consumption decisions, each consumer has the option to supply one unit of labor inelastically to either of the two types of R&D sectors or to final goods production.

Data, generated as a by-product of consumer activities, can be individually sold by consumers to the two types of R&D sectors, implying that consumers possess the property rights over their own data (Cong et al., 2021). For instance, when consumers engage in online shopping or use ride-hailing apps, their consumption patterns and behavior characteristics are recorded as data. R&D sectors can leverage this data to develop new business models, create innovative products, and enhance their ability to meet market demands.

However, when consumers sell their data to any R&D sector, their utility is impacted by concerns related to the leakage and misuse of personal information. As consumers can derive profits from selling their data, they strive to strike a balance between the financial gains and the associated privacy issues. Data subsidies can be viewed as additional bonuses beyond traditional income, enabling agents to optimize their utility based on their privacy sensitivity. Given the uncertainty surrounding how the data will be utilized, the disutility stemming from selling data to different R&D sectors varies among agents.

Each consumer's utility maximization problem can be represented as[1]:

$$\max_{c(t),D_H(t),D_V(t)} \int_0^{\infty} e^{-(\rho-n)\cdot t} \cdot \left[\frac{c(t)^{1-\gamma}-1}{1-\gamma} - \chi_H \cdot D_H(t)^{\sigma} - \chi_V \cdot D_V(t)^{\sigma}\right]dt; \quad (2.1)$$

subject to

$$\dot{a}(t) = (r(t) - n) \cdot a(t) + w(t) + p_{D,H}(t) \cdot D_H(t) + p_{D,V}(t) \cdot D_V(t) - c(t); \quad (2.2)$$

and

$$D_H(t) \leq \Theta_1(c(t)); \quad (2.3)$$

$$D_V(t) \leq \Theta_2(c(t)); \quad (2.4)$$

In the equations provided, $c(t)$ represents the per capita consumption level at time t, while $D_H(t)$ and $D_V(t)$ represent the quantities of data provided by a consumer

[1] To simplify calculation, this paper assumes that the marginal disutility of selling data to two different R&D sectors is the same. In order to distinguish them, the different weights are given to sell data to different sectors. Considering that we could distinguish clearly between the tradeoffs of data in two kinds of innovation, with avoid their interplay, the disutility equation adopts a linearly separable form.

to horizontal and vertical R&D sectors, respectively. The parameter ρ denotes the consumer's discount rate, and γ, which lies within the range $(1, \infty)$, represents the reciprocal of the elasticity of intertemporal substitution of consumption. The parameter σ parameterizes the disutility associated with data leakage, which depends on the quantity of data provided each time. The variables χ_H and χ_V represent the degrees of negative effect on utility when consumers sell data to horizontal and vertical R&D sectors, respectively. Furthermore, $\Theta_1(\cdot)$ and $\Theta_2(\cdot)$ are both increasing exogenous general functions that determine the generating process of data. The specific form of $\Theta_1(\cdot)$ and $\Theta_2(\cdot)$ reflects the constraints imposed on data generation, which can be influenced by factors such as the digital infrastructure, legal framework, and local privacy regulations. In the baseline model, it is assumed that $\Theta_1(c(t))$ and $\Theta_2(c(t))$ are sufficiently large, enabling consumers to have the autonomy to determine the quantity of data they wish to sell based on their preferences and constraints.

In the budget constraint Eq. (2.2), $a(t)$ represents the asset held by a consumer at time t, $r(t)$ represents the interest rate at time t, and $w(t)$ represents the wage for labor at time t. The variables $p_{D,H}(t)$ and $p_{D,V}(t)$ represent the time—t prices of data for horizontal and vertical R&D sectors, respectively. These prices are determined based on the nonrivalry and exclusivity of data. In order to simplify the model, it is assumed that consumers can directly sell the same data to both types of R&D sectors simultaneously, without the presence of competitive data intermediaries. This assumption aligns with previous studies such as Jones et al. (2020) and Cong et al. (2021). The disutility of data leakage caused by selling data is not constant and varies depending on the value of the parameter σ. If σ is larger than 1, the privacy cost associated with selling data will increase. Therefore, the price of data purchased by the R&D sectors is influenced by the quantity of data purchased by each sector. Constraints (2.3) and (2.4) impose limitations on the growth rate of data provision, ensuring that it remains bounded by the corresponding growth rate of consumption. This constraint reflects the idea that data, being by-products of economic activities, cannot exceed a certain proportion of consumption activities.

To obverse the relevant variables for transitional dynamics, we derive the system's evolution in the form of Euler equations from the Hamilton:

$$\frac{\dot{c}(t)}{c(t)} = \frac{r(t)-\rho}{\gamma}; \tag{2.5}$$

$$\frac{\dot{p}_{D,H}(t)}{p_{D,H}(t)} - (\sigma - 1) \cdot \frac{\dot{D}_H(t)}{D_H(t)} = r(t) - \rho; \tag{2.6}$$

$$\frac{\dot{p}_{D,V}(t)}{p_{D,V}(t)} - (\sigma - 1) \cdot \frac{\dot{D}_V(t)}{D_V(t)} = r(t) - \rho; \tag{2.7}$$

2.2.2 The Final Good Producer

A representative final good producer operates within a competitive environment, characterized by a production function:

$$Y(t) = L_E(t)^{\alpha} \cdot \int_0^{N(t)} A(v, t)^{\alpha} \cdot x(v, t)^{1-\alpha} dv; \tag{2.8}$$

In Eq. (2.8), $Y(t)$ represents the gross output, $L_E(t)$ denotes the amount of labor employed in the production of the final goods, $N(t)$ signifies the number of intermediate goods varieties utilized in the final goods production, and $A(v, t)$ represents the productivity parameter associated with the most recent version of intermediate good v at time t. Additionally, $x(v, t)$ refers to the total quantity of the intermediate good of variety v at time t, which can only be utilized in the production of final goods for a single period. The elasticity coefficient of labor in final goods production is denoted as α, and the rental fee for intermediate goods is denoted as $p_x(v, t)$. The first-order conditions derived from the profit maximization of the final goods producer, with respect to both labor employed and the quantity of each intermediate good, are as follows:

$$x(v, t) = \left[\frac{(1-\alpha)}{p_x(v, t)}\right]^{\frac{1}{\alpha}} \cdot A(v, t) \cdot L_E(t); \tag{2.9}$$

$$\alpha \cdot [L_E(t)]^{\alpha-1} \cdot \int_0^{N(t)} A(v, t)^{\alpha} \cdot x(v, t)^{1-\alpha} dv = w(t); \tag{2.10}$$

In Eq. (2.9), the quantity of intermediate good variety v at time t is determined by a combination of the rental fee, productivity parameter, and the amount of labor employed. Equation (2.10) represents the condition where the marginal productivity of labor in the final goods production is equal to the wage rate, denoted as $w(t)$.

2.2.3 Intermediate Producers

The decision-making process of potential intermediate producers in conducting research is not limited, allowing them to determine whether to engage in research activities and the extent of their investment. Successful horizontal innovation grants these producers a monopoly over the intermediate product they have developed. Consequently, the market will witness the emergence of a certain number of monopoly intermediate producers. Conversely, if vertical innovation proves successful, an existing monopoly intermediate producer will be replaced. Until the next instance of vertical innovation occurs, new intermediate producers can continue to enjoy monopoly profits. It is important to note that we assume that once previous innovators exit the market, they are unable to reenter. Therefore, the latest innovator will never face competition from past innovators (Howitt et al., 1998). To address the dynamics of intermediate producers, we employ a backward induction methodology, allowing for a comprehensive analysis of the problem.

2.2.4 Final Good Production Phase

For each monopoly intermediate producer entering the market, the profit obtained from the intermediate good of variety v in a single period, denoted as t is determined by the following profit-maximizing function:

$$\max_{p_x(v,t)}\left[p_x(v,t)\cdot x(v,t)-\psi\cdot x(v,t)\right]; \tag{2.11}$$

In Eq. (2.11), ψ represents the constant marginal cost associated with this production process in the economy.

Substituting Eq. (2.9) into Eq. (2.11) and taking the derivative with respect to $p_x(v,t)$ yields the optimal price for each variety of intermediate goods:

$$p_x(v,t)=\frac{\psi}{1-\alpha}; \tag{2.12}$$

It is evident that the optimal price of intermediate goods, $p_x(v,t)$, is independent of the specific intermediate good variety v and the time period.

Substituting Eqs. (2.12) and (2.9) into Eq. (2.11), we can derive the quantity of intermediate good of variety v:

$$x(v,t)=\frac{(1-\alpha)^{\frac{2}{\alpha}}}{\psi}\cdot A(v,t)\cdot L_E(t); \tag{2.13}$$

By substituting Eq. (2.13) into Eq. (2.11), the maximum profit obtained from the intermediate good of variety v can be expressed as:

$$\pi(v,t)=\frac{(1-\alpha)^{\frac{2}{\alpha}-1}}{\psi^{\frac{1}{\alpha}-1}}\cdot\alpha\cdot A(v,t)\cdot L_E(t); \tag{2.14}$$

Furthermore, the gross output, $Y(t)$, and the wage rate, $w(t)$, can be expressed as:

$$Y(t)=\left[\frac{(1-\alpha)^2}{\psi}\right]^{\frac{1}{\alpha}-1}\cdot L_E(t)\cdot\int_0^{N(t)}A(v,t)dv; \tag{2.15}$$

$$w(t)=\alpha\cdot\left[\frac{(1-\alpha)^2}{\psi}\right]^{\frac{1}{\alpha}-1}\cdot\int_0^{N(t)}A(v,t)dv; \tag{2.16}$$

In Eqs. (2.15) and (2.16), the gross output, $Y(t)$, is determined by the integral over all varieties of intermediate goods, denoted by $N(t)$, and their respective productivity parameter $A(v, t)$. The wage rate, $w(t)$, is a function of the integral over the same range.

2.2.4.1 Vertical Innovation Phase

This paper examines the vertical innovations that result in quality improvements. Vertical R&D sectors are capable of conducting research and development (R&D) activities by utilizing both labor, denoted as $L_V(t)$, and data acquired from consumers, represented as $D_V(t)\cdot L(t)$. The Poisson arrival rate of vertical innovations in any given sector is determined by $\Phi(t) = \mu\cdot\phi(t)$, $\mu > 0$, where μ is a parameter indicating the productivity of vertical R&D, and $\phi(t)$ represents the innovation success rate equation adjusted for productivity in vertical R&D within each sector (Howitt, 1999). The productivity-adjusted innovation success rate equation can be formulated as follows:

$$\frac{L_V(t)^{\beta}\cdot[D_V(t)\cdot L(t)]^{1-\beta}}{N(t)\cdot A^{\max}(t)}; \tag{2.17}$$

Equation (2.17) illustrates that vertical R&D sectors can enhance the success rate of innovation by utilizing a substantial amount of data during the scientific research process. In this equation, the leading-edge productivity parameter, $A^{\max}(t)$, represents the maximum value among all productivity parameters associated with the latest version of intermediate products. The parameter β signifies the contribution of labor in the vertical innovation process. $L_V(t)$ denotes the labor employed in vertical R&D sectors, while $l_V(t)$ represents the fraction of labor allocated to vertical R&D sectors. It is evident that as technology advances and the number of intermediate goods expands, vertical innovation becomes more intricate and challenging.[2]

Upon the successful completion of R&D, a new intermediate producer enters the monopolistic market, replacing the previous producer. The present value of the intermediate good with the leading-edge productivity parameter in a single period, denoted as t, can be calculated using the following expression:

$$V(t) = \int_t^{\infty} e^{-\int_t^{\tau}[r(s)+\Phi(s)]ds}\cdot\tilde{\pi}(\tau)d\tau, \tag{2.18}$$

In Eq. (2.18), $\tilde{\pi}(\tau)$ represents the profit obtained from the intermediate good with the leading-edge productivity parameter in a single period, given by:

$$\tilde{\pi}(t) = \frac{(1-\alpha)^{\frac{2}{\alpha}-1}}{\psi^{\frac{1}{\alpha}-1}}\cdot\alpha\cdot A^{\max}(t)\cdot L_E(t); \tag{2.19}$$

[2] Unlike Jones (1995), intermediate goods not only have spillover effect on horizontal innovation, but also have an inhibition effect vertical innovation.

The present value expression implies that higher investment in R&D leads to a greater success rate of innovation and a higher probability of becoming a monopoly producer of intermediate goods. However, it also implies that a higher success rate of innovation in the next phase results in a shorter cycle of replacement and a lower present value that can be obtained. This concept is rooted in the notion of creative destruction (Aghion et al., 1992).

Vertical R&D sectors determine the optimal allocation of labor, $L_R(t) = l_R(t) \cdot L(t)$, and data, $D_V(t) \cdot L(t)$, to maximize the expected net profit. This decision can be formulated as follows[3]:

$$\max_{D_V(t), l_V(t)} \left\{ \Phi(t) \cdot V(t) - w(t) \cdot L_V(t) - p_{D,V}(t) \cdot D_V(t) \cdot L(t) \right\}; \tag{2.20}$$

The first-order condition gives rise to two free-entry conditions:

$$\frac{\beta \cdot \mu \cdot l_V(t)^{\beta-1} \cdot D_V(t)^{1-\beta} \cdot \tilde{\pi}(t) \cdot [r(t)-n]}{w(t) \cdot [r(t)+\Phi(t)-n]^2 \cdot N(t) \cdot A^{\max}(t)} = 1; \tag{2.21}$$

and

$$\frac{(1-\beta) \cdot \mu \cdot l_V(t)^{\beta} \cdot D_V(t)^{-\beta} \cdot \tilde{\pi}(t) \cdot [r(t)-n]}{p_{D,V}(t) \cdot [r(t)+\Phi(t)-n]^2 \cdot N(t) \cdot A^{\max}(t)} = 1; \tag{2.22}$$

Equations (2.21) and (2.22) represent the two free-entry conditions derived from the first-order condition, which are integral to the decision-making process of vertical R&D sectors.

2.2.4.2 Horizontal Innovation Phase

Horizontal innovations are the result of R&D efforts aimed at creating new intermediate goods. In the horizontal R&D sector, both labor, $L_H(t)$, and data purchased from consumers, $D_H(t) \cdot L(t)$, are employed. The evolution of the aggregate innovation possibility frontier can be described by the following equation:

$$\dot{N}(t) = \frac{\eta \cdot N(t)^{\xi} \cdot (D_H(t) \cdot L(t))^{\theta} \cdot L_H(t)^{1-\theta}}{A^{\max}(t)}; \tag{2.23}$$

This equation can be simplified as:

$$\dot{N}(t) = \frac{\eta \cdot N(t)^{\xi} \cdot l_H(t)^{1-\theta} \cdot D_H(t)^{\theta} \cdot L(t)}{A^{\max}(t)}; \tag{2.24}$$

[3] According to Cong et al. (2021), if data processing cost is considered, the analysis of data transactions will be disrupted. Therefore, we will ignore this cost in the benchmark model.

From Eq. (2.24), we can observe that data can be transformed into digital knowledge in the process of horizontal innovation. Here, $\eta > 0$ is an efficiency term of innovation, $\theta \in (0, 1)$ represents the contribution of data in the horizontal innovation process, and $\xi \in (1, +\infty)$ represents the spillover effect of digital knowledge. $L_H(t)$ denotes the labor employed in the horizontal R&D sectors, and $l_H(t)$ represents the fraction of labor employed in the horizontal R&D sectors. Notably, digital knowledge is created through data spillovers to future periods by creating new varieties (Cong et al., 2021). The larger the leading-edge productivity parameter, the more complex the process of horizontal innovation becomes (Howitt, 1999).

Each horizontal innovation gives rise to a new intermediate product whose productivity parameter is randomly drawn from the distribution of existing intermediate products.

The expected value of a horizontal innovation can be expressed as:

In the decision-making process, horizontal R&D sectors determine the optimal allocation of labor, $L_H(t) = l_H(t) \cdot L(t)$, and data, $D_H(t) \cdot L(t)$, to maximize the expected net profit. This decision can be formulated as follows:

$$\max_{l_H(t), D_H(t)} \left\{ E\left[\frac{A(v,t)}{A^{\max}(t)}\right] \cdot V(t) \cdot N(t) - w(t) \cdot L_H(t) - p_{D,H}(t) \cdot D_H(t) \cdot L(t) \right\}; \quad (2.25)$$

The first-order condition leads to two free-entry conditions:

$$\eta \cdot (1-\theta) \cdot N(t)^{\xi} \cdot l_H(t)^{-\theta} \cdot D_H(t)^{\theta} \cdot V(t) \cdot E\left[\frac{A(v,t)}{A^{\max}(t)}\right] = w(t) \cdot A^{\max}(t); \quad (2.26)$$

and

$$\eta \cdot \theta \cdot N(t)^{\xi} \cdot l_H(t)^{1-\theta} \cdot D_H(t)^{\theta-1} \cdot V(t) \cdot E\left[\frac{A(v,t)}{A^{\max}(t)}\right] = p_{D,H}(t) \cdot A^{\max}(t); \quad (2.27)$$

Equations (2.26) and (2.27) represent the two free-entry conditions derived from the first-order condition, which play a crucial role in the decision-making process of horizontal R&D sectors.

2.2.4.3 Spillovers

The growth in the leading-edge parameter, $A^{\max}(t)$ occurs, due to the knowledge spillovers produced by vertical innovations. $A^{\max}(t)$ always grows at a rate proportional to the aggregate rate of vertical innovations (Caballero et al., 1993). The factor of proportionality, $\frac{\varphi}{N(t)}$, $N(t)$, by the flow of vertical innovations per sector. This relationship can be expressed as:

$$\frac{\dot{A}^{\max}(t)}{A^{\max}(t)} = \varphi \cdot \mu \cdot \Phi(t); \quad (2.28)$$

The distribution of productivity parameters among new intermediate goods mirrors the distribution across existing intermediate goods at time t. The distribution of relative productivity parameters, $b(v,t) = \frac{A(v,t)}{A^{\max}(t)}$, can be described by the following expression (Howitt, 1999)[4]:

In the long term, it follows that:

$$E\left[\frac{A(v,t)}{A^{\max}(t)}\right] = \frac{1}{1+\varphi}; \tag{2.29}$$

Equation (2.29) represents the expected value of the ratio of the productivity parameter of a new intermediate good to the leading-edge parameter in the long term.

2.3 Decentralized Economy on the Balanced Growth Path

In the decentralized economy on the Balanced Growth Path (BGP), an equilibrium is achieved where the evolution of the variable $\{N(t)\}_{t=0}^{\infty}$ is determined by free entry. Intermediate producers optimize their choices of $\{p_x(v,t), D_H(t), D_V(t),$

$L_H(t), L_V(t)\}_{t=0}^{\infty}$ to maximize the discounted value of profits. The evolution of $\{r(t), w(t), p_V(t), p_H(t)\}_{t=0}^{\infty}$ is consistent with market clearing, and the evolution of $\{L_E(t), x(v,t)\}_{t=0}^{\infty}$ is consistent with profit maximization by the final good producer.

The model is solved along the BGP, which assumes that all variables are growing at the same constant rate, denoted as $r(t) = r^*$. The relationships between the variables are as follows:

$$\frac{L_V(t)^{\beta} \cdot [D_V(t) \cdot L(t)]^{1-\beta}}{N(t) \cdot A^{\max}(t)} \to m; \tag{2.30}$$

$$\frac{\dot{D}_H(t)}{D_H(t)} = \frac{\dot{D}_V(t)}{D_V(t)}; \tag{2.31}$$

$$\frac{\dot{D}_H(t)}{D_H(t)} = \frac{1+\xi}{1-\beta-\theta} \cdot \frac{\dot{N}(t)}{N(t)}; \tag{2.32}$$

$$\frac{\dot{y}(t)}{y(t)} = \frac{\dot{c}(t)}{c(t)} = \frac{\dot{A}^{\max}(t)}{\int_0^{N(t)} A(v,t)dv} + \frac{A(v,t)}{\int_0^{N(t)} A(v,t)dv} \cdot \dot{N}(t); \tag{2.33}$$

Equation (2.30) states that on the BGP, the ratio of labor and data in vertical R&D sectors to the aggregate level of labor and the leading-edge productivity parameter tends to a certain value, represented as m in this paper.

[4] More detail can be acquired from the appendix of Howitt's paper (1999).

Equation (2.31) indicates that the growth rate of per capita data provision in horizontal R&D sectors is the same as the growth rate of per capita data provision in vertical R&D sectors.

Equation (2.32) further explains the relationship between the growth rate of per capita data provision and the growth rate of varieties of intermediate goods. On the BGP, it is determined by the parameter values and is given by a specific ratio.

Equation (2.33) decomposes the sources of per capita output growth on the BGP. It reveals that the growth in per capita output can be attributed to two factors: the quality improvements in production achieved by vertical R&D sectors and the growth rate of varieties of intermediate goods in horizontal R&D sectors. These factors contribute to the overall increase in output per capita.

2.3.1 Growth Rate in the Decentralized Economy

PROPOSITION 1. *The economic growth rates of the decentralized economy on the BGP can be expressed as follows*:

$$m = \frac{n}{\mu\cdot\varphi}\cdot\frac{(1+\xi)\cdot(\sigma-\beta)}{(1-\beta-\theta)\cdot(1-\gamma)+(1+\xi)\cdot\left[(\beta-1)\cdot(1-\gamma)+\sigma\right]} > 0; \tag{2.34}$$

$$\frac{\dot{D}_H(t)}{D_H(t)} = \frac{\dot{D}_V(t)}{D_V(t)} = (\mu\cdot\varphi\cdot m-n)\cdot\frac{1+\xi}{\theta+(1-\beta)\cdot\xi} < 0; \tag{2.35}$$

$$\frac{\dot{N}(t)}{N(t)} = (\mu\cdot\varphi\cdot m-n)\cdot\frac{1-\theta-\beta}{\theta+(1-\beta)\cdot\xi} > 0; \tag{2.36}$$

$$l_H^*(t) = \frac{1}{1+\frac{\beta\cdot\theta}{(1-\beta)\cdot(1-\theta)}+\frac{\left[\mu\cdot m\cdot(\gamma\cdot\varphi+1)+\rho-n\right]\cdot[\theta+(1-\beta)\cdot\xi]}{(\mu\cdot\varphi\cdot m-n)\cdot(\theta+\beta-1)\cdot(1-\theta)\cdot(1-\alpha)}}; \tag{2.37}$$

Equation (2.34) represents the expression for m on the BGP, and it can be easily proven that $(\mu\cdot\varphi\cdot m-n) < 0$ is tenable. Equation (2.35) indicates that in the decentralized economy, the per capita data provision of both types of R&D sectors will experience a downward trend, effectively alleviating the problem of consumer privacy disclosure. However, the aggregate data provision can still grow in the long term (similar to Cong et al., 2021).

In Eq. (2.36), it is necessary to assume that $\theta+\beta-1 > 0$.[5] The first partial derivatives of m with respect to key variables are as follows:

$$\frac{\partial m}{\partial\beta} = \frac{(1+\xi)\cdot\sigma\cdot(-1-2\cdot\xi+\gamma\cdot\xi)+(1-\gamma)\cdot(\theta+\xi)}{\{(1-\gamma)\cdot[(\beta-1)\cdot\xi-\theta]+\sigma\cdot(1+\xi)\}^2} < 0, \tag{2.38}$$

[5] Because the inhibition of the leading-edge parameter, $A^{max}(t)$, on the varieties of the intermediate goods expanding. If $\theta+\beta-1<0$, the varieties of the intermediate goods will gradually decrease, implying that the market scale will gradually decrease, which obviously violates the objective law of economics.

$$\frac{\partial m}{\partial \sigma} = \frac{(1+\xi)\cdot[(1-\gamma)\cdot(\beta\cdot\xi-\theta-\xi)+\beta\cdot(1+\xi)]}{\{(1-\gamma)\cdot[(\beta-1)\cdot\xi-\theta]+\sigma\cdot(1+\xi)\}^2} > 0; \tag{2.39}$$

PROPOSITION 2: *The innovation success rate of vertical R&D sectors is influenced by various factors. Specifically, it has a positive relationship with the parameter representing the disutility of data leakage and misuse* σ*, the natural population growth rate n, and a negative relationship with the contribution of labor in vertical innovation* β*, and the elasticity of intertemporal substitution of consumption* γ.

Most of the findings from Proposition 1 are in line with expectations. However, one notable result is the negative effect of the contribution of labor in the process of vertical innovation. This implies that a higher contribution rate of data to the success of innovation leads to a higher success rate. It demonstrates that data integration into vertical innovation processes can reduce uncertainty and improve the likelihood of success. There are two main reasons why data utilization can enhance the success rate of innovation. Firstly, according to Eq. (2.16), wages increase with the expansion of intermediate goods varieties and improvements in productivity parameters. Consequently, labor costs continue to rise. However, Eq. (2.7) shows that the price of data is dependent on per capita data usage. If data remains unused, the cost of utilizing it would be relatively low. Therefore, from a cost perspective, incorporating data can significantly reduce innovation costs, thereby increasing the monopoly profits of intermediate producers. Secondly, Eq. (2.14) reveals that monopoly profits are contingent on the labor used in final goods production. Consequently, if vertical R&D sectors replace some labor with data, there will be an increase in labor allocated to final goods production, resulting in improved monopoly profits. Hence, when data utilized in the innovation process offers greater revenue incentives, the success rate of innovation is substantially enhanced.

In contrast to the conclusion drawn by Howitt and Aghion (1998), data differs fundamentally from physical capital. While physical capital incurs production costs that affect the interest rate and consequently impact the monopoly profits of intermediate producers, data, as a byproduct of consumption, only entails the usage cost associated with privacy concerns and lacks production costs. Although both factors can enhance the success rate of innovation when incorporated into the innovation process, their mechanisms are distinct.

The innovation success rate is positively influenced by the parameter representing the disutility of data leakage and misuse. This suggests that in equilibrium, consumers require a higher success rate of innovation to compensate for the increased disutility resulting from heightened privacy concerns. Furthermore, the success rate of innovation is positively associated with the natural population growth rate. This implies that with a larger population, there is an increase in both the amount of labor involved in the innovation process and the overall availability of data for innovation purposes. Conversely, the success rate of innovation is negatively correlated with the elasticity of intertemporal substitution of consumption. This indicates that if individuals prefer substituting current consumption with future consumption, the amount of data accessible to vertical R&D sectors will be diminished, leading to a lower success rate of innovation.

2.4 Social Planner's Economy on the Balanced Growth Path

Subsequently, we proceed to derive the growth rate of key variables allocated under socially optimal allocations on the Balanced Growth Path (BGP). This serves as a benchmark for comparing the outcomes with those observed in the decentralized economy, given that the equilibrium in the decentralized economy is not socially optimal. In a social planner's economy, the objective of the social planner is to maximize the utility of representative consumers, subject to resource constraints. This implies that the aggregate net output, denoted as $\tilde{Y}(t)$, equals the aggregate total output minus the total cost of intermediate goods, and can be expressed as:

$$\max_{x(v,t)} \tilde{Y}(t) = \left\{ L_E(t)^{\alpha} \cdot \int_0^{N(t)} A(v,t)^{\alpha} \cdot x(v,t)^{1-\alpha} dv - \int_0^{N(t)} \psi \cdot x(v,t) dv \right\}; \tag{2.40}$$

The social planner optimizes the aggregate net output by selecting the optimal amount of intermediate goods input, denoted as $x^*(v,t)$, which can be calculated as:

$$x^*(v,t) = \left(\frac{1-\alpha}{\psi}\right)^{\frac{1}{\alpha}} \cdot L_E(t) \cdot A(v,t); \tag{2.41}$$

Consequently, the aggregate net output is given by:

$$\tilde{Y}(t) = \alpha \cdot \left(\frac{\psi}{1-\alpha}\right)^{1-\frac{1}{\alpha}} \cdot L_E(t) \cdot \int_0^{N(t)} A(v,t) dv; \tag{2.42}$$

As is widely recognized, the aggregate consumption, $C(t) = c(t) \cdot L(t)$, is equivalent to the aggregate net output. Thus, the average consumption can be represented as:

$$c(t) = \alpha \cdot \Delta \cdot l_E(t) \cdot \int_0^{N(t)} A(v,t) dv, \textit{ where } \Delta = \left(\frac{\psi}{1-\alpha}\right)^{1-\frac{1}{\alpha}}; \tag{2.43}$$

In comparison to the aggregate net output in the decentralized economy (2.15), the aggregate net output in the social planner's economy is consistently higher when labor and technology are held at the same level. This disparity can be attributed to the monopoly power prevailing in the decentralized economy.

The optimization problem faced by the social planner can be described as follows:

$$\max_{c(t), D_H(t), D_V(t)} \int_0^{\infty} e^{-(\rho-n)\cdot t} \left[\frac{c(t)^{1-\gamma}-1}{1-\gamma} - \chi_H \cdot D_H(t)^{\sigma} - \chi_V \cdot D_V(t)^{\sigma} \right] dt; \tag{2.44}$$

Subject to the following constraints:

$$\dot{N}(t) = \frac{\eta \cdot N(t)^{\xi} \cdot l_H(t)^{1-\theta} \cdot D_H(t)^{\theta} \cdot L(t)}{A^{\max}(t)}; \tag{2.45}$$

$$\dot{A}^{\max}(t) = \frac{\mu \cdot \varphi \cdot l_V(t)^{\beta} \cdot D_H(t)^{1-\beta} \cdot L(t)}{N(t)}; \tag{2.46}$$

$$c(t) = \alpha \cdot \Delta \cdot l_E(t) \cdot \int_0^{N(t)} A(v, t)dv; \tag{2.47}$$

$$l_H(t) + l_V(t) + l_E(t) = 1; \tag{2.48}$$

Here, Eq. (2.45) represents the horizontal innovation possibility frontier, Eq. (2.46) represents the vertical innovation possibility frontier, Eq. (2.47) represents the resource constraint, and Eq. (2.48) signifies labor market equilibrium. To solve this problem, a current-value Hamiltonian equation can be defined as:

$$\begin{aligned} G = & \frac{c(t)^{1-\gamma} - 1}{1-\gamma} - \chi_H \cdot D_H(t)^{\sigma} - \chi_V \cdot D_V(t)^{\sigma} \\ & + \kappa(t) \cdot \left[\alpha \cdot \Delta \cdot l_E(t) \cdot \int_0^{N(t)} A(v, t)dv - c(t)\right] \\ & + \omega(t) \cdot \frac{\eta \cdot N(t)^{\xi} \cdot l_H(t)^{1-\theta} \cdot D_H(t)^{\theta} \cdot L(t)}{A^{\max}(t)} \\ & + \varepsilon(t) \cdot \frac{\mu \cdot \varphi \cdot l_V(t)^{\beta} \cdot D_H(t)^{1-\beta} \cdot L(t)}{N(t)}, \end{aligned} \tag{2.49}$$

Here, $\kappa(t)$, $\omega(t)$ and $\varepsilon(t)$ represent the shadow prices corresponding to constraints (2.49), (2.51), and (2.52), respectively. The first-order conditions are derived with respect to $c(t), D_H(t), D_V(t), l_H(t), l_V(t), A^{\max}(t), N(t)$.

2.4.1 Growth Rate in the Social Planner's Economy

In the analysis of the social planner's economy on the Balanced Growth Path (BGP), the paper examines the relationship between key variables. The following relationships are established:

$$\frac{l_V(t)^{\beta} \cdot D_V(t)^{1-\beta} \cdot L(t)}{N(t) \cdot A^{\max}(t)} \to M; \tag{2.50}$$

$$\frac{\dot{D}_H(t)}{D_H(t)} = \frac{\dot{D}_V(t)}{D_V(t)}; \tag{2.51}$$

$$\frac{\dot{N}(t)}{N(t)} = \frac{1-\beta-\theta}{\xi} \cdot \frac{\dot{D}_H(t)}{D_H(t)}; \tag{2.52}$$

$$\frac{\dot{c}(t)}{c(t)} = \frac{\sigma}{1-\gamma} \cdot \frac{\dot{D}_H(t)}{D_H(t)}; \tag{2.53}$$

Equation (2.50) indicates that on the BGP, the success rate of the vertical innovation approaches a specific value denoted as M. Equations (2.51) and (2.52) demonstrate that on the BGP, the growth rate of per capita data provision is the same for both types of R&D sectors, and it relates the growth rate of per capita data provision to the growth rate of varieties of intermediate goods. Equation (2.53) reveals that on the BGP, the growth rate of per capita consumption is determined by the growth rate of per capita data provision.

PROPOSITION 4. *The economic growth rates of the social planner's economy on the BGP can be expressed as follows:*

$$M = \frac{n}{\mu \cdot \varphi} \cdot \frac{\sigma \cdot \xi}{\sigma \cdot \xi - (1-\gamma) \cdot [(1-\beta) \cdot (\xi - 1) + \theta]} > 0; \tag{2.54}$$

$$\frac{\dot{N}(t)}{N(t)} = n \cdot \frac{(1-\gamma) \cdot (1-\beta-\theta)}{\sigma \cdot \xi - (1-\gamma) \cdot [(1-\beta) \cdot (\xi - 1) + \theta]} > 0; \tag{2.55}$$

$$\frac{\dot{D}_H(t)}{D_H(t)} = \frac{\dot{D}_V(t)}{D_V(t)} = n \cdot \frac{(1-\gamma) \cdot \xi}{\sigma \cdot \xi - (1-\gamma) \cdot [(1-\beta) \cdot (\xi - 1) + \theta]} < 0; \tag{2.56}$$

$$l^*_{H,s}(t) = \frac{1-\theta}{\frac{(1+\beta) \cdot \theta}{(1-\beta)} + \frac{(1-\sigma-\beta) \cdot n \cdot (1-\gamma) \cdot \xi + \rho \cdot \Lambda}{n \cdot (1-\gamma) \cdot (1-\theta-\beta)} - (\theta + \xi)}, \tag{2.57}$$

where $\Lambda = \sigma \cdot \xi - (1-\gamma) \cdot [(1-\beta) \cdot (\xi - 1) + \theta]$;

According to Eq. (2.59), it is evident that $\frac{\partial M}{\partial \beta} < 0$ holds, indicating that in the social planner's economy, a higher success rate of innovation is achieved with a greater contribution of data in the vertical innovation process. This is primarily because fewer labor resources are employed in the R&D sectors, allowing for more labor in the final goods production sector and a looser resource constraint, as indicated by Eq. (2.14). On the other hand, Eq. (2.56) demonstrates that in the social planner's economy, the per capita data provision in both types of R&D sectors continues to decline, indicating that the issue of consumer privacy disclosure does not deteriorate over time.

2.4.2 Misallocation in the Decentralized Economy

In this section, we examine the misallocation of resources in a decentralized economy. By using standard values from the existing literature, with $n = 0.02, \gamma = 2.5, \sigma = 3, \theta = 0.5$, and$\xi = 0.85$, as well as reasonable discretionary values, Fig. 2.1 illustrates the difference between the success rate of vertical innovation in two cases, as per Eqs. (2.35) and (2.54). The observed difference varies with the contribution of labor in the process of vertical innovation.

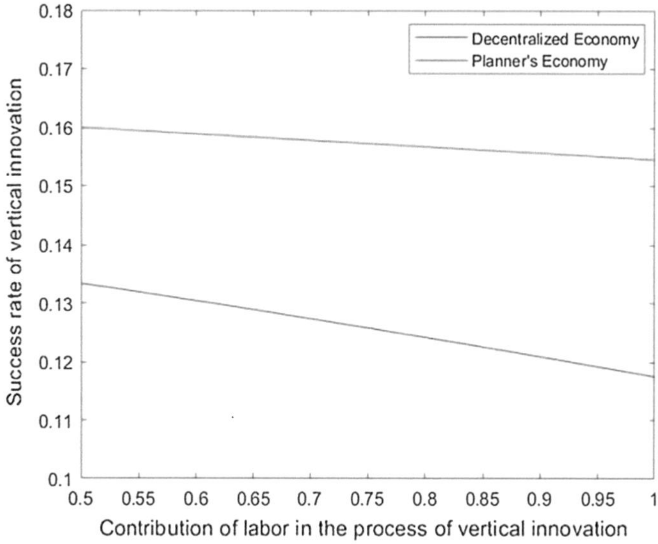

Fig. 2.1 Success rate of the vertical innovation in both types of economies

Similarly, utilizing $n = 0.02, \gamma = 2.5$ (standard values from existing literature), $\sigma = 3, \beta = 0.7, \xi = 0.85$ (reasonable discretionary values), Fig. 2.2 displays the difference between the growth rate of varieties of intermediate goods in the two cases, according to Eqs. (2.36) and (2.55). This observed difference varies with the contribution of data in the process of horizontal innovation.

As depicted in Figs. 2.1 and 2.2, both the success rate of vertical innovation and the growth rate of varieties of intermediate goods in the social planner's economy surpass those in the decentralized economy. Intuitively, due to the inherent competition and lack of coordination between the two types of research and development (R&D) sectors, each sector independently maximizes its own profits in the decentralized economy, resulting in negative externalities between them. Conversely, in the social planner's economy, the R&D intensity of both sectors is determined by the maximization of total utility, effectively mitigating the negative externalities.

To further investigate the misallocation within the decentralized economy, this paper examines the differences in the ratio of labor employed in R&D sectors and the growth rate of data provision. By employing standard values ($n = 0.02, \gamma = 2.5, \rho = 0.03, \alpha = \frac{2}{3}, \beta = 0.7, \theta = 0.5, \xi = 0.85, \mu = 0.1$, and$\varphi = 10$) from the existing literature, Fig. 2.3 presents the difference between the ratios of labor employed in horizontal R&D sectors in the two cases, as per Eqs. (2.37) and (2.57). The observed difference varies with the disutility effect of data. Notably, since the ratio of labor employed in vertical R&D sectors is the same proportion in both economies on the balanced growth path (BGP), our analysis focuses solely on the ratio of labor employed in horizontal R&D sectors.

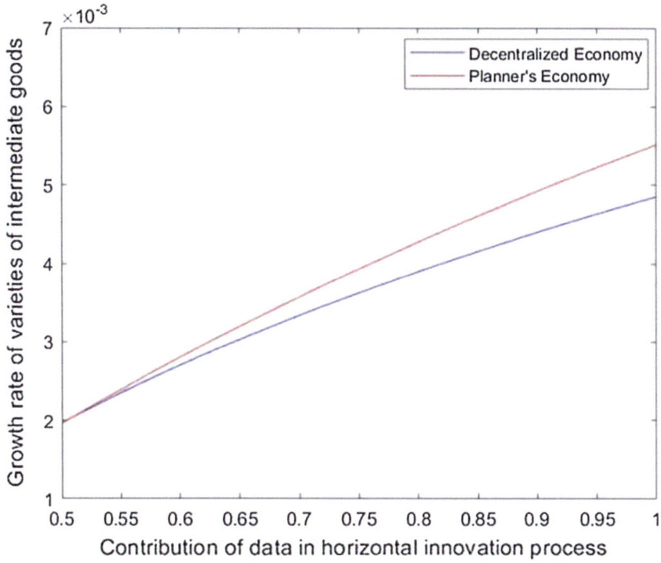

Fig. 2.2 Growth rate of varieties of intermediate goods in both types of economies

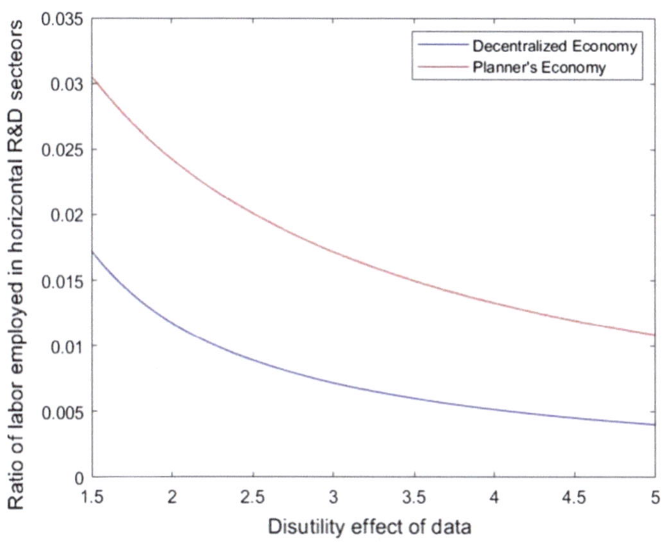

Fig. 2.3 Ratio of labor employed in horizontal R&D sectors in both types of economies

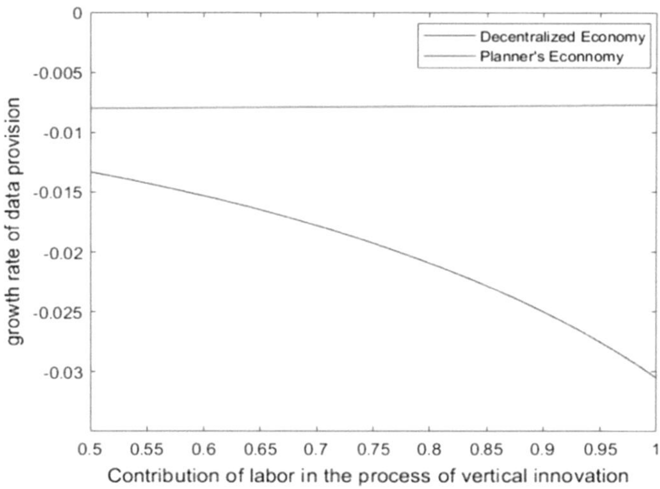

Fig. 2.4 Growth ratio of data provision in R&D sectors in both types of economies

With $n = 0.02, \gamma = 2.5, \rho = 0.03, \alpha = 0.67$ taking on standard values from the existing literature, as well as $\sigma = 3, \theta = 0.5, \xi = 0.85, \mu = 0.1, \varphi = 10$ as reasonable discretionary values, Fig. 2.4 is presented to analyze the difference in the growth rate of data provision employed in R&D sectors between the two cases, as per Eqs. (2.35) and (2.56). The observed difference varies with the contribution of labor in the vertical innovation.

Notably, Fig. 2.3 illustrates that on the balanced growth path (BGP), the ratio of labor employed in horizontal R&D sectors in the decentralized economy is consistently lower than that in the social planner's economy, regardless of the disutility effect of data. This outcome arises due to the high prices set by monopoly intermediate producers for their intermediate goods, which prompts final goods producers to substitute labor for some intermediate goods. Consequently, there is an undersupply of labor employed in R&D sectors, aligning with the findings of Jones (1995).

Furthermore, Fig. 2.4 demonstrates that on the BGP, the growth ratio of data provision in R&D sectors is consistently lower in the decentralized economy compared to the social planner's economy, regardless of the contribution of labor in the process of vertical innovation. This discrepancy primarily arises because, in the decentralized economy, R&D sectors need to purchase data using financial resources instead of receiving direct allocations for innovation. Moreover, according to Eqs. (2.6) and (2.7), the price of data is positively influenced by data provision and per capita consumption, indicating that the price of data introduces distortions in data provision. Consequently, on the BGP, both types of R&D sectors employ less labor and data in the decentralized economy. There are two underlying reasons for this, which imply that the R&D intensity in the decentralized economy is lower compared to the planned economy.

2.5 Data Ownership: Innovators Versus Consumers

In the benchmark model, consumers possess ownership of their data, allowing them to enhance their utility by selling the data. However, per capita data usage gradually declines on the balanced growth path (BGP) due to privacy concerns among consumers. In this chapter, we examine the growth rate of the digital economy and data usage on the BGP when innovators assume ownership of data.

When innovators own the data, they no longer need to compensate consumers. To determine the amount of data usage, we introduce a data processing cost for innovators. Consequently, the profit maximization problem for the vertical R&D sector becomes:

$$\max_{D_V(t),l_V(t)} \left\{\Phi(t)\cdot V(t) - w(t)\cdot L_V(t) - [D_V(t)\cdot L(t)]^{\Gamma 1}\right\}; \tag{2.58}$$

Likewise, the profit maximization problem for the horizontal R&D sector becomes:

$$\max_{l_H(t),D_H(t)} \left\{E\left[\frac{A(v,t)}{A^{\max}(t)}\right]\cdot V(t)\cdot N(t) - w(t)\cdot L_H(t) - [D_H(t)\cdot L(t)]^{\Gamma 2}\right\}; \tag{2.59}$$

Here, $\Gamma 1$ parameterizes the processing cost of data for the vertical sectors, which depends on the quantity of data usage. Similarly, $\Gamma 2$ parameterizes the processing cost of data for the horizontal sectors, also contingent on the quantity of data usage.

Consequently, Eqs. (2.22) and (2.27) are modified as follows[6]:

$$\frac{(1-\beta)\cdot\mu\cdot l_V(t)^{\beta}\cdot D_V(t)^{1-\beta-\Gamma 1}\cdot\tilde{\pi}(t)\cdot L(t)^{1-\Gamma 1}\cdot[r(t)-n]}{\Gamma 1\cdot[r(t)+\Phi(t)-n]^2\cdot N(t)\cdot A^{\max}(t)} = 1; \tag{2.60}$$

$$\eta\cdot\theta\cdot N(t)^{\xi}\cdot l_H(t)^{1-\theta}\cdot D_H(t)^{\theta-\Gamma 2}\cdot V(t)\cdot L(t)^{1-\Gamma 2}\cdot E\left[\frac{A(v,t)}{A^{\max}(t)}\right] = \Gamma 2\cdot A^{\max}(t); \tag{2.61}$$

Moreover, the consumers' budget constraint (2.2) becomes:

$$\dot{a}(t) = (r(t)-n)\cdot a(t) + w(t) - c(t); \tag{2.62}$$

Combining Eqs. (2.21), (2.26), (2.28), (2.60), and (2.61), we derive the following results:

[6] Obviously, $\Gamma 1$ and $\Gamma 2$ should be greater than 2. On one hand, $N(t)$ and $A^{max}(t)$ need to ensure positive growth rates on the BGP, and on the other hand, the sufficient convexity of processing cost is quite reasonable.

$$\frac{\dot{N}(t)}{N(t)} = \frac{n\cdot(\Gamma2-\theta)\cdot(\Gamma1-2)\cdot(1-\beta)}{1-\beta+(1+\xi)\cdot(\beta+\Gamma1-1)} > 0; \tag{2.63}$$

$$\frac{\dot{A}^{\max}(t)}{A^{\max}(t)} = \frac{-n\cdot[\xi\cdot\Gamma1\cdot\Gamma2\cdot(2-\Gamma1)+\Gamma1(\Gamma2-\theta)-\Gamma2\cdot\xi\cdot(1-\Gamma1)\cdot(\beta+\Gamma1-1)]}{1-\beta+(1+\xi)\cdot(\beta+\Gamma1-1)} > 0; \tag{2.64}$$

$$\frac{\dot{D}_H(t)}{D_H(t)} = \frac{n\cdot\xi\cdot(1-\beta)\cdot(2-\Gamma2)}{1-\beta+(1+\xi)\cdot(\beta+\Gamma1-1)} > 0; \tag{2.65}$$

$$\frac{\dot{D}_V(t)}{D_V(t)} = \frac{n\cdot(2-\Gamma1)\cdot[\Gamma2\cdot(1+\xi)-\theta]}{1-\beta+(1+\xi)\cdot(\beta+\Gamma1-1)} > 0; \tag{2.66}$$

Consequently, if innovators have ownership of data, both of them will use more data to maximize their profits on the BGP, irrespective of consumers' privacy concerns. This finding deviates from the conclusion of the baseline model. Even if intermediate goods (digital knowledge) exhibit dynamic non-rivalry and the data processing cost is convex, the quantity of data usage continues to increase. Intuitively, as the marginal contribution of data to innovation diminishes, innovators need to utilize more data to ensure maximum profit. Thus, it becomes evident that only when data belongs to consumers, can privacy concerns be adequately addressed, preventing them from becoming increasingly severe in the long run.[7]

2.6 The Role of Human Capital

In the previous discussion, we identified a significant issue in the development of the digital economy, namely the conflicting relationship between economic growth and the quantity of data usage. However, in the era of the digital economy, the rapid advancement of digital technology has had a positive impact on the dissemination and preservation of digital knowledge (Xie & Yang, 2022). This, in turn, generates a notable positive externality effect on the accumulation of human capital, offering a potential solution to address both economic growth and privacy concerns simultaneously.

Drawing from the work of Lucas (1988) and Wu and Zhang (2022), the cumulative growth equation for human capital for each worker can be represented as follows:

$$\dot{h}(t) = h(t)^{\delta} \cdot N(t)^{\lambda}; \tag{2.67}$$

Here, $\delta \in (0, 1)$ represents the coefficient of workers' self-learning ability. It signifies that the agents with stronger self-learning abilities experience a faster cumulative growth rate of human capital, assuming they spend the same amount of time on learning. On the other hand, $\lambda \in (0, 1)$ denotes the coefficient of digital knowledge in

[7] Cong et al. (2021) mentioned that data create knowledge spillovers to future periods by creating new intermediate goods, which is namely dynamic nonrivalry.

promoting the accumulation of human capital. It represents the quality of local digital infrastructure and digital technology, indicating that better digital infrastructure and technology contribute to a faster cumulative growth rate of human capital under the condition of the same learning time. Clearly, the growth of human capital is influenced by both workers' self-learning ability and the digital knowledge generated by the horizontal R&D sectors.

In order to examine the role of human capital in R&D, we now consider a disaggregated model based on the benchmark model. The consumer's budget constraint (2.2) is modified as follows:

$$\begin{aligned}\dot{a}(t) = (r(t) - n) \cdot a(t) + w(t) \cdot h(t) + p_{D,H}(t) \cdot D_H(t) \\ + p_{D,V}(t) \cdot D_V(t) - c(t);\end{aligned} \tag{2.68}$$

Additionally, the production function (2.8) of the representative final goods producer becomes:

$$Y(t) = [u(t) \cdot h(t) \cdot L_E(t)]^{\alpha} \cdot \int_0^{N(t)} A(v,t)^{\alpha} \cdot x(v,t)^{1-\alpha} dv; \tag{2.69}$$

The profit optimization problem (2.20) of the vertical R&D sectors is modified as:

$$\max_{D_V(t), l_V(t)} \left\{ \Phi(t) \cdot V(t) - h(t) \cdot w(t) \cdot L_V(t) - p_{D,V}(t) \cdot D_V(t) \cdot L(t) \right\}; \tag{2.70}$$

Similarly, the profit optimization problem (2.25) of the horizontal R&D sectors becomes:

$$\max_{l_H(t), D_H(t)} \left\{ \begin{array}{c} E\left[\frac{A(v,t)}{A^{\max}(t)}\right] \cdot V(t) \cdot \dot{N}(t) - h(t) \cdot w(t) \cdot L_H(t) \\ - p_{D,H}(t) \cdot D_H(t) \cdot L(t) \end{array} \right\}; \tag{2.71}$$

By following the same optimization process as in the baseline model, we can derive the growth rates of various variables under BGP. The growth rate of the success rate of vertical innovation in the two cases can be obtained as:

$$m' = \frac{n}{\mu \cdot \varphi} \cdot \frac{(1-\delta)\cdot(1+\xi)\cdot(\sigma-\beta)+\lambda\cdot(\beta+\theta-1)\cdot(1+\beta-\gamma-\sigma)}{Q+K}, \tag{2.72}$$

where $Q = (\beta + \theta - 1)\left[\lambda(2 - \sigma - 2\gamma) - (1 - \delta)(1 - \gamma)\right]$,
and $K = (1 - \delta)(1 + \xi)\left[(\beta - 1)(1 - \gamma) + \sigma\right]$;

$$\frac{\dot{D}_H(t)}{D_H(t)} = \frac{\dot{D}_V(t)}{D_V(t)} = \frac{(\mu\cdot\varphi\cdot m-n)\cdot[\lambda\cdot(\beta+\theta-1)-(1+\xi)\cdot(1-\delta)]}{(\lambda+\delta-1)\cdot(\beta+\theta-1)-(1+\xi)\cdot(1-\beta)\cdot(1-\delta)}; \tag{2.73}$$

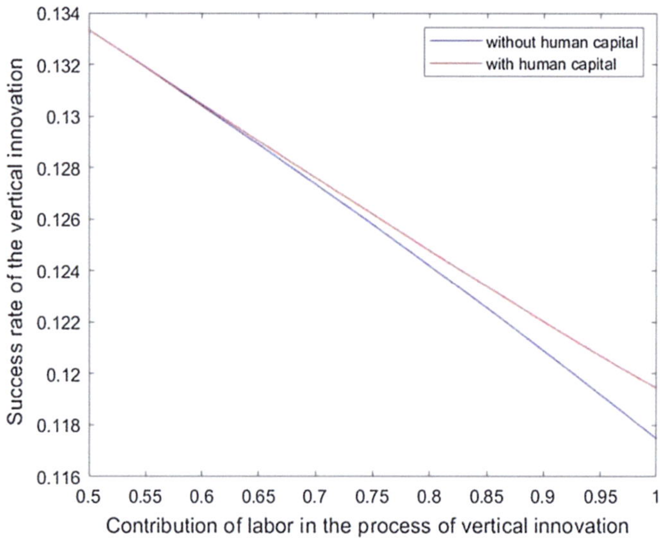

Fig. 2.5 Success rate of the vertical innovation with (without) human capital

$$\frac{\dot{N}(t)}{N(t)} = \frac{(\mu\cdot\varphi\cdot m-n)\cdot[(\beta+\theta-1)\cdot(1-\delta)]}{(\lambda+\delta-1)\cdot(\beta+\theta-1)-(1+\xi)\cdot(1-\beta)\cdot(1-\delta)}; \tag{2.74}$$

Using the reasonable values ($n = 0.02, \gamma = 2.5, \sigma = 3, \theta = 0.5, \xi = 0.85, \lambda = 0.3, \delta = 0.8$) from existing literature, Fig. 2.5 illustrates the difference between the success rates of vertical innovation in the two cases according to Eq. (2.34) and (2.72). The difference varies with the contribution of labor in the process of vertical innovation.

Clearly, when considering human capital, the success rate of vertical innovation is higher compared to the case without human capital, given the same contribution of labor in the innovation process. Furthermore, even with the accumulation of human capital, the data used in the innovation process can still enhance the success rate of innovation. Unlike the conclusion drawn by Zeng (2003), we highlights that the accumulation of human capital relies on the positive externality of digital knowledge rather than physical capital.

Digital knowledge plays a crucial role in promoting human capital due to its vertical nonrivalry, which means that its utilization in the production process and data in the innovation process does not lead to their depletion. Thus, data can still improve the success rate of vertical innovation even when human capital is accumulated.

The first partial derivative of m with respect to λ (the coefficient of digital knowledge) is:

$$\frac{\partial m}{\partial \lambda} = \frac{n}{\mu \cdot \varphi} \cdot \left\{ \begin{array}{c} \frac{-(\beta+\theta-1)^2(1+\beta-\gamma-\sigma)(1-\delta)(1-\gamma)}{(Q+K)^2} \\ +\frac{K-(\beta+\theta-1)(2-\sigma-2\gamma)(1-\delta)(1+\xi)(\sigma-\beta)}{(Q+K)^2} \end{array} \right\} > 0; \quad (2.75)$$

This derivative indicates that the success rate of vertical innovation is positively influenced by the coefficient of digital knowledge for promoting the accumulation of human capital. Therefore, a better digital infrastructure and digital technology will result in a higher the success rate of vertical innovation.

Using the reasonable values ($n = 0.02, \gamma = 2.5, \sigma = 3, \theta = 0.5, \xi = 0.85, \lambda = 0.3, \delta = 0.8$) from existing literature, Fig. 2.6 illustrates how parameters related to human capital affect the growth rate of per capita data provision according to Eq. (2.75).

As depicted in Fig. 2.6, the growth rate of per capita data provision is negatively influenced by the coefficient of digital knowledge for promoting the accumulation of human capital. Essentially, the promotion of digital knowledge on human capital can be seen as another way of utilizing past data. This implies that the more effectively historical data is utilized, the higher the labor productivity, and the lower the current demand for data. Consequently, this approach effectively mitigates the issues of data leakage and misuse.

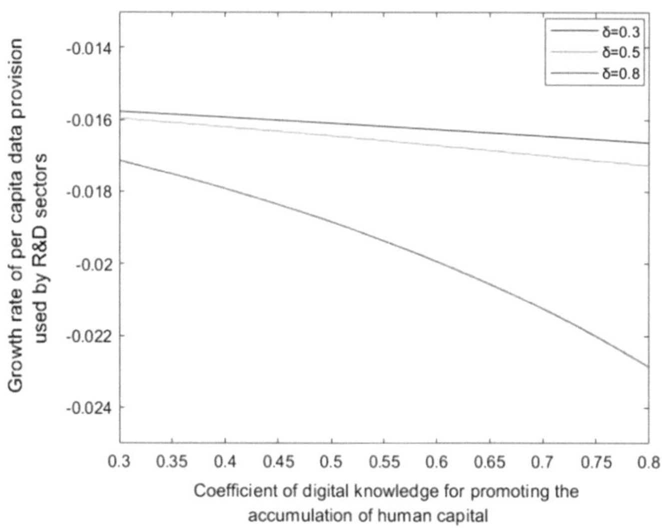

Fig. 2.6 Relationship between human capital's parameters and the growth rate of per capita data provision

2.7 Transitional Dynamics: Numerical Analysis

In the preceding sections, the analysis revealed that the development of the digital economy leads to a decline in data usage in two types of R&D sectors, indicating a gradual easing of concerns regarding data privacy as regulations and digital infrastructure become less restrictive. This section focuses on examining the transitional dynamics of the digital economy from the initial state to the balanced growth path (BGP). Additionally, considering the limited provision of data for vertical and horizontal innovation, we explore the transitional dynamics of the digital economy in contrast to the benchmark model.

2.7.1 *Methodology and Calibration*

To facilitate tractability, this paper employs a numerical method based on the social planner's economy, following a similar approach to Jones (2016). Instead of undertaking formal calibration to replicate the circumstances of a specific country, this analysis aims to demonstrate the basic transitional dynamics achievable within the theoretical framework.[8] By deriving the first-order conditions with respect to variables such as $c(t), D_H(t), D_V(t), l_H(t), l_V(t), A^{\max}(t), N(t)$ from Eq. (2.49) in Sect. 2.4, the dynamical systems can be expressed as a set of differential equations.[9] Since $l_H(t), l_V(t), A^{\max}(t), N(t)$ are all state variable, this paper sets their initial values to a sufficiently small ε to drive economic growth.[10]

Table 2.1 provides a summary of the parametrization choices made in this study. Based on estimates from Antras (2004), the elasticity of substitution falls within the range of approximately 0.6 to 0.8. Therefore, we set the contribution of labor in final goods production α to 2/3. Considering estimates from Vissing-Jørgensen (2002), which suggest that the elasticity of intertemporal substitution (EIS) ranges from 0.3 to 0.4, we select the reciprocal of EIS γ as 2.5. Drawing from estimates in Krupka and Stephens (2013), the subjective discount factor ρ is set at 0.025. Population growth is estimated at around 1 percent per year according to Jones (2020), and the growth rate of R&D labor in developed economies is approximately 4 percent. Hence, we

[8] Due to the inability to precisely calibrate some parameters, this article will use the parameters from previous articles for numerical simulation. On the one hand, it can help us better understand the evolution process of this economy, and on the other hand, it can be compared with the results of previous articles.

[9] Using these differential equations in Sect. 2.4, we could obtain the dynamical system of all variables, which could help us understand the transition dynamics of each variable from initial state to steady state.

[10] Here, ε takes the value of 0.0001. Because it is small enough, we could approximate that the growth rate of digital economy starts at zero.

Table 2.1 Parameters for studying transitional dynamics

Variable	Meaning	Value	Source
α	Contribution of labor in final good production	2/3	Antras, 2004
γ	Reciprocal of elasticity of intertemporal substitution	2.5	Vissing-Jørgensen, 2002
ρ	Subjective discount factor	0.025	Krupka and Stephens, 2013
ξ	Spillover effect of knowledge in horizontal innovation	0.85	Cong et al., 2021
θ	Contribution of data in horizontal innovation	0.5	Cong et al., 2021
β	Contribution of labor in vertical innovation	0.7	Discretionary
n	Population growth rate	0.02	Jones, 2020
η	Efficiency term in horizontal innovation	1	Jones, 1995
σ	Severity of consumers' privacy concern	1.8	Cong et al., 2021
μ	Productivity of vertical innovation	10	Caballero et al., 1993
Φ	Marginal impact of vertical innovation on the stock of public knowledge	0.1	Caballero et al., 1993

choose the value n to be 0.02. Considering estimates from Caballero et al. (1993), the productivity of vertical innovation μ is chosen as 10, and the marginal impact of vertical innovation on the stock of public knowledge φ as 0.1.

Because they could not be accurately estimated, the following parameter values are selected from Jones (1995) and Cong et al. (2021): the contribution of data in horizontal innovation θ as 0.5, the spillover effect of knowledge in horizontal innovation ξ as 0.85, the efficiency term in horizontal innovation η as 1, and the severity of consumers' privacy concern σ as 1.8. To meet the requirement $\theta + \beta\text{-}1 > 0$, the contribution of labor in vertical innovation β is set at 0.7.

In the forthcoming figures, we examine the potential impact on the economy when the quantity of data available to either of the R&D sectors is limited.[11] To incorporate this constraint, we reformulate Eqs. (2.3) and (2.4) as Eqs. (2.76) and (2.77) respectively. To enforce the constraint on data provision for each R&D sector, we set the values of s_1 or s_2 as 0.01. This ensures that the provision of data used by the respective sectors adheres to the constraint. Conversely, if we do not intend to impose a constraint on the data provision used by the R&D sectors, we set the values of s_1 and s_2 as 100, rendering the constraint (2.3) or (2.4) ineffective.

[11] Since this is a numerical simulation, the time period does not have realistic meaning, such as one year or one month. In reality, data has been a key factor in business (or product) innovation for decades, but it has not been fully utilized yet. There are grounds to believe that the digital economy in a period of transition from an initial state to a steady state. Therefore, we could analyze the impact of data restrictions on economic growth by comparing the time required for the economy to enter a steady state under different circumstances.

$$\frac{\dot{D_H}(t)}{D_H(t)} \leq \frac{\dot{c}(t)}{c(t)} + s_1; \tag{2.76}$$

$$\frac{\dot{D_V}(t)}{D_V(t)} \leq \frac{\dot{c}(t)}{c(t)} + s_2; \tag{2.77}$$

Equation (2.76) states that the growth rate of $\frac{\dot{D_H}(t)}{D_H(t)}$ should not exceed the growth rate of $\frac{\dot{c}(t)}{c(t)} + s_1$, while Eq. (2.77) imposes a similar constraint for $\frac{\dot{D_V}(t)}{D_V(t)}$ compared to $\frac{\dot{c}(t)}{c(t)} + s_2$.

2.7.2 *Results and Discussions*

In Panel (a) of Fig. 2.7, the paper reveals that in the absence of constraints, different types of innovations play distinct roles during different periods of economic growth. In the early stage, vertical innovation assumes greater significance due to the limited availability of intermediate goods varieties. However, as the number of intermediate goods varieties gradually increases, horizontal innovation becomes more crucial in the later stage. In comparison to the findings of Cong et al. (2021), by placing greater emphasis on vertical innovation, this economy achieves a higher economic growth rate along the transitional path in the long run.

Panel (b) of Fig. 2.7, as per Eq. (2.6), illustrates the performance of the two types of innovations during different stages of economic growth when a constraint is imposed on horizontal innovation. The constraint implies insufficient data usage in the horizontal R&D sectors. It is evident that there is more pronounced fluctuation during the early period of economic development. Moreover, an economy constrained by horizontal innovation requires additional time to reach the balanced growth path (BGP). Intuitively, when the data usage in horizontal R&D sectors is inadequate, the rate at which labor moves away from final goods production slows down. This can be observed in both Panel (a) and (b) of Fig. 2.8, similar to the findings of Cong et al. (2021). The insufficient data provision and labor in horizontal R&D sectors result in a lack of driving force for horizontal innovation. Consequently, vertical innovation assumes a more prominent role in the later stage. However, as per capita consumption increases and the constraint on data usage becomes more significant, the speed of intermediate goods variety expansion accelerates. The impact of vertical innovation is subject to a certain spillover effect, leading to greater fluctuations.

In Panel (c) of Fig. 2.7, it is observed that the economy with a constraint on vertical innovation reaches the BGP in approximately the same period as the economy without any constraints. Intuitively, due to the spillover effect of the expansion of intermediate product varieties, vertical innovation has minimal influence on the timing of reaching the BGP. Although the economy performs smoothly without significant fluctuations

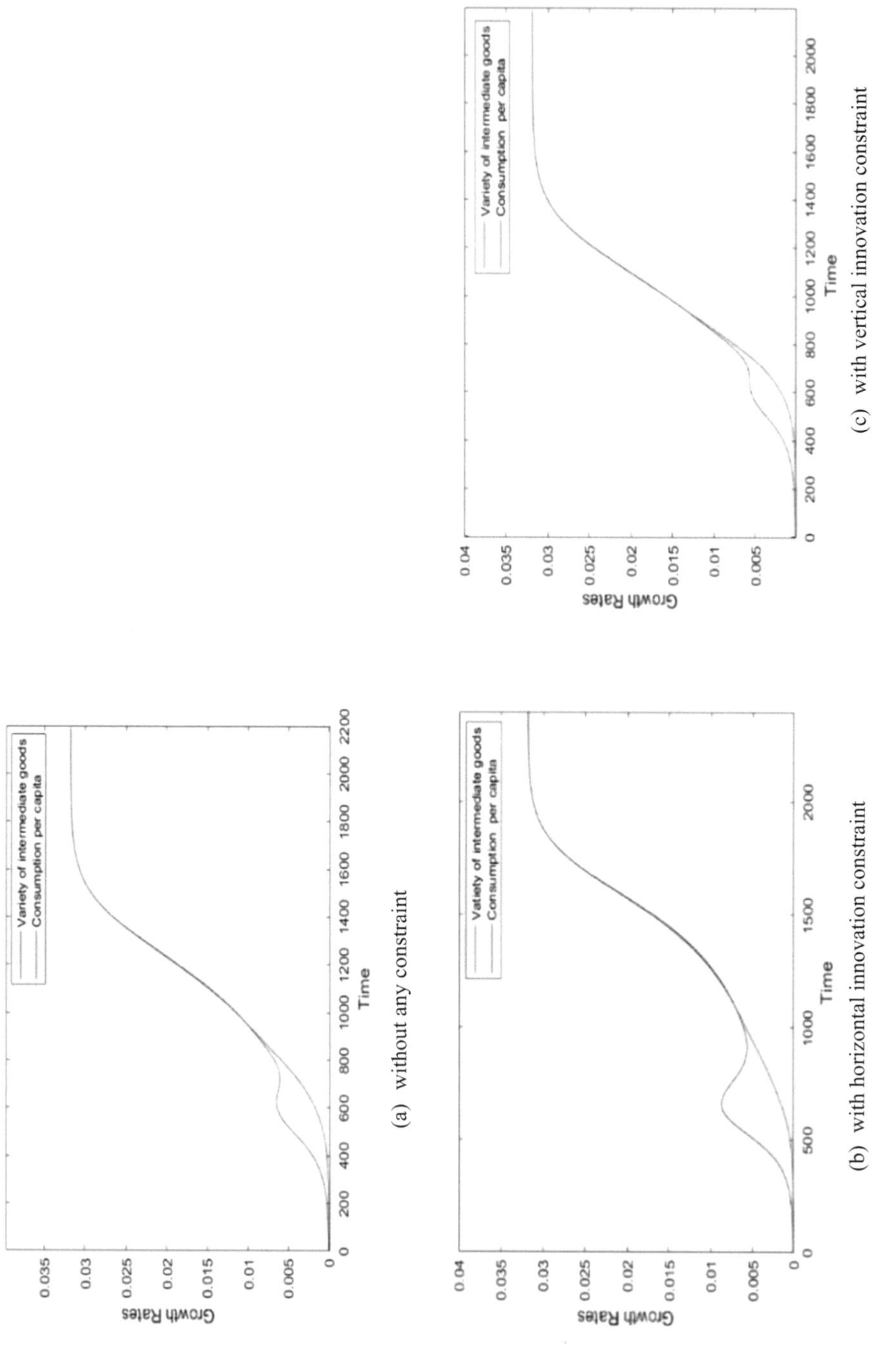

(a) without any constraint

(b) with horizontal innovation constraint

(c) with vertical innovation constraint

Fig. 2.7 Growth rates of consumption and intermediate goods varieties

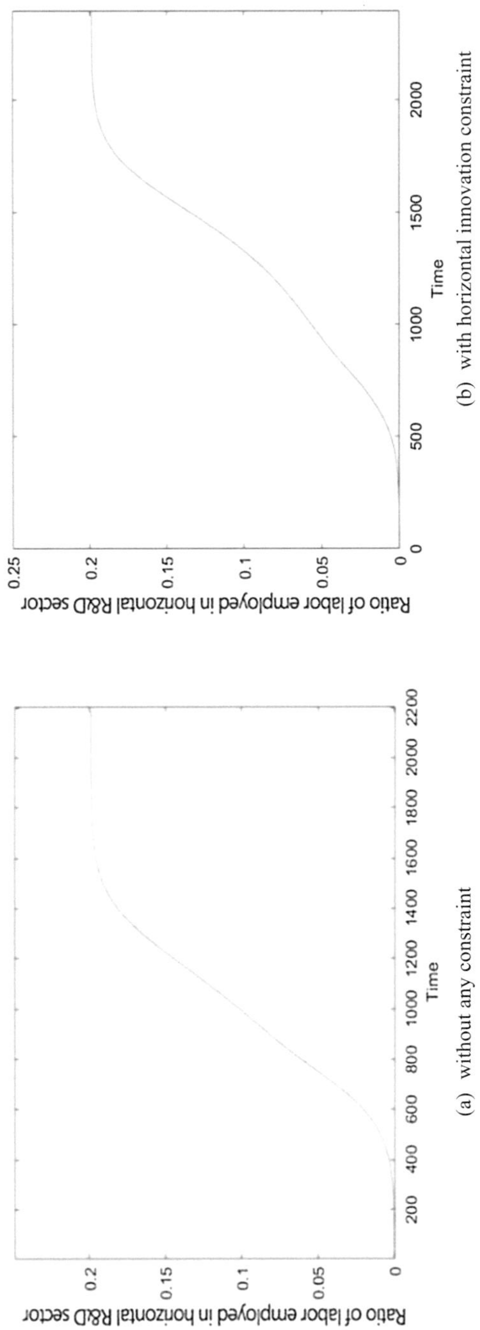

(a) without any constraint

(b) with horizontal innovation constraint

Fig. 2.8 Rate of labor employed in horizontal R&D sector

in this scenario, the growth rate of per capita consumption along the transitional path is lower compared to Panel (a) of Fig. 2.7.

For further analysis, Fig. 2.9 is examined. Both images demonstrate that the growth rate of the leading-edge productivity parameter initially increases to a maximum and then stabilizes. This suggests that when there are relatively few varieties of intermediate goods, vertical innovation is more easily realized. Additionally, Fig. 2.10 shows an increasing number of laborers swiftly transitioning from final goods production to vertical R&D sectors.

However, as the scale of intermediate goods gradually expands, vertical innovation becomes more complex and plays a less significant role. Consequently, the growth rate of the leading-edge productivity parameter gradually slows down, with some laborers in vertical R&D sectors transitioning to other sectors. Furthermore, an economy with limited data usage requires additional time to reach the maximum value of the growth rate of the leading-edge productivity parameter, influenced by the stronger spillover effect. This is why such an economy experiences smoother progress along the traditional path with minimal fluctuation.

In summary, when the data provision in horizontal R&D sectors is limited, the economy exhibits more severe fluctuations along the transitional path, resulting in increased uncertainty during the development process and requiring additional time to reach the BGP. If the data usage in vertical R&D sectors is constrained, the economy experiences a lower growth rate without significant fluctuations, indicating that the welfare level of the local population is relatively lower in the early stages of development.

2.8 Conclusion

First, accelerating China's transition from a traditional factor-driven growth model to an innovation-driven development paradigm requires fully leveraging existing digital infrastructure while moderately relaxing privacy-related regulations on data use within controlled, institutionalized frameworks. This does not imply neglecting individual privacy; rather, it entails establishing scientifically grounded data utilization mechanisms that enable data to act as a more efficient, productive input in technological R&D. By lowering barriers to data access, research departments can obtain higher-quality datasets, thereby enhancing both the success rate of technological innovations and their practical implementation efficiency. For instance, in the healthcare sector, allowing controlled access to non-sensitive clinical data for AI training can significantly improve the accuracy of diagnostic assistance and personalized treatment, ultimately enhancing overall public health outcomes. Consequently, privacy policies must strike a balance between protecting citizens' fundamental rights and supporting technological innovation. Approaches such as "usable but invisible" data frameworks and tiered, classified data governance provide feasible pathways to achieve this balance.

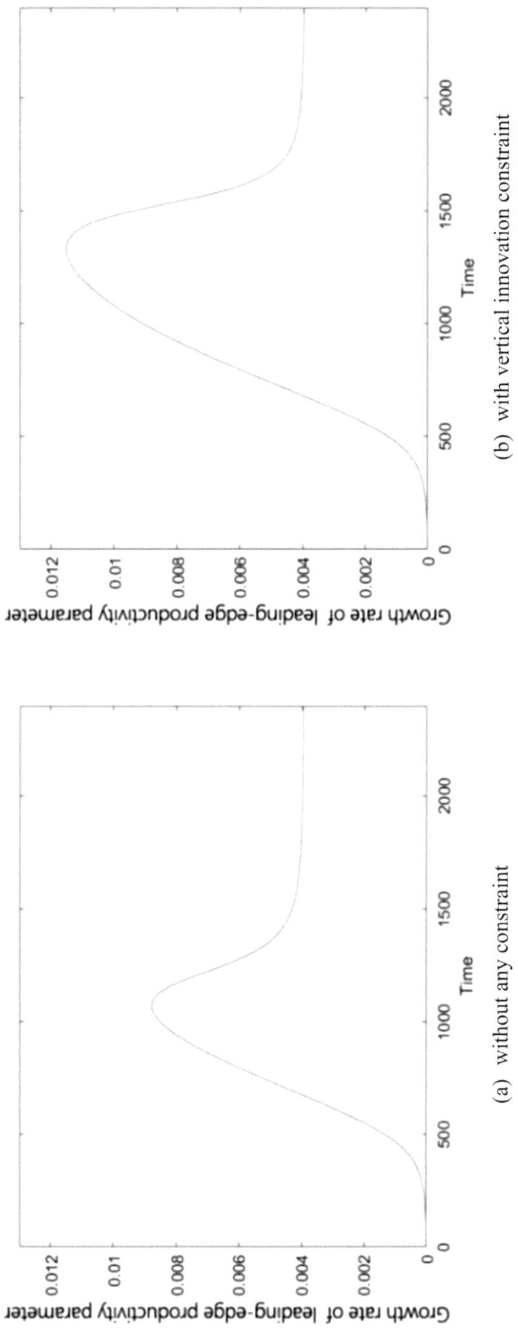

(a) without any constraint

(b) with vertical innovation constraint

Fig. 2.9 Growth rate of leading-edge productivity parameter

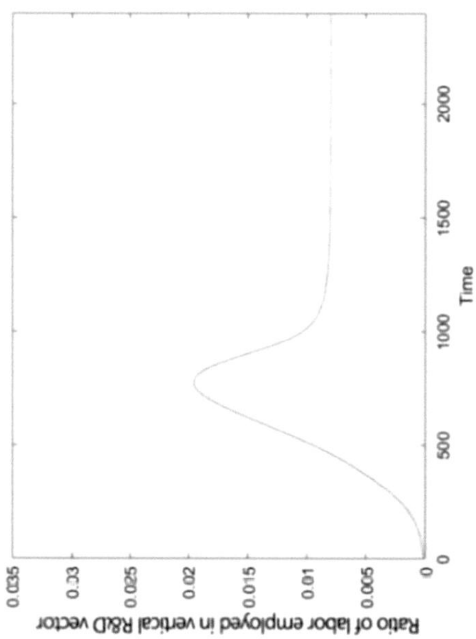

(a) without any constraint

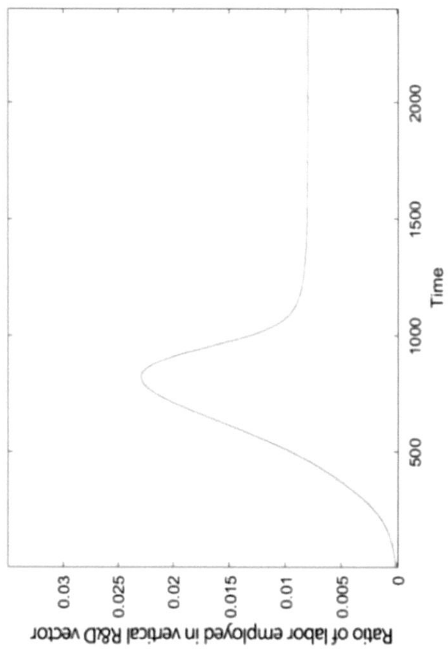

(b) with vertical innovation constraint

Fig. 2.10 Rate of labor employed in vertical R&D sector

Second, it is essential to harness China's increasingly sophisticated digital infrastructure to activate and amplify the positive spillover effects of digital knowledge. As a new type of productive knowledge resource, digital knowledge is non-rival, highly permeable across sectors, and capable of freely circulating across industries, thereby facilitating diverse collaborative innovation mechanisms. With continuous advancements in 5G, industrial internet, and computational hubs, the timeliness and breadth of digital knowledge dissemination have been significantly enhanced, enabling the integration of previously fragmented datasets across regions and sectors. This integration drives both technological synergy and institutional innovation. Moreover, digital knowledge can mitigate privacy concerns through human capital accumulation: as societal digital literacy improves, public understanding of data increases, raising social acceptance of data utilization. Simultaneously, enterprises and research institutions, driven by high-quality human capital, can better address ethical and compliance issues, achieving a dynamic equilibrium between technological gains and privacy protection.

Finally, from a medium- to long-term development perspective, reducing economic volatility, enhancing resilience, and sustaining stable high growth necessitate further acceleration of digital infrastructure construction and upgrading, coupled with complementary legal and regulatory frameworks. A forward-looking and inclusive national privacy supervision system is essential. At the infrastructure level, strategic initiatives such as East Data–West Computing, urban computing hubs, and edge computing nodes should continue to ensure the efficient nationwide flow and sharing of data, providing robust support for R&D activities. Institutionally, the delineation and enforcement of data ownership rights must clarify the responsibilities and rights of firms, individuals, and the government in data use. Critically, a nationally coordinated, tiered, transparent, and auditable privacy regulatory framework should enable vertical and horizontal R&D units to optimize resource allocation while remaining compliant. Introducing flexible governance mechanisms such as regulatory sandboxes and industry self-regulatory alliances can effectively manage risks without constraining innovation. Only when infrastructure and institutional frameworks advance in coordination can data factors be fully activated and intelligent technologies continuously break through, providing a strong foundation for China's transition to high-quality development.

2.9 Summary

In the context of the global wave of digitalization and intelligent technologies, data has evolved from a mere technical resource into a core production factor that fundamentally reshapes economic structures, industrial boundaries, and governance paradigms. This chapter, centered on the theme of "data as a production factor, creative destruction, and digital economic growth," systematically examines, from both theoretical and empirical perspectives, how data functions as a catalyst for innovation and drives the process of creative destruction in continuous technological replacement and organizational renewal. Using policy experiments under the national big data strategy and firm-level behavioral data, this chapter not only validates the practical pathways of data-driven technological change but also demonstrates how data interacts with traditional production factors such as human capital and firm capabilities to enhance total factor productivity (TFP).

At the theoretical level, the key distinction of data from traditional factors lies in its non-rivalry, renewability, and strong externalities. Data can be infinitely replicated and widely distributed, and through algorithmic learning, transformed into knowledge, insights, and predictive capability. Based on this, the chapter constructs a "data–AI–innovation–growth" technological change pathway, emphasizing that data serves both as an input for knowledge production and as a signal for forecasting future trends. Particularly under AI, data becomes a dynamic learning and feedback network, profoundly influencing organizational structures, technology trajectories, and resource allocation patterns—manifesting as a process of creative destruction.

"Creative destruction" refers to the continuous updating, marginalization, or elimination of legacy technologies, organizations, and market mechanisms, while new technologies, applications, and organizational models rapidly emerge and dominate. This phenomenon is especially pronounced in internet platforms, smart manufacturing, and digital healthcare. For example, traditional retail industries faced extensive capacity restructuring, organizational realignment, and value chain redefinition under big-data-driven e-commerce platforms, whereas digital-native firms leveraged data capabilities to enhance agile decision-making and customer responsiveness, reflecting the ongoing dynamic interplay between old and new forces.

Unlike Schumpeter's original notion of creative destruction as discrete or sporadic breakthroughs, this process represents systemic transitions driven by continuous data accumulation and learning. In case studies from big data pilot zones, industry technology lifecycles were significantly shortened, with new product development cycles reduced from an average of 24 months to less than 12, while traditional processes were rapidly marginalized, reflecting a cyclical pattern of innovation → substitution → diffusion → obsolescence. These empirical findings not only complement the assumptions of Chapter 1 but also link data-driven vertical technological change to real-world economic restructuring.

Data's value is not intrinsically realized but depends on the cognitive and transformation capabilities of its recipients. By introducing the human capital dimension, this chapter shows how data is "activated" into innovative outputs through skill structures, human resource allocation, and organizational learning mechanisms—a data–cognition–knowledge conversion pathway. In regions or firms with high human capital density, the marginal effect of data policies on innovation is significantly enhanced. For instance, the elasticity between data acquisition capacity and technological innovation reaches 0.56 in high-skill firms but only 0.21 in low-skill firms, highlighting substantial heterogeneity and validating the hypothesis that data policy effectiveness depends on internal cognitive structures. Without a compatible human capital configuration, data remains a "silent resource," incapable of generating productive knowledge and innovation.

This chapter further proposes a "decoupling–synergy" theoretical mechanism to explain the dynamic interplay between data and human capital. Decoupling occurs when algorithms partially replicate workers' experience, substituting for mid- and low-skill tasks. Synergy occurs when data and human capital collaborate on complex tasks, improving overall system output. Practically, this manifests as: data-driven automation displaces certain jobs, yet simultaneously equips high-skill workers with richer analytical and predictive tools, enhancing their marginal productivity and functional scope. This dual mechanism constitutes the micro-foundation of creative destruction, showing that the interaction between data and human capital is not one-dimensional substitution but structural collaboration.

From a policy perspective, using multiple national big data pilot zones with differentiated strategies, the chapter systematically evaluates the causal effects of data policies on innovation and industrial restructuring. Results reveal time-lagged and regionally heterogeneous effects: innovation gains are limited during the first two years post-implementation but accelerate significantly from the third year onward, reflecting the "incubation period" needed for infrastructure and firm capability to translate into technological dividends. Particularly in central and western regions, pilot zones achieved a strategic leap from resource-following to data-driven growth, leveraging national data centers and edge computing nodes to form localized data–application–market loops, facilitating regional transitions from manufacturing-to-service-led economies.

However, the chapter also notes the boundedness of externalities: sustained data policy benefits depend on institutional capacity. Ambiguous property rights, platform monopolies, and lagging privacy regulations may impede corporate dynamism, triggering governance issues such as "data fear" and "data idling." Future data policies must therefore emphasize nested institutional structures and feedback mechanisms to prevent policy ineffectiveness.

If the first half of this chapter focused on data-driven technological leaps and macroeconomic growth paths, the latter half transitions to the micro-level, asking how data shapes firm behavior and risk preferences. In a big data environment, firms are no longer concerned with whether they have information but how to process and respond to massive data streams. Firms with strong data capabilities exhibit sharper market judgment, enhanced resource allocation, and more aggressive strategies—e.g., accelerated M&A, higher leverage, and increased R&D investment—which simultaneously raise exposure to market and financial uncertainties. This establishes the "data-driven behavioral intensification → risk exposure increase" mechanism, laying the foundation for Chapter 3 on corporate risk. It demonstrates that data, while enhancing efficiency, may also promote strategic aggressiveness, which is fully realized only under robust institutional constraints and sound corporate governance.

Through this analysis, a cohesive framework emerges: data, as a new production factor characterized by platform effects, network externalities, and non-rivalry, is reshaping technological trajectories and driving endogenous productivity growth. In traditional growth models, technology is treated as exogenous, largely dependent on research, policy incentives, and capital investment. In the era of big data, cloud computing, and AI, the capacity to acquire, process, and utilize data becomes an endogenous variable, driving TFP gains through feedback loops, self-iteration, and scale externalities.

Data-driven technological progress operates on multiple dimensions:

- Production processes: precise monitoring of workflows, resource allocation, and risk alerts, promoting process intelligence and resource optimization;
- R&D and innovation: reducing uncertainty and trial-and-error costs, accelerating product iteration and technology diffusion;
- User interaction: massive behavioral data informs demand forecasting, design adjustments, and feedback triggers.

Data is thus no longer an auxiliary input but a core driver of technological evolution and production function transformation.

Importantly, the implications extend beyond efficiency gains or production expansion. Data-driven technologies fundamentally reshape labor division, skill structures, and job paradigms. Unlike traditional industrial technologies that replace physical or repetitive labor, digital economy technologies increasingly permeate medium- and high-skill cognitive work, continuously expanding the boundaries of "replaceable" labor. Labor is deconstructed into tasks, processes, and modules, coordinated algorithmically, and worker capabilities must now be quantifiable (e.g., efficiency, accuracy, collaboration metrics). This "tagged labor" model transforms traditional labor valuation and embeds work within platform and algorithmic governance.

Consequently, laborers' identities evolve: employment becomes more task- or platform-oriented, less stable, and often de-organized, increasing flexibility but also vulnerability, disrupting skill accumulation, and weakening employment protections. The employment transformation is non-linear and structurally differentiated: high-skill labor demand surges, middle-skill jobs face fragmentation or automation, and low-skill labor occupies flexible or informal positions with limited upward mobility. Globally, this manifests as platform-based labor expansion, skill and regional polarization, and structural decoupling of middle- and low-skill workers.

These structural changes carry profound economic and social implications: declining job stability, fragmented career paths, and algorithmic labor control raise ethical, legal, and social concerns. Labor marginalization may suppress consumption, weaken social cohesion, and threaten macroeconomic stability.

Thus, technology–labor interactions must be seen as systemic restructuring rather than simple substitution or augmentation. Data-driven technological progress shapes not only economic growth but also labor paradigms and employment structures. Workers become both contributors to and subjects of data systems, presenting complex challenges for research and policy.

In summary, understanding how data reshapes technological progress requires re-examining labor as a production factor. Efficiency gains alone cannot ensure a sustainable, inclusive, and socially stable digital economy. The logic of data-driven creative destruction must extend to labor-market analysis, including dynamic skill evolution, job redistribution, and the institutional adaptation of employment relations.

The following chapters will explore these issues in depth, focusing on how data and AI co-shape labor market structures, skill demand paths, and social division of labor.

We will examine platform-mediated labor participation, AI-driven task replacement, cross-generational and regional disparities, and how education, training, and labor policies can adapt, providing actionable policy insights.

Whereas this chapter highlights data's role in driving technological logic and productivity, the next chapter centers on labor, revealing how data and AI jointly restructure labor markets. Technology and data redefine not only machine operations but also human roles, values, and future trajectories. In a data-driven economy, labor reorganization is both a challenge and an opportunity to redefine production and growth. Only by viewing technological progress and labor restructuring as a continuous logic chain can we fully understand the panoramic impact of data on economic growth.

References

Aghion, P., & Howitt, P. W. (1992). A model of growth through creative destruction. *Econometrica, 60*(2), 323–351.

Caballero, R. J., & Jaffe, A. B. (1993). How high are the giants' shoulders: An empirical assessment of knowledge spillovers and creative destruction in a model of economic growth. *NBER macroeconomics annual, 8*, 15–74.

Cong, L. W., Xie, D., & Zhang, L. (2021). Knowledge Accumulation, Privacy, and Growth in a Data Economy. *Management Science, 67*(10), 6480–6492.

Farboodi, M., & Veldkamp, L. (2021). A growth model of the data economy. NBER working paper w28427.

Howitt, P. W., & Aghion, P. (1998). Capital accumulation and innovation as complementary factors in long-run growth. *Journal of Economic Growth 3*(2), 111–130.

Howitt, P. (1999). Steady endogenous growth with population and R&D inputs growing. *Journal of Political Economy, 107*(4), 715–730.

Ichihashi, S. (2020). Online privacy and information disclosure by consumers. *American Economic Review ,110*(2), 569–95.

Ichihashi, S. (2021a). Competing data intermediaries. *The RAND Journal of Economics, 52*(3), 515–537.

Ichihashi, S. (2021b). The economics of data externalities. *Journal of Economic Theory 196*, 105316.

Jones, C. I. (2016). Life and growth. *Journal of Political Economy, 124*(2), 539–578.

Jones, C. I., & Tonetti, C. (2020). Nonrivalry and the Economics of Data. *American Economic Review ,110.*

Krupka, E. L., & Stephens, M., Jr. (2013). The stability of measured time preferences. *Journal of Economic Behavior & Organization, 85*, 11–19.

Lucas, R. E. (1988). On the mechanics of economic development. *Journal of Monetary Economics, 22*(1), 3–42.

Murphy, R. S. (1996). Property rights in personal information: An economic defense of privacy. *Georgetown Law Journal, 84*(7), 2381–2417.

Vissing-Jørgensen, A. (2002). Limited asset market participation and the elasticity of intertemporal substitution. *Journal of Political Economy, 110*(4), 825–853.

Wu, M., & Zhang, L. (2022). *Endogenous growth and human capital accumulation in a data economy* (SSRN Working Paper No. 4248918).

Xie, D., & Yang, B. (2022). *Endogenous information carrier technology* (SSRN Working Paper No. 4114985).

Zeng, J. (2003). Reexamining the interaction between innovation and capital accumulation. *Journal of Macroeconomics, 25*(4), 541–560.

Chapter 3
Differentiation and Skill Reallocation in the Era of Artificial Intelligence

3.1 The Logic of Employment Restructuring Driven by Generative Artificial Intelligence

With the rapid development of Generative Artificial Intelligence (GAI), its powerful "generative capabilities" have been demonstrated in fields such as automated office work, content creation, product design, and personalized marketing, making it a crucial driver of the digital economic transformation. The market value of Chinese AI enterprises has continued to grow, indicating the explosive expansion of related industries. In this process, GAI's demand for data factors has increased exponentially. China's total data output reached 8.1 zettabytes (ZB) in 2023, providing unique resource advantages for technological development (Fig. 3.1).

Unlike traditional AI, which mainly replaces low-skilled labor, GAI possesses more complex capabilities in content creation and problem-solving. It may affect medium and high-skilled jobs, reshape the division of labor and production organization, and bring about skill differentiation and structural adjustments. Some studies argue that GAI will stimulate demand for high-skilled labor and spawn new occupations, while others point out that it may exacerbate income inequality. Meanwhile, numerous literatures emphasize the significant role of data's non-rivalry and increasing returns to scale in long-term growth, but often overlook the impact of labor supply elasticity. Based on this, this chapter constructs an endogenous growth model incorporating GAI, data factors, and an elastic labor supply mechanism to reveal the interactive relationship between technological change, data supply, and labor choices.

In the model, residents can sell their personal data to enterprises for training and innovation to obtain additional income, but they also bear utility losses due to privacy leakage; enterprises use data to conduct research and development (R&D) and improve productivity; labor supply is no longer exogenously fixed but dynamically determined based on residents' trade-offs among data transactions, leisure, and labor income. We analyze three types of equilibrium scenarios: first, when data supply is

X. Li et al., *Data as a New Factor of Production*, Applied Economics and Policy Studies, https://doi.org/10.1007/978-981-95-9985-1_3

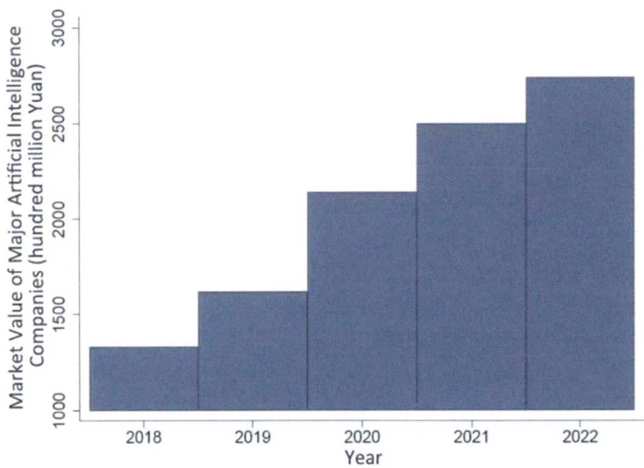

Fig. 3.1 Market value of major artificial intelligence manufacturers

sufficient and labor is fixed, growth and welfare steadily improve; second, when labor supply is elastic, part of the labor is converted into data sales—although labor input decreases, technological efficiency drives output growth; third, if data supply is insufficient due to privacy constraints, innovation is hindered, growth momentum declines, and welfare is suppressed.

Numerical simulation results show that when GAI has high marginal innovation returns, moderate labor elasticity can promote data supply and drive output; however, if privacy losses are excessively high or property rights are ill-defined, data market failure will significantly hinder R&D and economic growth.

The policy implications of this chapter include: first, constructing a unified, efficient, and trustworthy data market, promoting confirmation of rights, hierarchical management, and cross-border circulation to provide stable data supply for GAI; second, improving privacy protection mechanisms, reducing social costs through authorization mechanisms and privacy-enhancing technologies such as privacy-preserving computation, and enhancing residents' willingness to engage in data transactions; third, paying attention to the dynamics of labor supply, strengthening skill training and education reform while promoting technological substitution to mitigate the impact on employment structure.

The structure of the chapter is arranged as follows: the second part reviews relevant literatures, sorting out the research context of GAI and data factors, labor market impacts, and elastic labor supply; the third part introduces the theoretical model, analyzing the mechanism of interaction among GAI, data supply, and labor choices; the fourth part presents numerical simulations and dynamic comparisons; the fifth part puts forward implications combined with institutions and policies; the sixth part summarizes and looks forward to future research.

3.2 Literature Review

With the continuous advancement of technological progress, the profound impact of automation and artificial intelligence on the labor market has become a hot topic among academics and policymakers in recent years. Especially against the backdrop of the Fourth Industrial Revolution, new-generation information technologies are increasingly integrating with production and living scenarios. The application of Artificial Intelligence (AI), especially Generative AI (GAI), has become more widespread, reshaping the employment structure, labor demand, and social division of labor systems. Existing literatures have extensively focused on the employment effects of traditional AI and automation technologies, indicating that technological progress may both replace low-skilled workers and create new job opportunities. These two effects show significant heterogeneity across different industries, groups, and time dimensions.

From a micro perspective, "reactive machines" represented by robots and automated equipment have both creative and substitution effects. For example, Wang Yongqin and Dong Wen (2020) pointed out that the promotion of robotic automation technology can simultaneously create new jobs and replace existing ones. The scales of the two effects are relatively close, resulting in an insignificant impact on the total employment volume. From a structural perspective, the degree to which employment in different industries and groups is affected by automation varies. Mann and Püttmann (2023) noted that employment and wage levels in the manufacturing sector are more affected by automation shocks, while the service sector can achieve positive employment growth through technological improvements in service efficiency in some scenarios. Based on Chinese labor market data, Zhou Guangsu et al. (2021) found that automation shocks have a more significant negative impact on low-educated and low-skilled workers, suggesting that skill upgrading has a buffering effect on employment stability.

Gender and family role factors are also affected by automation shocks. Wang Linhui et al. (2023a) found that under the impact of robot substitution, female workers face higher labor market risks, especially the phenomenon of "motherhood penalty"—that is, their wage income and career advancement are significantly affected after becoming mothers. Furthermore, based on Chinese microdata, Wang Linhui et al. (2023b) found that the widespread deployment of AI technology has reduced the long-term nature of labor contract signings, increasing the uncertainty and flexibility of the labor market, as manifested by shorter contract terms and a decline in the proportion of stable employment. From a macro-policy perspective, Wu Liyuan et al. (2023) pointed out that AI investment has changed the central bank's monetary policy reaction function. Policy rules overly focusing on the output gap will exacerbate employment volatility risks in the context of AI technology diffusion. In summary, automation and traditional AI technologies have been widely proven to bring redistribution effects to the labor market structure, and their impacts present complex interactions due to multiple factors such as industrial sectors, skill levels, gender roles, and institutional design.

In contrast, research on the impact of generative AI on the labor market is still in its infancy. Unlike traditional AI, which focuses on executive tasks, generative AI possesses advanced functions such as content generation, design optimization, and decision support, thus having stronger potential for complementing cognitive tasks and replacing knowledge-based work. Studies by Acemoglu and Restrepo (2024), Autor and Dorn (2013), Böhm (2020, 2024), etc., point out that generative AI also has dual effects of creating new occupations and replacing existing jobs. However, due to its task complexity and algorithmic embedding capabilities, its impact paths on labor productivity and job attributes are more diverse.

In terms of task collaboration, generative AI can expand the production boundaries of human workers and improve the efficiency of cognitive tasks. Acemoglu and Restrepo (2018, 2019) proposed that AI tools can enable workers to enter higher skill spaces based on their original tasks, promoting work restructuring and value creation. Based on an empirical study in customer service scenarios, Brynjolfsson et al. (2023) found that after introducing generative AI tools, the average number of problems solved by employees per hour increased by approximately 14%, with the productivity of low-skilled workers increasing by as much as 34%, significantly narrowing the performance gap. Such collaborative effects are reflected not only at the efficiency level but also in the optimization of workers' learning curves and knowledge accumulation. Research by Noy and Zhang (2023) also shows that generative AI can significantly shorten the completion time of copywriting and data processing tasks, improve the quality of outcomes, and enhance the work capabilities of workers, especially vulnerable groups.

However, current research generally points out that in the short term, generative AI is more likely to replace labor time (i.e., reduce labor intensity) rather than directly create new skills. In other words, its marginal contribution to total employment remains to be observed over time, and its current advantages are more reflected in improving the marginal output of human capital and reducing skill thresholds. Therefore, it is necessary to expand the research on generative AI from micro productivity to the perspective of macro growth and employment structure changes, exploring its long-term institutional effects and dynamic general equilibrium paths.

Parallel to the research on AI, economic research on data factors has been emerging. As the basic resource and training material for generative AI, the value structure and allocation mechanism of data have gradually become research hotspots. Cong et al. (2021, 2022), Jones and Tonetti (2020), etc., introduced data factors into the endogenous growth framework, pointing out that the non-rivalry and replicability of data can bring increasing returns to scale, effectively improving total factor productivity. The model by Jones and Tonetti (2020) shows that systematically integrating consumer behavior data into the innovation system helps form a virtuous cycle of knowledge accumulation and technology diffusion.

However, most macro models assume labor supply as a fixed variable, ignoring the possibility of elastic responses of labor supply to changes in economic incentives. This assumption limits our comprehensive understanding of how data and labor jointly affect the growth path. Arrieta-Ibarra et al. (2018) proposed the view that "data is labor," arguing that data should be regarded as an economic contribution produced by individuals rather than an exogenous public good. They advocated incentivizing data providers through rights confirmation and profit-sharing mechanisms. This view contrasts with the reality of centralized monopoly of data platforms and ambiguous personal rights and interests, pointing out that the lack of institutional design inhibits the willingness to supply data resources.

Domestic scholars such as Chen Xiaohong and Wu Mengtao also pointed out that data factors have a positive role in promoting workers' skill upgrading. Especially in the context of vocational education and online platforms, data mining can be used to accurately identify individual abilities and matching degrees, thereby improving the efficiency of person-job matching and labor market transparency. The synergistic mechanism between data and human capital indicates that digital skills, as an important source of growth for new-type human capital, their allocation efficiency largely determines the evolution of economic structure and the speed of employment upgrading.

In terms of labor supply mechanisms, classic growth models mostly adopt the exogenous setting of labor supply, ignoring workers' right to choose among disposable time, work intensity, and non-wage income. Studies by Turnovsky (2000) and others have shown that after introducing elastic labor supply, the growth path will have more endogenous adjustment mechanisms, and may even trigger multiple equilibria or path dependence. In the context of the digital economy, the substitution relationship between labor time and data transaction time has become increasingly prominent. The trade-off between individuals selling data to obtain income and providing labor constitutes a new household decision-making problem. This study models this and verifies the significant impact of labor supply elasticity on growth rate and welfare evolution path through simulations.

In summary, existing studies have revealed how digital technologies reshape the economic and employment patterns from the perspectives of automation, AI, data factors, and labor supply. Compared with existing literatures, this book incorporates two core variables—generative AI and data factors—into a unified endogenous growth framework, establishing a dynamic economic model considering elastic labor supply, thereby systematically studying the synergistic mechanism among the three. The main innovations of this study are reflected in the following aspects:

It identifies the task complementarity effect of generative AI on the labor market, emphasizing that its impact on workers' performance and distribution patterns through efficiency improvement and skill integration paths is different from that of traditional AI; we treat data as an independent production factor and clarify its non-rivalry, endowing it with incentive mechanisms and institutional environment dependence in the model, reflecting its interactive relationship with AI R&D activities; we introduce the setting of elastic labor supply, depicting the dynamic trade-off process of workers in the ternary choice of "data sales—work—leisure," filling the gap in existing research on the labor-data time allocation mechanism; on the basis of theoretical modeling, we conduct numerical simulations, systematically analyzing the differences in the impact of different data property rights arrangements, privacy sensitivity, and AI technology diffusion paths on economic growth and employment structure.

Through the above modeling and empirical strategies, this study not only expands the economics of AI and the theory of data factors but also provides a new research path for understanding the employment change mechanism and policy design in the context of generative AI, laying a theoretical foundation for future digital economic governance and sustainable development strategies.

3.2.1 *Decentralized Economic Model and Balanced Growth Path*

Based on Romer's (1990) endogenous growth model, this chapter constructs a benchmark decentralized economic model incorporating data elements, generative artificial intelligence, and elastic labor supply. We present model assumptions and decision-making processes for the household sector, final goods production sector, and generative artificial intelligence R&D sector respectively, and clarify the conditions for market equilibrium. All mathematical formulas retain their original numbering to accurately express the model structure.

3.2.2 *Representative Households*

Assume that in period t, a decentralized economy consists of N_t infinitely-lived representative households, with the population growing at a constant rate n, i.e., $\dot{N}_t/N_t = n.$. Households own the ownership of their data factors. Drawing on studies such as Jones and Tonetti (2020), we assume that households selling data factors will incur privacy leakage, resulting in utility loss, and set the utility loss from privacy leakage as d_t, where d_t is the privacy sensitivity coefficient. Additionally, referring to Heckman et al. (1998), we no longer assume that labor supply is perfectly inelastic; the leisure gained by households reducing labor supply also brings utility loss. Thus, we set the utility loss caused by labor supply as $\theta, l_t^{1+\eta}/(1+\eta)$, where $\theta > 0$ measures the importance of leisure and is the reciprocal of the Frisch labor supply elasticity $\eta > 0$. The instantaneous utility function of households is expressed as:

$$U_t = \frac{c_t^{1-\sigma} - 1}{1-\sigma} - \theta \frac{l^{1+\eta}}{1+\eta} - d_t \tag{3.1}$$

where c_t is per capita consumption, l_t is per capita labor supply, and $\sigma > 0$ is the relative risk aversion coefficient (reciprocal of the intertemporal elasticity of substitution in consumption). In Eq. (3.1), the first term represents consumption utility, the second term is the marginal utility loss of labor, and the third term is the privacy loss caused by data sales.

In period t, households face the following budget constraint:

$$a_t = (r_t - n)a_t + w_t l_t + P_{d,t} d_t - c_t \tag{3.2}$$

where a_t is per capita assets, r_t is the real interest rate, w_t is the real wage rate, and $P_{\{d,t\}}$ is the price of data factors (the price of the final product is normalized to 1). Equation (3.2) indicates that households' total current income includes capital returns $(r_t - n)a_t$, labor income w_t l_t, and income from data sales $P_{d,t}d_t$; the change in assets is equal to total income minus consumption expenditure c_t. Considering that data factors originate from consumption behavior, we introduce the data generation constraint:

$$d_t \leq \Gamma(c_t) \tag{3.3}$$

where $\Gamma(\cdot)$ is a non-negative and monotonically increasing function, satisfying $\Gamma(0) = 0$ and $\lim_{x \to +\infty} \Gamma(x) = +\infty$, , which characterizes the property that the amount of data factors increases with consumption. In the benchmark model of this chapter, we do not explicitly discuss Constraint (3) for the time being, and its impact can be further relaxed or characterized in subsequent transitional dynamic analysis.

Representative households maximize the present value of utility by choosing c_t,l_t,d_t:

$$\frac{\dot{c}_t}{c_t} = \frac{r_t - \rho}{\sigma} \tag{3.4}$$

$$\frac{\dot{w}_t}{w_t} - \eta \frac{\dot{l}_t}{l_t} = r_t - \rho \tag{3.5}$$

$$\frac{\dot{P}_{d,t}}{P_{d,t}} - (\varphi - 1)\frac{\dot{d}_t}{d_t} = r_t - \rho \tag{3.6}$$

3.2.3 Representative Final Good Firms

In period t, representative final good firms operate in a perfectly competitive market environment. Their production function considers the impact of labor and the types of existing generative AI products on output. Let x(v,t) be the input quantity of the $v \in [0, A_t]$ type of generative AI product, A_t be the total number of existing technology types, and L_t be the labor demand of the final good sector (given by labor market clearing $L_t = l_t N_t$). The production function of the final good is assumed to be:

$$Y_t = L_t^{\beta} \int_0^{At} x(v, t)^{1-\beta} dv \tag{3.7}$$

where $0 < \beta < 1$ measures the contribution rate of labor in the production process. Equation (3.7) indicates that the output Y_t of the final good exhibits increasing returns to scale with respect to labor and AI product inputs; meanwhile, the contributions of different types of generative AI products to output exhibit constant returns to scale. Firms maximize profits by choosing the input x(v,t) of various types of generative AI products and hiring labor L_t:

$$\max_{L_t, x(v,t)} Yt - w_t L_t - \int_0^{A_t} P(v,t)x(v,t)dv \tag{3.8}$$

where P(v,t) is the price of the v type of AI product, and the price of the final good is

$$w_t = \beta (l_t N_t)^{\beta - 1} \int_0^{A_t} x(v,t)^{1-\beta} dv \tag{3.9}$$

$$P(v,t) = (1-\beta)(l_t N_t)^{\beta} x(v,t)^{-\beta} \tag{3.10}$$

3.2.4 *Generative AI Product Firms*

Generative AI product firms obtain monopoly profits by developing new product types. The R&D process requires data factor inputs and is affected by the spillover effect of existing product types.

3.2.4.1 Manufacturing Procedure

For any type $v \in [0, At]$ of generative AI product, the firm earns $P(v,t)$ for each unit of product sold and incurs a cost $\phi(v)$. This paper assumes that the marginal cost of the production department of generative AI firms is a constant, i.e., $\phi(v) \equiv \phi$. The production department chooses the product output $x(v,t)$ to maximize profits:

$$\max P(v,t)x(v,t) - \phi x(v,t) \tag{3.11}$$

Substituting Equation $P(v,t) = (1-\beta)(l_t N_t)^{\beta} x(v,t)^{-\beta}$ and solving the profit maximization problem, the first-order condition is obtained:

$$x(v,t) = [\frac{(1-\beta)^2}{\phi}]^{\frac{1}{\beta}} l_t N_t := x_t \tag{3.12}$$

$$P(v,t) = \frac{\phi}{1-\beta} := P_t \tag{3.13}$$

Combining the above conditions and the production function of final good firms, the expressions for the monopoly profit of generative AI products, household wage rates, and final good output are derived:

$$\Pi(v,t) = \beta[\frac{(1-\beta)^2}{\varphi}]^{(\beta-1)/\beta} l_t N_t = \Pi_t \tag{3.14}$$

$$w_t = \beta[\frac{(1-\beta)^2}{\varphi}]^{(\beta-2)/\beta} At \tag{3.15}$$

$$Y_t = [\frac{(1-\beta)^2}{\varphi}]^{(1-\beta)/\beta} A_t\, l_t N_t \tag{3.16}$$

3.2.4.2 R&D Process

In the R&D process of generative AI, the role of labor is relatively limited. Data factors and current generative AI technologies have an important impact on the R&D of new-generation products. This paper constructs a model for expanding the types of generative AI products. The increment in product types can be expressed as:

$$\dot{A}_t = \gamma\, A_t^{\zeta}\, (d_t N_t)^{\alpha} \tag{3.17}$$

where γ is R&D efficiency, ζ is the spillover effect of product stock, and α is the contribution degree of data factors.

The R&D department focuses on whether it can maximize the monopoly profit of generative AI product firms after successful R&D. Define the total value $V(v,t)$ that successfully developed products can achieve in the future, i.e., the total value of future continuous profits discounted to period t:

$$V(v,t) = \int_t^{\infty} e^{-\int_t^s r(\tau)\,d\tau}\, \Pi(v,s)\, ds := V_t \tag{3.18}$$

The R&D department chooses the quantity of data factors $d_t N_t$ required for R&D to maximize profits:

$$P_{d,t} = \alpha\,\gamma\, A_t^{\zeta}\, (d_t N_t)^{\alpha-1}\, V_t \tag{3.19}$$

3.2.5 Equilibrium Definition

In equilibrium, generative AI product firms choose product prices and data factor demand to maximize profits; final good firms choose labor and generative AI product demand to maximize profits; representative households choose consumption volume, data supply volume, and labor supply volume to maximize utility. All markets (labor market, capital market, product market, and data factor market) clear.

3.2.6 Parameter Calibration

The parameter values of the benchmark model are mainly set based on previous literature (see Table 3.1). Among them, the relative risk aversion coefficient σ is set to 2, referring to the setting of Mei and Gong (2011). The Frisch labor supply elasticity is estimated to be 0.75 according to Chetty et al. (2011), soη is set to 1.33 in this paper. In addition, referring to the study of Cong et al. (2021), the parameters affecting the increment in generative AI product types are set: the privacy sensitivity coefficient φ is set to 1.5, the spillover effect ζ of generative AI product stock is set to 0.85, and the contribution degree α of data factors in the R&D process is set to 0.5. Meanwhile, according to the study of Jones and Tonetti (2020), the growth rate n of the representative household population is set to 0.02. Finally, referring to the study of Jones (2016), the discount factor ρ of representative household utility is set to 0.03.

Table 3.1 Parameter settings of the model

Parameter meaning	Parameter symbol	Calibrated value	Reference literature
Relative risk aversion coefficient	σ	2	Mei and Gong (2011)
Reciprocal of Frisch labor supply elasticity	η	1.33	Chetty et al. (2011)
Privacy sensitivity coefficient	$\in$	1.5	Cong et al. (2021)
Spillover effect of generative AI product stock	ζ	0.85	Cong et al. (2021)
Contribution degree of data factors in the R&D process	α	0.5	Cong et al. (2021)
Growth rate of representative household population	g	0.02	Jones and Tonetti (2020)
Discount factor of representative household utility	ρ	0.01	Jones (2016)

Table 3.2 Steady-state growth rates of economic variables in the decentralized economy

g_A	g_l	g_d	g_c (g_y)
0.0391	-0.0118	-0.0183	0.0274

Source Calculated based on the benchmark parameter values in Table 3.1 and Eqs. (3.19) to (3.22)

3.2.7 Balanced Growth Path of the Decentralized Economy

On the balanced growth path, the growth rates of various variables reach constant values. Define the steady-state growth rate expression of the decentralized economy as $g(\cdot)$. Combining the above equations and market clearing conditions, the expressions for the growth rates of per capita labor supply, per capita data supply, per capita consumption (per capita output growth rate), and the growth rate of generative AI product types on the balanced growth path are obtained as follows:

$$g_l = -\frac{\alpha\,\varphi\,(\sigma - 1)\,n}{(1-\zeta)\,(\sigma+\eta)\,\varphi + \alpha\,(\sigma-1)\,(1+\eta)} \tag{3.20}$$

$$g_d = -\frac{\alpha\,(\sigma - 1)\,(1+\eta)\,n}{(1-\zeta)\,(\sigma+\eta)\,\varphi + \alpha\,(\sigma-1)\,(1+\eta)} \tag{3.21}$$

$$g_c = g_y = \frac{\alpha\varphi(1+\eta)n}{(1-\zeta)(\sigma+\eta)\varphi + \alpha(\sigma-1)(1+\eta)} \tag{3.22}$$

$$g_A = \frac{\alpha\,\varphi\,(\sigma+\eta)\,n}{(1-\zeta)\,(\sigma+\eta)\,\varphi + \alpha\,(\sigma-1)\,(1+\eta)} \tag{3.23}$$

Based on the benchmark parameter values, the steady-state growth rates of various variables on the balanced growth path are obtained as shown in Table 3.2.

Conclusion 1: On the balanced growth path of the decentralized economy, the increase in the types of generative AI reduces the labor demand required for unit output. When the ownership of data factors belongs to households, households can increase consumption while reducing labor supply and data supply.

3.2.8 Comparative Static Analysis

By changing household characteristic parameters and generative AI product characteristic parameters, we explore their impacts on the balanced growth path.

Conclusion 2: On the balanced growth path of the decentralized economy, the growth rate of per capita data factor supply decreases with the increase in the reciprocal of labor supply elasticity, slowing down the growth rates of per capita output and consumption; while the improvement of the privacy sensitivity coefficient, the spillover effect of generative AI product stock, and the contribution degree of data factors in the R&D process can significantly promote the growth rate of generative AI product types, increase the growth rates of per capita output and consumption, and reduce the growth rate of labor supply.

The specific analysis is as follows: On the balanced growth path of the decentralized economy, the impact of households' labor supply elasticity on per capita output is not obvious. The increase in the privacy sensitivity coefficient can accelerate the expansion rate of generative AI product types, thereby increasing the growth rate of per capita output. The greater the contribution degree of data factors in the R&D process, the higher the efficiency of generative AI firms' R&D departments in using current data factors. The higher the spillover effect of generative AI product stock, the higher the efficiency of R&D departments in using past data factors. Changes in both parameters can effectively improve the R&D efficiency of generative AI products, promote per capita output growth, and reduce the growth rates of labor supply and data supply.

Figure 3.2 shows the impact of household characteristic parameters on the balanced growth path, and Fig. 3.3 shows the impact of generative AI product characteristic parameters on the balanced growth path.

The horizontal axis of Fig. 3.2 represents the reciprocal of labor supply elasticity, and the vertical axis represents the growth rate of per capita data factor supply, per capita output growth rate, and consumption growth rate. It can be seen from the figure that as the reciprocal of labor supply elasticity increases, the growth rate of per capita data factor supply decreases, and the growth rates of per capita output and consumption also slow down accordingly.

The horizontal axis of Fig. 3.3 represents the contribution degree of data factors in the R&D process, and the vertical axis represents the growth rate of generative AI product types, per capita output growth rate, and labor supply growth rate. It can be seen from the figure that as the contribution degree of data factors increases, the growth rate of generative AI product types accelerates, the per capita output growth rate increases, and the labor supply growth rate decreases.

3.3 Central Planner Economy Model and Transitional Dynamics

3.3.1 Central Planner Economy

The central planner economy model aims to further explore the impact of limited data factor supply on the dynamic process of economic growth. Under resource constraints, the central planner maximizes the utility of representative households. According to the final good market clearing principle, total household consumption equals net output:

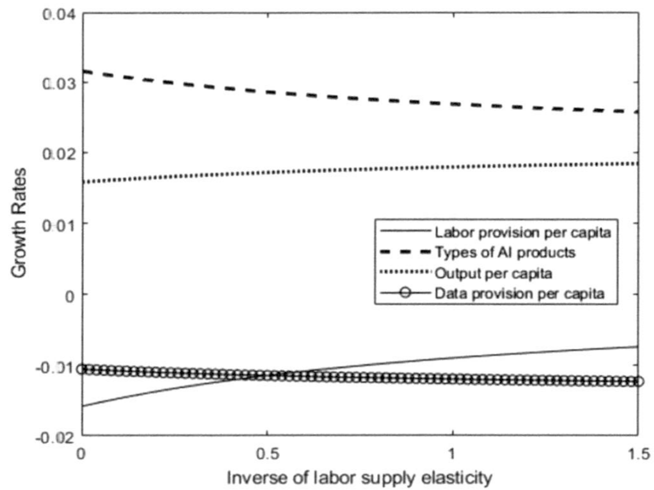

a. The Impact of the Reciprocal of Labor Supply Elasticity on the Balanced Growth Path

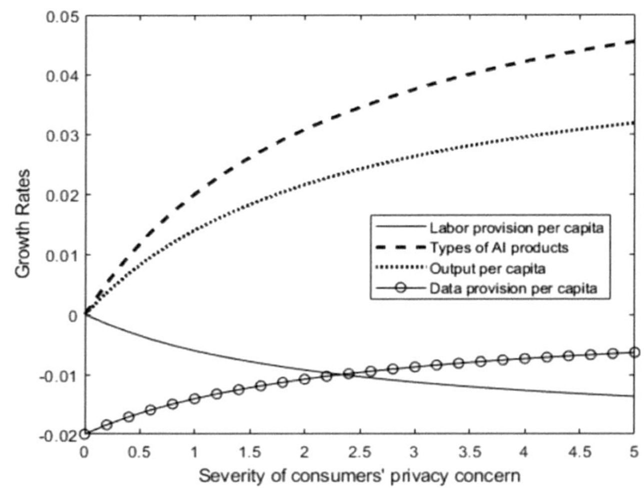

b. The Impact of the Privacy Sensitivity Coefficient on the Balanced Growth Path

Fig. 3.2 Impact of household characteristic parameters on the balanced growth path

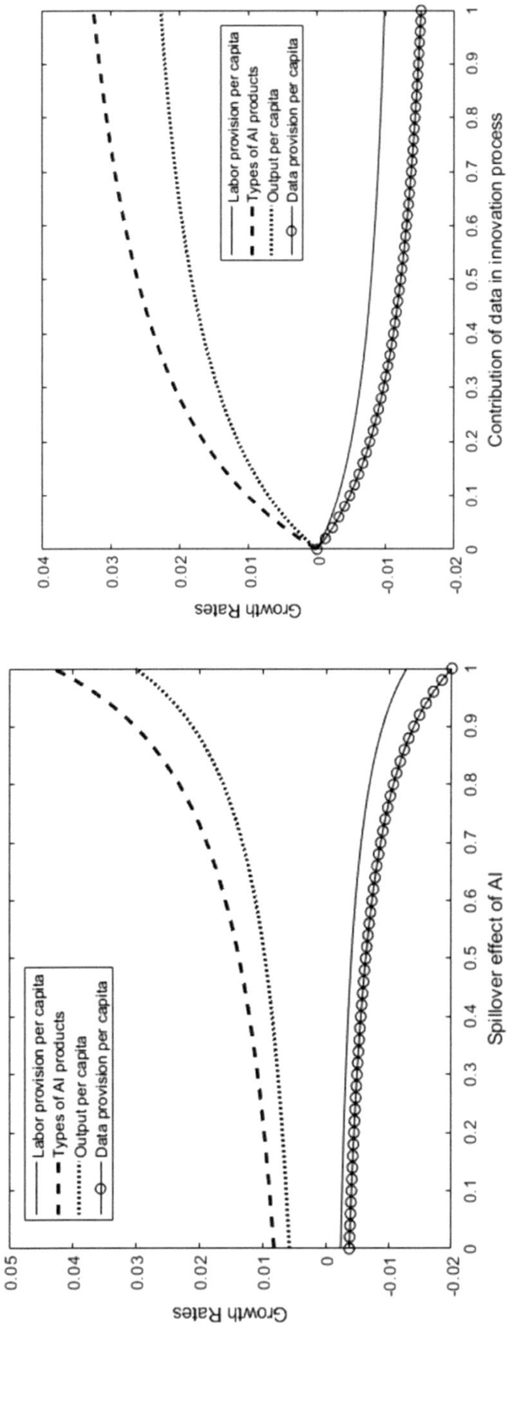

a. The Impact of the Spillover Effect of the Stock of DT Artificial Intelligence Products on the Balanced Growth Path

b. The Impact of the Contribution Degree of Data Elements in the R&D Process on the Balanced Growth Path

Fig. 3.3 Impact of generative AI product characteristic parameters on the balanced growth path

$$N_t c_t = (l_t N)^{\beta} \int_0^{A_t} x(v,t)^{1-\beta} dv - \int_0^{A_t} \phi x(v,t) dv \tag{3.24}$$

The central planner chooses the quantity of generative AI products to maximize net output. Solving yields the first-order condition:

$$x(v,t) = \beta(1-\beta)\phi^{\frac{1}{\beta}} A_t N_t \tag{3.25}$$

Substituting the above condition into the net output expression, the resource constraint expression is obtained:

$$c_t = \beta(1-\beta)\phi^{\frac{1}{\beta}-1} A_t l_t \tag{3.26}$$

The problem of the central planner maximizing the utility of representative households can be expressed as:

$$max \int_0^{+\infty} e^{-(\rho-nt)} \left(\frac{c^{1-\sigma}}{1-\sigma} - \theta \frac{l^{1+\eta}}{1+\eta} - d \cdot \phi \right) dt \tag{3.27}$$

subject to the following constraints:

$$c_t = \beta(1-\beta)\phi^{\frac{1}{\beta}-1} A_t l_t \tag{3.28}$$

$$A_t = \gamma A_t^{\zeta} (d_t N_t) \alpha \tag{3.29}$$

Construct the present-value Hamiltonian function and take partial derivatives with respect to c_t, l_t, d_t, A_t respectively to obtain the first-order conditions:

$$c_t^{-\sigma} = \lambda_t \tag{3.30}$$

$$\theta l_t^{\eta} = \beta(1-\beta)^{\frac{1}{\beta-1}} \lambda_t A_t \tag{3.31}$$

$$\varepsilon d_t^{\phi-1} = \alpha \gamma A_t^{\zeta} d_t^{\alpha-1} N_t^{\alpha} \tag{3.32}$$

$$\lambda_t \beta(1-\beta)^{\frac{1}{\beta-1}} l_t + \gamma \zeta \mu_t A_t^{\zeta-1} (d_t N_t)^{\alpha} = -\dot{\mu}_t + (\rho - n)\mu_t \tag{3.33}$$

where λ_t and μ_t are the shadow prices corresponding to the resource constraint and the increment in product types, respectively.

3.3.2 Balanced Growth Path of the Central Planner Economy

Define the steady-state growth rate expression of the main variables in the central planner economy as $g \sim (\cdot)$. Combining the above equations, the steady-state growth rate expressions on the balanced growth path are obtained: $\tilde{g}_A$

$$\tilde{g}_A = \frac{\alpha\phi(\sigma+\eta)n(1-\zeta)}{(\sigma+\eta)\phi+\alpha(\sigma-1)(1+\eta)} \tag{3.34}$$

$$\tilde{g}_l = -\frac{\alpha(\sigma-1)(1+\eta)n(1-\zeta)}{(\sigma+\eta)\phi+\alpha(\sigma-1)(1+\eta)} \tag{3.35}$$

$$\tilde{g}_d = -\frac{\alpha(\sigma-1)(1+\eta)n(1-\zeta)}{(\sigma+\eta)\phi+\alpha(\sigma-1)(1+\eta)} \tag{3.36}$$

$$\tilde{g}_c = \frac{\alpha\phi(1+\eta)n(1-\zeta)}{(\sigma+\eta)\phi+\alpha(\sigma-1)(1+\eta)} \tag{3.37}$$

Conclusion 3: On the balanced growth path of the central planner economy, the growth rate of generative AI product types is positive, the growth rates of labor supply and data supply are negative, and the consumption growth rate is positive.

Comparing the decentralized economy and the central planner economy, it is found that due to the monopoly markup behavior of generative AI product firms in the decentralized economy, the per capita output of the decentralized economy $w_t l_t = \beta\left(\frac{(1-\beta)^2}{\phi}\right)^{\frac{1}{\beta-1}} A_t l_t$ is less than that of the central planner economy $c_t = \beta\left(\frac{1-\beta}{\phi}\right)^{\frac{1}{\beta-1}} A_t l_t$. In addition, the monopoly pricing strategy of generative AI product firms is fixed-proportion cost-plus pricing, which affects the level of per capita output but not the per capita output growth rate on the balanced growth path.

3.3.3 Transitional Dynamics of the Central Planner Economy

To explore the impact of limited data factor supply on the dynamic process of economic growth, we further analyze the transitional dynamics of the central planner economy. The circulation volume of data factors is affected by both supply and demand sides and consumption volume. The impact of limited data factor supply is simulated through the transitional dynamic process of the central planner economy. Based on the above equations, the dynamic system is obtained:

$$-\sigma g_c(t) = g_\lambda(t) \tag{3.38}$$

$$\eta g_l(t) = g_\lambda(t) + g_A(t) \tag{3.39}$$

$$(\varepsilon - \alpha)g_d(t) = g_\mu(t) + \zeta g_A(t) + \alpha n \tag{3.40}$$

$$\dot{g}_\mu(t) = [(1+\eta)g_l(t) - g_A(t) - g_\mu(t)][\zeta g_A(t) + g_\mu(t) - \rho + n] - \zeta \dot{g}_A(t) \tag{3.41}$$

$$g_c(t) = g_A(t) + g_l(t) \tag{3.42}$$

$$\dot{g}_A(t) = g_A(t)[(\zeta - 1)g_A(t) + \alpha g_d(t) + \alpha n] \tag{3.43}$$

where $g(\cdot)(t)$ represents the growth rate of a variable or shadow price in period t. Starting from the steady-state values of the central planner economy, the transitional dynamic process of the economy is simulated.

Conclusion 4: In the production mode where data factors train generative AI, when the supply of data factors is unrestricted, the economy will start growing earlier and quickly enter a steady state. Households' labor supply will also show a downward trend earlier, with a faster decline rate. When the supply of data factors is restricted, the start time of economic growth will be delayed, and the time to enter the steady state will be later. Households need to provide more labor for a long time until the economic growth starts, after which the growth rate of labor supply begins to decline.

Conclusion 5: After introducing the elastic labor setting, the convergence speed of the dynamic system is significantly reduced. Comparing the transitional dynamic results of this paper with those of Cong et al. (2021), regardless of whether data factors are restricted, the dynamic system of Cong et al. (2021) converges in about 400 periods, while after introducing the elastic labor supply setting in this paper, the dynamic system converges in about 1000 periods. The reason is that the labor supply and data sales of representative households are mutually substitutable; limited data factors will increase the labor demand of enterprises, thereby inducing households to increase labor supply and reduce data factor supply, ultimately reducing the technical accumulation rate of generative AI R&D enterprises.

Figure 3.4 shows the transitional dynamic process of the economy with (without) data factor supply constraints.

The horizontal axis represents time, and the vertical axis represents the growth rate of various economic variables. It can be seen from the figure that when the supply of data elements is restricted, the growth rate of the economy is low in the initial stage, gradually rises over time, and finally enters a steady state; when there are no restrictions on the supply of data elements, the economy grows at a faster rate and quickly enters a steady state.

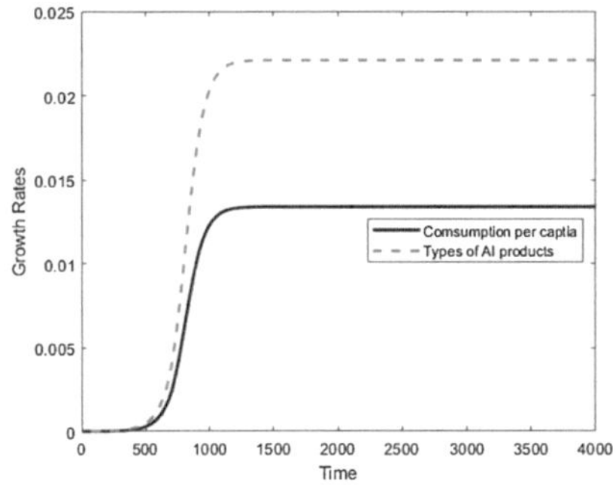

a. The Growth Rate of Per Capita Consumption and the Expansion Speed of Types of DT Artificial Intelligence Products (with Data Element Supply Constraints)

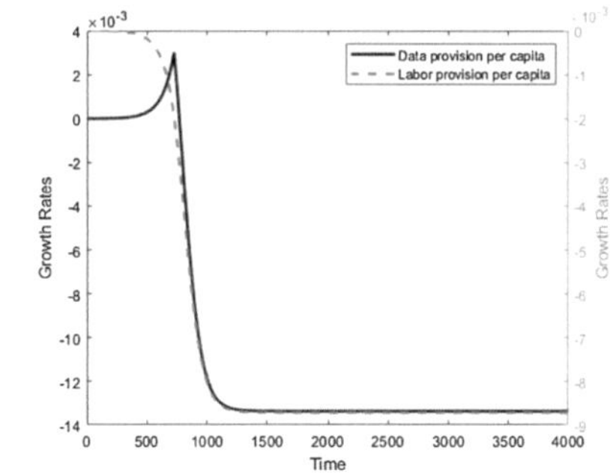

b. The Growth Rates of Per Capita Labor Supply and Per Capita Data Supply (with Data Element Supply Constraints)

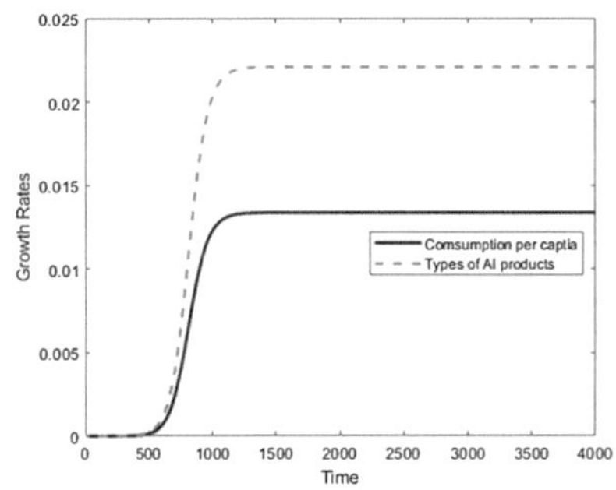

c. The Growth Rate of Per Capita Consumption and the Expansion Speed of Types of DT Artificial Intelligence Products (without Data Element Supply Constraints)

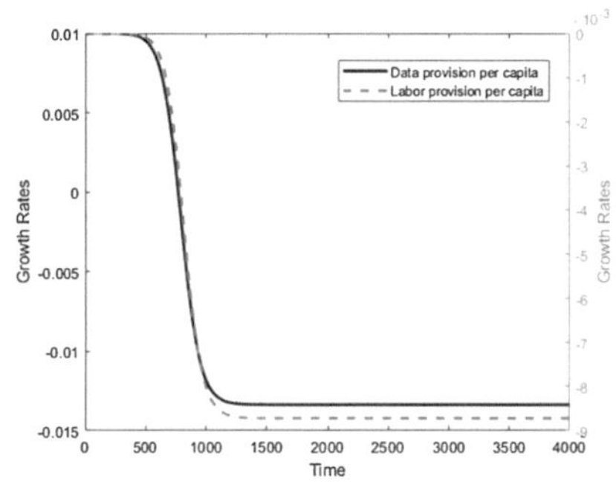

d. The Growth Rates of Per Capita Labor Supply and Per Capita Data Supply (without Data Element Supply Constraints)

Fig. 3.4 Transitional dynamic process of the economy with (or without) restrictions on data element supply

3.4 Conclusions and Policy Recommendations

Based on the theoretical deduction and numerical simulation analysis of the above model, we draw several important research conclusions, which not only expand the current growth theory in the context of the combination of data elements and generative artificial intelligence but also provide theoretical support and practical enlightenment for real-world policy formulation.

The ownership arrangement of data elements has a crucial impact on the path of economic growth and the level of residents' welfare. In the model setting, data can be owned either by residents or directly acquired by innovators. Simulation results show that when data is owned by residents, they can balance data sales and labor time allocation according to their own privacy preferences, thereby increasing leisure time and consumption levels while reducing labor supply, and ultimately achieving welfare improvement. Under this setting, although labor input decreases slightly, benefiting from the enhanced efficiency of AI technology and income compensation brought by data transactions, the overall output and residents' utility levels can still maintain a positive evolutionary trend. Conversely, if data supply is constrained—especially in scenarios with unclear property rights, inadequate privacy protection, or lack of incentive mechanisms—innovators struggle to obtain sufficient data to train AI models, which will directly inhibit the accumulation of AI products and technological progress, leading to slower economic growth and reduced residents' welfare.

Privacy sensitivity, the technological spillover effect of AI products, and the marginal contribution rate of data to technological progress jointly determine the speed of AI development and the level of steady-state growth rate. When residents have weak demand for privacy protection, or when the regulatory framework allows a higher degree of data sharing, the supply capacity of the data market is significantly enhanced, which is conducive to the rapid training and iterative update of AI algorithms, thereby increasing the variety and usage efficiency of AI products. At the same time, the external characteristics of AI technology itself determine its positive feedback effect on the entire economic system: AI products not only improve the efficiency of direct users but also provide platforms and tools for other innovators, driving subsequent technological breakthroughs. This multi-level technological spillover mechanism accelerates the overall speed of knowledge accumulation, thereby increasing the steady-state growth rate of the economy and residents' long-term utility.

Loose and clear data usage rules can effectively promote the diffusion and application of AI technology, helping the economic system enter a high-growth stage earlier. Simulation results show that in scenarios without strict data restrictions, the accumulation speed of AI products is faster, the time for economic convergence is significantly shortened, and residents can enjoy higher levels of consumption, leisure, and welfare earlier. This indicates that reasonably relaxing excessive restrictions on data usage and seeking a balance between privacy protection and efficiency improvement is a key path to promoting the high-quality development of the digital economy. Especially in the technical system of generative artificial intelligence, which is highly dependent on data accumulation, institutional constraints on data usage directly affect technological paths and industrial layout, and the phenomenon of "data silos" should be avoided to prevent inhibiting innovation vitality.

The labor supply elasticity mechanism introduced in the model significantly prolongs the time for the economic system to reach a steady state, indicating that there is an in-depth interaction between labor and data elements. With the adjustment of work methods, labor remuneration, and living structures brought about by AI development, residents' preference for choices among labor, leisure, and data transactions will undergo structural changes. Against the background of the overall downward trend in labor supply coupled with population aging, how to alleviate labor shortages and improve the overall well-being of residents by optimizing data allocation and enhancing AI efficiency has become an important issue in macroeconomic governance.

Based on the above research findings, this paper puts forward the following policy recommendations:

Clarify the ownership and transaction mechanism of data elements. Efforts should be made to promote legislation on data right confirmation, clarify residents' ownership of their personal data, and make data a freely tradable asset category. Institutionally, technical means such as smart contracts and blockchain should be encouraged to ensure the traceability and credibility of data transactions, while supporting the construction of a unified and standardized data trading platform to improve market transparency and trust. In terms of income distribution mechanisms, establishing an incentive subsidy mechanism for data transaction income can not only increase residents' willingness to participate but also help create new income sources for residents in the process of AI technology replacing some labor positions, alleviating social pressure brought by the adjustment of employment structure.

Strengthen residents' privacy protection and digital literacy development. Policy formulation should strengthen institutional protection of personal information security while ensuring technological innovation. Cutting-edge technologies such as "privacy computing", "differential privacy", and "multi-party secure computing" can be considered to improve the utilization efficiency of data under the condition of "usable but invisible". At the same time, public awareness of data rights and privacy protection should be raised through education and publicity to enhance consumers' trust in the data circulation process. Studies have shown that the more perfect the privacy protection mechanism, the higher residents' willingness to supply data, the faster technological progress, and the more efficient and stable the overall economic operation.

Improve data processing efficiency and core technology R&D capabilities. Against the backdrop of an increasingly large volume of data, extracting effective information from complex data has become a key bottleneck in AI development. Investment in core technologies such as data cleaning, semantic understanding, model compression, and edge computing should be increased, and enterprises and research institutions should be encouraged to strengthen joint research to break through computing power constraints and algorithm bottlenecks, achieving more efficient AI system training and deployment. In addition, efforts should be made to promote the industry to build an integrated "data-model-application" ecosystem, forming an efficient, collaborative, and positive-cycle AI innovation system.

Build an efficient, open, and credible data element market. As the infrastructure of the data market, data trading platforms should take "fairness, standardization, and security" as core principles, and coordinate data pricing mechanisms, transaction compliance mechanisms, and cross-subject data circulation rules. The government can promote the construction of data element market systems by setting up data transaction pilots and encouraging local governments to explore data asset listing systems; at the same time, on the premise of protecting privacy, moderately relax restrictions on cross-industry and cross-regional data circulation, provide AI enterprises with a wider range of model training materials, and expand the boundaries of their algorithm performance and commercial application scenarios.

Coordinate and promote the coordinated development of AI and the labor market. Facing the future, a new employment ecosystem driven by both "human–machine collaboration" and "data sharing" should be built. On the one hand, optimize the education system, lay out new vocational skills training and lifelong learning mechanisms in advance, and improve workers' adaptability to AI impacts; on the other hand, the government should strengthen reemployment support and social security coverage for groups affected by technological unemployment, providing an institutional buffer zone for group differences in the digital transformation.

In summary, by constructing an endogenous growth model integrating generative artificial intelligence, data elements, and elastic labor supply, this paper reveals the complex and critical interaction logic among technology, data, and labor, and verifies the far-reaching impact of data resource allocation efficiency on AI development, economic growth, and residents' welfare. In the future, further deepening the construction of the data element market, optimizing data property rights and transaction mechanisms, improving privacy system protection, and promoting the accelerated evolution of AI technology are expected to fully release the data multiplier effect, form a new growth paradigm centered on data and intelligence, and help China's economy move forward steadily on the path of high-quality development.

3.5 Chapter Summary

With the core theme of "Data Elements, Generative Artificial Intelligence, and Residents' Employment", this chapter further extends the discussions from previous chapters on the impacts of data and artificial intelligence on technological innovation, corporate risks, and regional entrepreneurship to the critical social issue of employment structure. It systematically reveals how data and intelligent technologies restructure the structure and dynamics of the labor market in the context of the digital economy. Through dual approaches of theoretical modeling and empirical analysis, this chapter not only sorts out the mechanisms by which data and AI act on both sides of labor supply and demand but also explores in depth the institutional conditions and behavioral logic behind such changes, providing solid theoretical support and empirical evidence for understanding how digital technologies transmit from the production side to the employment side.

This chapter first focuses on a classic yet evolving issue: How does technological progress affect employment structure? Against the backdrop of the continuous advancement of automation and artificial intelligence technologies, this question has become increasingly complex. Traditional technologies, typically represented by "reactive" machines, mainly undertake process automation and standard task substitution, with their core role being to improve efficiency and reduce costs. However, a new generation of technologies represented by generative artificial intelligence exhibits stronger "creative" characteristics, capable of performing unstructured tasks such as language generation, image recognition, and content creation, with potential impacts far exceeding previous technologies.

From the perspective of substitution logic, AI directly impacts medium and low-skilled positions, particularly in repetitive roles such as customer service, copywriting, and data entry, where its substitution effect is evident; from the perspective of creation logic, emerging positions such as data annotators, AI trainers, and algorithm evaluators have gradually emerged, forming new employment growth points. This "crowding out-compensation" mechanism is not one-to-one corresponding but presents high heterogeneity in dimensions such as job types, skill structures, and industry attributes, thereby exacerbating the differentiation of the employment structure.

More importantly, the impact of AI on employment structure is not limited to quantitative changes but is also reflected in qualitative transformation. Trends such as the rising proportion of high-skilled positions, increased demand for interdisciplinary capabilities, and shortened career lifecycles have already emerged. This requires workers to possess stronger adaptability and lifelong learning abilities, while traditional education and vocational training systems face obvious challenges in adaptation.

An important contribution of this chapter is expanding "labor" from a single physical or mental effort to a ternary choice mechanism of "labor-data-leisure". In the digital economy, individuals can engage in "data labor" by authorizing data usage, participating in the platform economy, and remotely participating in AI training—i.e., using personal data as a production factor to participate in the value creation process. Such behaviors transcend the definition of the traditional labor market and constitute a new form of economic participation in the data era.

The theoretical model depicts the dynamic allocation choices of representative residents among working hours, data sales, and leisure by introducing the setting of elastic labor supply. Numerical simulation results show that in scenarios where data property rights are unclear or data incentives are insufficient, individuals tend to maintain traditional labor methods, leading to limited data accumulation speed of AI enterprises, which in turn inhibits the overall speed of technological evolution and economic growth efficiency. This mechanism reveals the profound impact of institutional design on the path of technological diffusion.

In addition, the behavioral logic of labor suppliers is influenced by multiple factors such as privacy sensitivity, income elasticity, and institutional incentives. If the returns from data sales are significantly higher than labor wages, individuals may reduce working hours and instead rely on data income; conversely, they tend to choose traditional employment methods. This phenomenon reflects the increased substitutability between data and labor, also making labor supply itself an outcome variable of technological and institutional evolution rather than an exogenous setting.

In the dynamic path analysis, this chapter demonstrates the impact of data elements on the operation trajectory of the economy under different institutional constraints by introducing two supply scenarios: data-constrained and data-free. Results show that in scenarios with sufficient data element supply, the per capita consumption growth rate can reach 2.74%, the speed of AI technology accumulation accelerates significantly, while labor supply decreases by 1.18%, presenting a macro mechanism of "efficiency improvement-labor reallocation". This mechanism echoes the regional analysis results of "entrepreneurship-driven employment" in Chapter 4, forming a complete chain of data impacting production factors.

However, in data-constrained supply scenarios, AI R&D enterprises face training bottlenecks, technological iteration slows down, which in turn feeds back to slower growth in employment and income levels. This mechanism once again emphasizes the linkage logic between "institutional foundation-technological capabilities-employment structure", suggesting that policy designers should optimize data governance systems while strengthening dynamic management of the path of AI technology diffusion.

Notably, although technological progress is generally conducive to improving social welfare, the distribution of its benefits is extremely uneven. Platform enterprises and capital owners concentrate on enjoying benefits due to their algorithmic advantages and data resources, while workers are often at the bottom of the data value chain. If this structural imbalance is not intervened in a timely manner, it may exacerbate income gaps, trigger social instability, and become a "backlash" force against technological evolution.

Based on the above analysis, this chapter further proposes a series of institutional and policy recommendations to build an employment governance system adapted to the development of the digital economy. First, the construction of a data element market should become the core of policies, improving data supply efficiency and breaking information barriers between AI enterprises and workers by clarifying data property rights, optimizing data transaction mechanisms, and establishing data trading platforms.

Second, structural reforms in the education system should be promoted. Most existing education systems are oriented towards knowledge indoctrination and lack the cultivation of emerging skills such as data governance, algorithm understanding, and cross-platform collaboration capabilities. Against the backdrop of "human–machine collaboration" becoming the norm, it is necessary to comprehensively adjust curriculum settings and evaluation standards from basic education to vocational training, build a lifelong learning mechanism, and provide an institutional buffer zone for workers to cope with technological impacts.

Third, a more flexible social security system should be constructed, focusing on reemployment support, income compensation, and career transition guidance for groups marginalized by AI technologies. Especially for medium and low-skilled workers, special job transfer channels and skill training mechanisms should be set up to prevent the accumulation of "structural unemployment" brought about by technological evolution.

Finally, the responsibilities of platform enterprises should be strengthened, and a "data dividend sharing mechanism" should be explored—i.e., feeding back part of the benefits to data producers through technology taxes, data dividends, AI income regulation, etc., to truly realize the inclusiveness of technological progress.

The conclusion of this chapter actually lays the groundwork for understanding the issues in the next chapter: Data not only reshapes the structure of the labor market but also deeply intervenes in enterprises' re-understanding, re-classification, and re-control of "labor" itself. In this process, enterprise organizations are both users of data and "platforms and executors" of data-driven labor structure restructuring. Enterprises with stronger data capabilities have more detailed perceptions of labor, more sensitive responses to behaviors, and more forward-looking control of risks, thus being more likely to achieve optimal solutions for human resource allocation in complex environments.

The following chapters will adopt a perspective with more micro-organizational characteristics to analyze how enterprises use data technologies to enhance their labor governance capabilities against the backdrop of increased uncertainty, with a particular focus on how enterprises identify and respond to risks, formulate labor-related policies, and achieve flexible, efficient, and sustainable organizational operation methods through data-driven management systems. Enterprises are not passive recipients of data technologies but core nodes that actively use data to address challenges in complex external environments. Only by deeply understanding the interaction mechanism between enterprise data capabilities and labor governance can we truly grasp the complex process of "how data elements affect K"—starting from labor governance, mapping the underlying logic between capital returns and organizational stability.

References

Jones, C.I., Tonetti, C. (2020). Nonrivalry and the Economics of Data. *Am. Econ. Rev. 110* (9), 2819–2858. https://doi.org/10.1257/aer.20191330

Kabir Hassan, M., Chiaramonte, L., Dreassi, A., Paltrinieri, A., Pisera, S. (2021). The crossroads of ESG and religious screening on firm risk. *Res. Int. Bus. Financ. 58* https://doi.org/10.1016/j.ribaf.2021.101500

Mei D., and Gong L. (2011). "Exchange Rate System Choices in Emerging Market Economies", *Economic Research*, No. 11, pp. 73–88.

Romer, P. M. (1990). Endogenous technological change. *Journal of Political Economy, 98*(5, Pt. 2), S71–S102.

Wang Y. and Dong W. (2020). "How is the rise of robots affecting China's labor market? — Evidence from listed manufacturing companies," *Economic Research*, No. 10, pp. 159–175.

Wang L., Qian Y., Song D., and Dong Z. (2023a). "Job Transition Effects of Robot Applications and Characteristics of Employment-Sensitive Groups—Empirical Evidence from the Micro-Individual Level," *Economic Research Journal*, No. 7, pp. 69–85.

Wang L., Qian Y., Zhou H., and Dong Z. (2023b). "The Impact of Artificial Intelligence Technology and the Direction of Occupational Changes in China," *Management World*, No. 11, pp. 74–95.

Wu L., Wang C., Fu C., and Gong L. (2023). "Artificial Intelligence, Employment and Monetary Policy Objectives", Economic Research, No. 1, pp. 56-72. Acemoglu, D., & Robinson, J. A. (2015). Why Nations Fail: The Origins of Power, Prosperity and Poverty. *Profile Books.*

Zhou G., Li L., and Meng L. (2021). "The Impact of Intelligentization on China's Labor Market: An Analysis Based on Employment Breadth and Intensity," *Financial Research*, No. 6, pp. 39–58.

Chapter 4
Big Data Analytics, Firm Risk and Corporate Policies: Evidence from China

4.1 Big Data Analytics Capability and Corporate Risk Decision-Making

In recent years, Big Data Analytics (BDA) has emerged as a critical tool for firms to identify market trends, optimize resource allocation, and manage risks, driving profound transformations in management models (Ghasemaghaei, 2021; Jones & Tonetti, 2020). However, despite extensive research exploring the applications of BDA in marketing, supply chain management, and user behavior analysis, systematic studies on its relationship with corporate risk remain notably scarce. As a resource with both technical and strategic attributes, the deployment of BDA may fundamentally alter firms' decision-making models and influence risk levels through multiple channels. This chapter aims to fill this research gap by investigating the internal logic and transmission mechanisms between firms' BDA capabilities and risk-taking behavior.

To this end, this chapter first constructs a firm-level BDA capability index covering A-share listed companies. Unlike previous literature that predominantly adopts questionnaire surveys (e.g., Akter et al., 2016; Wamba et al., 2017), this study employs an unstructured text mining approach: leveraging deep learning algorithms to expand "big data"-related vocabulary, extracting the frequency of relevant keywords from annual reports, and assigning differentiated weights based on semantic similarity to establish a comprehensive measurement. This method not only avoids the subjectivity of manual word selection but also enhances the stability and explanatory power of the index, enabling a more comprehensive and objective capture of firms' dynamic practices in big data applications.

Within a framework integrating theory and empirics, this chapter further examines the impact of BDA capabilities on firms' strategic decisions and verifies their mediating effect in the relationship between BDA and risk. Drawing on the research of Ferris et al. (2017) and Bernile et al. (2018), this study analyzes the mechanisms

X. Li et al., *Data as a New Factor of Production*, Applied Economics and Policy Studies, https://doi.org/10.1007/978-981-95-9985-1_4

of three types of strategic behaviors: investment, R&D, and mergers and acquisitions (M&As). The results indicate that firms with stronger BDA capabilities exhibit significantly higher investment scales, R&D expenditures, and M&A frequencies, demonstrating greater strategic initiative and risk preference. Combined with existing literature on the positive association between strategic behaviors and corporate risk, this study reveals the transmission path of "BDA capability → decision-making behavior → corporate risk," suggesting that while BDA enhances firms' innovation vitality, it may also exacerbate operational and market risks.

The remainder of this chapter is structured as follows: Sect. 4.2 reviews the theoretical foundation and proposes research hypotheses; Sect. 4.3 introduces data sources, variable construction, and tests of indicator validity; Sects. 4.4 to 4.7 sequentially present the empirical model, regression results, robustness tests, and heterogeneity analysis; Sect. 4.8 summarizes the main findings and puts forward policy recommendations and future research directions that balance innovation and risk management.

4.2 Literature Review and Hypotheses

4.2.1 Big Data Analytics

Existing research often discusses how BDA aids in value creation for enterprises by examining its impact on three aspects: firm performance, decision-making, and innovation. Based on the Resource-Based Theory, researchers define different types of big data analytical resources and explore their role in enhancing the capability of firms to create value (Gupta & George, 2016; Mikalef et al., 2019; Müller et al., 2018). Similarly, drawing from the Dynamic Capabilities perspective, Yasmin et al. (2020) categorize BDA capabilities into infrastructure capabilities, management capabilities, and human resource capabilities, and discuss their positive effects on firm performance.

In exploring the relationship between big data and corporate decision-making, Shamim et al. (2019) suggest that excellent big data management is a prerequisite for leveraging big data capabilities, positively influencing the quality of big data-driven decision-making. Awan et al. (2021a, 2021b) also confirm the positive relationship between big data analytical capabilities and decision-making quality. Acharya et al. (2018) found that knowledge co-creation within an organization is a mediating variable in how big data facilitates effective decision-making. Furthermore, Merendino et al. (2018) discovered that if there is a lack of awareness, cognitive bias, or overestimation of big data at the senior management level, it can affect the cohesion of the board of directors and negatively impact their decisions.

Given the uniqueness of big data technology, companies that adopt BDA typically exhibit superior innovation performance compared to those that do not. Ghasemaghaei and Calic (2019) found that data velocity, diversity, and accuracy all enhance a firm's insights, thereby improving its innovation capability, although they did not detect a role for data volume in this relationship. Further research by Ghasemaghaei and Calic (2020) revealed that data diversity and velocity positively impact business innovation performance, with data velocity being particularly crucial.

Previous studies have linked BDA with corporate performance, showing that companies adopting BDA have higher decision quality and innovation capabilities than their peers. We expand the literature on the corporate-level impact of BDA by investigating how it influences corporate decision-making and further affects firm risk.

4.2.2 *Firm Risk*

The relationship between firm risk and return is important in financial economics. Risk represents potential harm and encompasses opportunities and profits; appropriate firm risk is the foundation for a company to earn returns. Previous research has provided ample evidence on the determinants of firm risk. These studies have largely focused on micro aspects such as management, board, and company levels, with occasional reference to macro aspects.

The literature generally indicates that CEOs and boards of directors are usually the primary decision-makers regarding whether a company adopts risky decisions. Therefore, factors such as the gender diversity of company executives and boards of directors (P. A. A. et al., 2016; Bernile et al., 2018), social experiences (Neyland, 2020), personality traits (Harrison et al., 2020), and social network relationships (Fan et al., 2021) can all affect firm risk. Company-level factors influencing firm risk include corporate governance structure (Abdoh & Liu, 2021; Kini & Williams, 2012), company nature (Batten et al., 2021; Graddy-Reed, 2021) (whether multinational or non-profit), corporate social responsibility (Albuquerque et al., 2019), tax avoidance strategies (Perryman et al., 2016), risk disclosure (Kim & Yasuda, 2018), non-financial disclosure (Rossi & A, 2020), and brand assets (Rego et al., 2009). Additionally, researchers have examined the impact of macro-environmental factors on firm risk, such as national macro policies (Huang et al., 2021), religious culture (Kabir Hassan et al., 2021), and the application of RFID technology (Tang and Zhang, 2019).

Although the studies mentioned above provide rich and interesting insights into the determinants of firm risk, the evidence on how the application of emerging technologies, such as BDA, affects firm risk has not been fully discussed. This technology has already reached a proliferation of about 90% at the corporate level. We contribute to this literature by exploring the relationship between BDA and firm risk, providing a more comprehensive reference for this body of research.

4.2.3 Hypothesis Development

Classical Financial Economic Theory suggests that firm risk and returns are positively correlated over time (Merton, 1987; Sharpe, 1964). Firm risk is the inherent risk of internal and external factors that affect the profitability of a firm and it accompanies the whole life cycle of a firm's existence (Huang et al., 2021; Jo & Na, 2012). We believe the main reasons BDA affects firm risk are as follows.

On the one hand, we conjecture that BDA leads to lower levels of firm risk for several reasons. First, BDA reduces information asymmetry and subjective interferences faced by decision-makers within firms, thereby improving the quality of managerial decision-making. Researchers such as Awan et al. (2021a, 2021b) propose that BDA enhances decision-making quality through data-driven insights, business intelligence, and analytics capabilities. Drawing on dynamic capability theory, Li et al. (2022) find that the positive impact of BDA on decision-making enables firms to gain a competitive advantage. Other studies indicate that firms adopt BDA tools to transform large volumes of data into knowledge, aiding effective decision-making and strategy formulation in dynamic market scenarios (Chatterjee et al., 2023; Voort et al., 2021). In summary, BDA facilitates organizations in gaining new knowledge, enabling managers to make high-quality, data-based decisions and reducing firm risk arising from decision-making blind spots.

Second, BDA has the ability to uncover patterns, trends, and correlations hidden within vast amounts of data. In-depth analysis of big data sets allows for the identification of market and business environment changes. This empowers organizations to adapt their products, services, and business models to meet evolving market demands. Côrte-Real et al. (2017) find that BDA fosters dynamic capabilities through knowledge management, thereby impacting processes and competitive advantage. Additionally, Mikalef et al. (2020) suggest that BDA enables firms to generate insights that strengthen their dynamic capabilities. Other studies demonstrate that BDA tools provide firms with information regarding customer preferences, likes, dislikes, and more. This information facilitates more accurate forecasting and prediction (Chatterjee et al., 2023; Tseng et al., 2022). Consequently, the discovery of insights through big data empowers companies to enhance their competitiveness, achieve business growth, and maintain a leading position in the market, thereby reducing firm risk. Accordingly, we propose the following hypothesis.

Hypothesis 1a. Big data analytics reduces firm risk.

Conversely, we conjecture that BDA may lead to over-investment, data analysis capability or changes in corporate policies that increase firm risk. First, achieving value from BDA necessitates a synergistic integration of data, algorithms, and computational capabilities. For instance, in the automotive industry, substantial datasets are employed to fine-tune algorithms, enhancing the safety features of self-driving cars (Jones & Tonetti, 2020). This underscores the considerable investment required in terms of corporate resources, encompassing the cultivation of specialized technical talent and the establishment of robust data infrastructure (Singh, 2022; Yasmin et al.,

2020). This investment may, however, inadvertently divert resources from other ventures with more predictable returns, creating a potential crowding-out effect. Moreover, the adoption of cutting-edge big data technologies by firms introduces heightened uncertainty and intricacies into their operational processes (Low et al., 2011). Consequently, challenges emerge in the realm of BDA (Sivarajah et al., 2017). Despite the rapid evolution of BDA at a technical level, there remains room for improvement in the accuracy and security of practical applications. At an organizational level, executives' decision-making using big data is contingent not solely upon its predictive and analytical prowess but also on the adept coordination and management of big data resources (Gupta et al., 2020).

Second, BDA induces a transformation in managerial decision-making patterns through two primary mechanisms. On one hand, predicated on the Bounded Rationality Hypothesis (Simon, 1996), which posits that managers, faced with numerous outcome possibilities, operate within constraints and make decisions that are satisficing rather than perfectly rational. This implies a threshold beyond which decisions with uncertainties exceeding managerial acceptance cannot be embraced. Yet, leveraging the robust analytical and predictive capabilities of big data empowers managers to obtain more predictive information. This heightened predictability, in turn, increases the likelihood that managers will embrace decisions associated with higher risks and rewards. Furthermore, the Resource Integration-Based View (RIBV) theory posits that efficient corporate resource integration fosters the development of core competencies (Bruce et al., 2019; Peters, 2016), the judicious allocation of limited corporate resources forms the bedrock for optimizing firms' economic performance. Literature has confirmed that there is no doubt that BDA can improve the ability of firms to allocate resources and analyze and predict the internal and external environment (Ciampi et al., 2021; Yasmin et al., 2020), which may lead firms to engage in more risky activities to obtain higher returns. Therefore, we posit a converse hypothesis.

Hypothesis 1b. Big data analytics increases firm risk.

The conceptual model of this study is shown in Fig. 4.1.

4.3 Data and Methodology

4.3.1 Sample and Data Collection

We selected all A-share listed companies from 2003 to 2019 as the initial research sample and processed the data as follows: (I) the observations of ST, *ST and delisted firms; (II) the observations with missing values of variables; and (III) the observations of listed companies in the IT industry. Because the BDA belongs to the IT industry, the impact of BDA on them may be different from that of other industries, so it is excluded. Ultimately, our sample comprises 19,116 observations from 2,226 listed

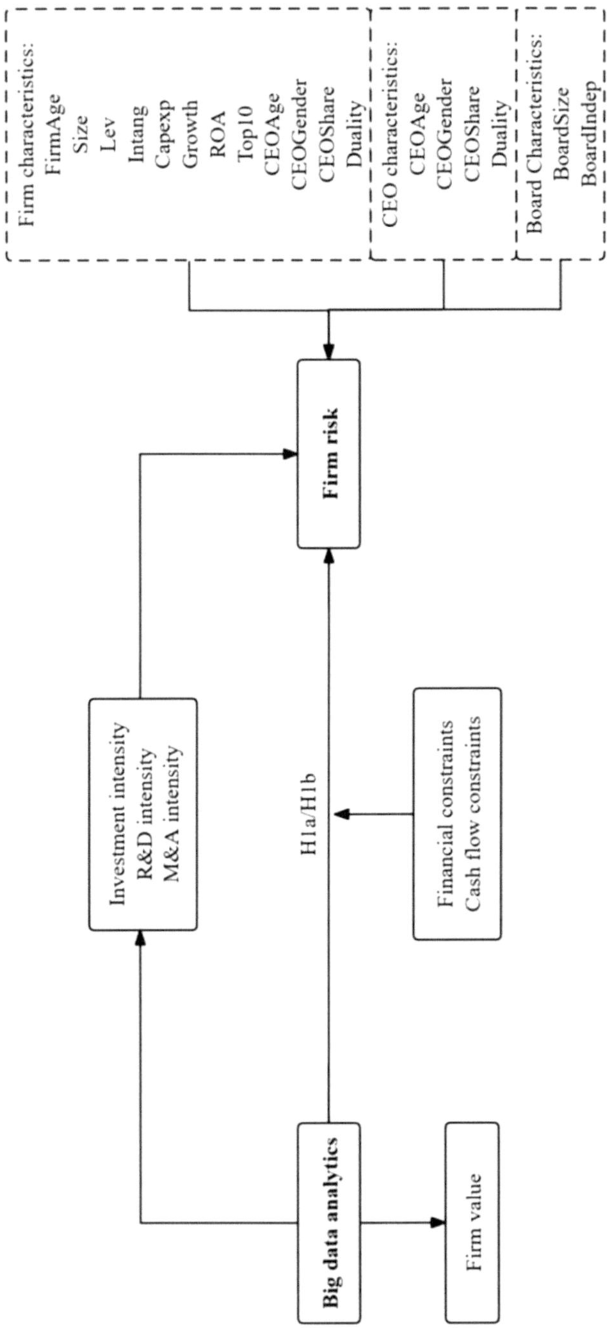

Fig. 4.1 Conceptual model

companies. The BDA measures are based on the analysis of annual reports of listed companies. The annual reports are obtained from the Shanghai Stock Exchange, the Shenzhen Stock Exchange, the Cninfo database and other public websites. We use the financial data from the China Stock Market Accounting Research (CSMAR) database. All continuous variables are winsorized at their 1% and 99% values. Standard errors of all regression results are adjusted for firm-level clustering.

4.3.2 Big Data Analytics Capability

The measurement of BDA capability has become a hot frontier issue of common concern in academia and industry. Since BDA capability is an abstract concept, it is not easy to find an indicator to measure it in reality accurately. The annual report disclosed by listed companies is an objective summary and statement based on the actual operation of listed companies. Therefore, we believe that the frequency of big data-related terms in annual reports reflects firms' BDA capability (Zhang et al., 2021a, b). Based on the above basic assumptions, we think it is scientifically feasible to use the frequency statistics of the words related to "big data" in firms' annual reports to measure BDA capability. However, unlike Zhang et al. (2021a, b), we believe that it is unreasonable to measure the BDA capability with the same weight for different "big data" keywords.

The process of constructing the BDA capability index is as follows:

(1) Download all annual reports disclosed by A-share listed companies from the Shanghai Stock Exchange, Shenzhen Stock Exchange and Cninfo database, and manually collect and supplement the missing annual reports from other public websites. (2) Extract all text information in the annual reports through the Python PDFMiner, which is used as the information pool for Chinese word separation.[1] (3) Based on jieba,[2] separate the text of annual reports and transform the continuous, unstructured Chinese paper into a discrete, distributed word vector. Subsequently, we clean the word vector, eliminating keywords preceded by "none", "not" and "non-" in front of the expressions, and remove deactivated words. (4) The term "big data" first appeared in the 1980s and is generally translated as big data or massive data in China. Therefore, our study chooses to include "big data" and "massive data" as seed words in the dictionary. (5) Expand the seed word set with the Continuous Bag of Words (CBOW) model in Word2Vec to obtain similar words and their corresponding similarity; (6) Capturing the frequencies of keywords and the total number of words in the separate annual report word vector set based on the seed word set and the expanded word set. (7) Calculate the BDA capability index.

[1] Chinese word separation is a process of grouping a sequence of characters into a sequence of words. Unlike English, which uses spaces as natural separators, Chinese characters need to be grouped into words for semantic recognition to convey their true meaning.

[2] The Chinese word segmentation module for Python.

A single word can often describe only part of the information of a feature of a thing, and we often need to use different words with similar semantics when describing the same feature of a thing. Therefore, we need to expand the seed word set in our study, and use the obtained expanded word set as a proxy variable for BDA. Word2Vec is a model for efficient training of word vectors proposed by Mikolov et al. (2013). The core concept of the model is that similar words in a sentence are related to each other, and two words with similar contexts should also have similar word vectors. Based on such a basic assumption, we can use words to predict words. We use the Continuous Bag-of-words (CBOW) Model in the Word2Vec neural network model to obtain similar words and their corresponding similarity, which is trained on the massive Chinese text corpus disclosed by listed companies. The massive text corpus includes financial reports, board reports, management discussion and analysis (MD&A), audit reports, notes to financial statements, IPO prospectuses, internal control evaluation reports, transcripts of earnings presentations, social responsibility reports, interactive Q&A data, inquiry function data, interim announcements, and other announcements. The formula for CBOW is

$$\max \sum_{\omega \in C} \log p(\omega | Context(\omega)) \tag{4.1}$$

where C is all words in the corpus, ω is the central word, and $Context(\omega)$ is the context word of the central word. The task of CBOW is to give the words within a certain neighborhood radius of the central word, which is the context word of the central word. Then, predict the probability of the output word being that central word.

Following Wei et al. (2022), we calculate BDA capabilities using the following model:

$$Bigdata_{it} = \frac{\sum Freq_{itn} \times Sim_n}{Totalwords_{it}} \tag{4.2}$$

where $Bigdata_{it}$ is the BDA capability. $Freq_{itn}$ is the exact word frequency of the nth word in the dictionary in the annual report of firm i in year t. Sim_n is the similarity between the nth word in the dictionary and the seed word. We assign the similarity of the seed word to 1. $Totalwords_{it}$ is the total number of words in the annual report of firm i in year t after excluding English and numbers.

4.3.3 Firm Risk

Following Sila et al. (2016), Chaivisuttangkun and Jiraporn (2021), Fan et al. (2021) and Kabir Hassan et al. (2021), we use three different ways to measure firm risk: Total Risk, Systematic Risk and Idiosyncratic Risk. First, we calculate the annualized standard deviation of daily stock returns. To make the estimated coefficients more intuitive, we multiply the calculations by 100 as a proxy variable for total risk, which will not fail to affect the significance of the estimates. Second, based on the capital asset pricing model (CAPM), we calculate the regression coefficient of market returns, β, to measure systematic risk. β is the degree of change in a firm's daily stock returns in response to changes in market returns. Third, we calculate the annualized standard deviation of the regression residuals, a variable that represents idiosyncratic risk since the risk in the broad market has been eliminated. The CAPM is shown below:

$$R_{it} = \alpha_i + \beta_i R_{mt} + \varepsilon_{it} \tag{4.3}$$

where R_{it} is the stock return of firm i on day t; R_{mt} is the stock market return on day t.

4.3.4 *Control Variables*

Following Sila et al. (2016), Bernile et al. (2018), Fan et al. (2021), we include three vectors of variables that control for firm characteristics, CEO characteristics, and board characteristics in the regression model, including FirmAge, Size, Lev, Intang, Capex, Growth, ROA, Top10; CEOAge, CEOGender, CEOShare, Duality; BoardSize, BoardIndep. Industry and year dummy variables are also set in this study to control for industry and year fixed effects. Industry classification refers to the *Guideline on Industry Classification of Listed Companies* issued by the China Securities Regulatory Commission in 2012.

4.3.5 *Validity Testing of Big Data Analytics*

Prior to the empirical analysis, we will test the constructed BDA to ensure that it is valid.

4.3.5.1 The Cut-Off Points for Growth Trends in Big Data Analytics Capabilities

Most media believe that 2013 is the first year of big data. Along with 2013 comes the explosion of data, a big data revolution that brings unprecedented innovation and challenges to business development and decision-making. We predict that the growth of enterprise BDA capabilities will be slow until 2012 and rapid from 2013 onwards. We calculated the mean value of BDA capability for the full sample of enterprises and plotted it on Panel A in Fig. 4.1. It can be seen that the BDA capability has been growing slowly from 2003 to 2012 and growing rapidly since 2013, which is exactly in line with our prediction and proves the validity of our constructed BDA capability. Further, we show the trend of the broad BDA capability (see below for the construction process) through Panel B of Fig. 4.2, and the result is similar to Panel A. Therefore, big data can better reflect the BDA capability.

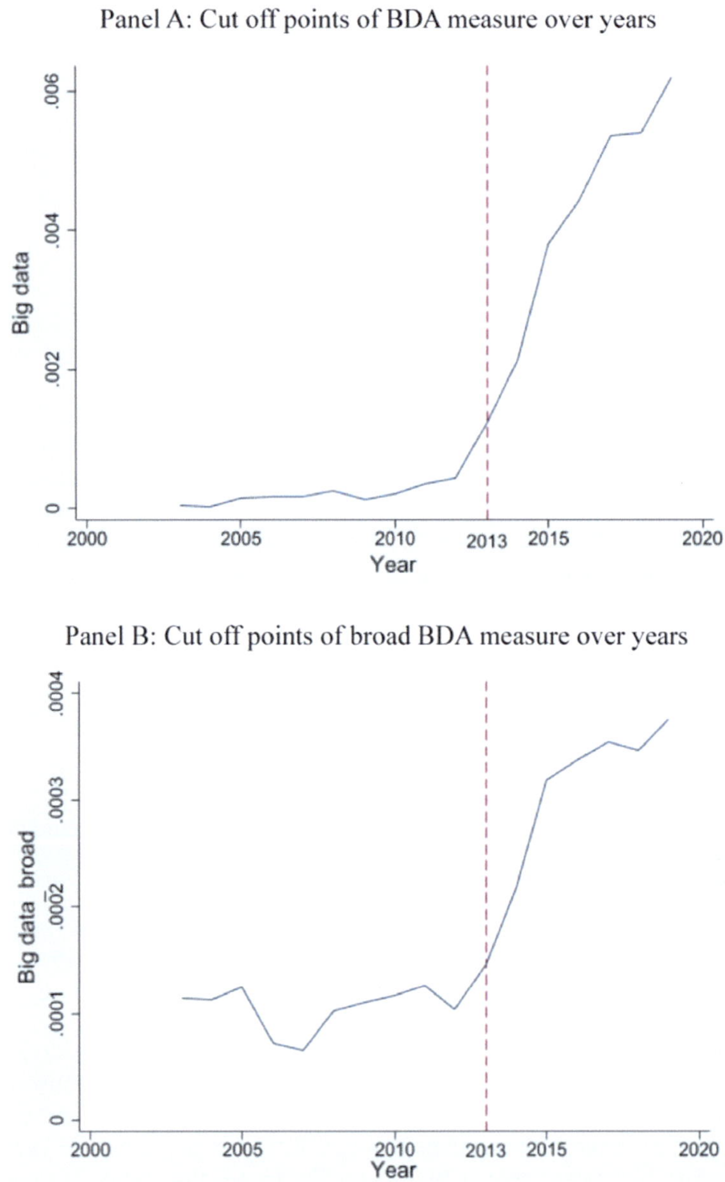

Fig. 4.2 Growth trends in BDA capabilities

4.3.5.2 Persistence of BDA Capabilities in the Time Dimension

The implementation of the company's big data development strategy cannot be completed in a short period. Therefore, we believe that BDA capabilities are persistent in the time dimension. In this study, we use the internal consistency reliability to test the persistence of BDA capability. Specifically, we screened out 706 companies that consistently performed BDA during the sample period 2013 to 2019. Based on Cronbach (1951), we calculated Cronbach's Alpha coefficients for each company's BDA capability over the sample period, thus analyzing the persistence of the time dimension. In general, in a basic study, the Alpha coefficient of no less than 0.8 indicates high consistency and confidence in the data, while for an exploratory study, the Alpha coefficient should be at least 0.7. Our results show that the Alpha coefficient of big data analytic capability corresponding to companies that have continuously conducted BDA for seven years is 0.9176, which indicates the validity of our constructed BDA capability index.

4.4 Empirical Results and Analysis

4.4.1 Descriptive Statistics

Table 4.1 reports the descriptive statistics for all variables. The table shows that, on average, total risk is 2.9413, systematic risk is 1.1480, and idiosyncratic risk is 2.3668. In terms of firm characteristics, our sample firms have a moderate average age, large average size, moderate leverage, and good growth, ranging from 0 to 29 years old, with an average value of 9.83. Specifically, the average firm size, measured as the natural logarithm of total assets, is 22.17, which implies that the average sample firm has total assets of RMB 4.25 billion. On average, the leverage ratio is 46.01%, the intangible assets ratio is 4.62%, the capital expenditure ratio is 5.44%, the firm growth is 0.2017. Overall, these values are consistent with those reported by Fan et al. (2021) and Huang et al. (2021).

4.4.2 Does Big Data Analytics Affect Firm Risk?

In this section, we investigate whether the adoption of BDA is associated with heightened levels of firm risk. Table 4.2 presents the estimated values from the baseline regression. Columns (1)–(3) employ total risk, systematic risk, and idiosyncratic risk as independent variables, integrating two-way fixed effects for both year and industry. The Ordinary Least Squares (OLS) regression outcomes reveal that the coefficient estimates for BDA are all statistically significant at the 1% level. Extending the analysis in columns (4)–(6) with interacted industry-year fixed effects, the coefficients for

Table 4.1 Descriptive statistics

	(1)	(2)	(3)	(4)	(5)	(6)
Variables	N	Mean	SD	Min	Median	Max
Risk measures						
Total Risk	19,116	2.9413	0.9203	1.3138	2.7663	5.6386
Systematic Risk	19,116	1.1480	0.2709	0.3897	1.1484	2.0583
Idiosyncratic Risk	19,116	2.3668	0.7475	1.0269	2.2693	4.7819
Bigdata measures						
Bigdata	19,116	0.0000	0.0001	0.0000	0.0000	0.0006
Bigdata_b	19,116	0.0002	0.0004	0.0000	0.0001	0.0023
Firm characteristics						
FirmAge	19,116	9.8347	6.6333	0.0000	9.0000	29.0000
Size	19,116	22.1704	1.3292	19.3707	21.9899	27.0700
Lev	19,116	0.4601	0.2069	0.0553	0.4618	0.9879
Intang	19,116	0.0462	0.0503	0.0000	0.0334	0.3123
Capex	19,116	0.0544	0.0506	0.0003	0.0397	0.2412
Growth	19,116	0.2017	0.4652	-0.6292	0.1248	3.2243
ROA	19,116	0.0004	0.0006	-0.0022	0.0004	0.0019
Top10	19,116	0.5857	0.1529	0.2331	0.5957	0.9160
CEO characteristics						
CEOAge	19,116	48.8656	6.6564	25.0000	49.0000	81.0000
CEOGender	19,116	0.9337	0.2488	0.0000	1.0000	1.0000
CEOShare	19,116	0.0409	0.1031	0.0000	0.0000	0.5143
Duality	19,116	0.2407	0.4275	0.0000	0.0000	1.0000
Board characteristics						
BoardSize	19,116	8.8187	1.7730	1.0000	9.0000	19.0000
BoardIndep	19,116	0.3693	0.0538	0.0000	0.3333	0.5714

BDA remain significantly positive at the 1% level. Consequently, BDA demonstrates a positive correlation with firm risk.

Assessing the economic significance, for instance, in column (1), the estimated coefficient for BDA is 324.8696. This implies that a one standard deviation increase in BDA capability corresponds to an approximately 0.0325 increase in total risk relative to its sample mean. In column (4), the estimated coefficient for BDA is 260.4473, signifying that a one standard deviation increase in BDA capability results in a 0.0260 increase in total risk. Thus, the positive impact of BDA on firm risk is both statistically and economically substantial, corroborating the support for hypothesis 1b.

Considering control variables, Size and Return on Assets (ROA) exhibit a significant negative association with firm risk across all three metrics. This suggests that larger firms and those with better operating conditions tend to exhibit lower levels

Table 4.2 Big data analytics and firm risk

	(1)	(2)	(3)	(4)	(5)	(6)
Variables	Total risk	Systematic risk	Idiosyncratic risk	Total risk	Systematic risk	Idiosyncratic risk
Bigdata	324.8696***	124.8821***	339.0454***	260.4473***	82.8463***	297.4890***
	(5.4134)	(4.3058)	(5.4643)	(4.0769)	(2.6973)	(4.5207)
FirmAge	-0.0091***	-0.0044***	-0.0076***	-0.0078***	-0.0039***	-0.0064***
	(-8.0143)	(-7.7794)	(-6.6819)	(-6.6987)	(-6.7128)	(-5.5224)
Size	-0.1724***	-0.0154***	-0.2040***	-0.1751***	-0.0171***	-0.2061***
	(-27.5273)	(-4.5869)	(-34.8092)	(-27.3313)	(-4.8988)	(-34.3952)
Lev	0.3893***	-0.0352*	0.5189***	0.3910***	-0.0303	0.5155***
	(10.7329)	(-1.9247)	(15.0089)	(10.6783)	(-1.6192)	(14.6786)
Intang	-0.2617**	-0.1633***	-0.0736	-0.2057	-0.1635***	-0.0396
	(-2.0736)	(-2.6084)	(-0.6407)	(-1.6400)	(-2.6132)	(-0.3414)
Capex	0.1544	0.1428***	0.0821	0.2379**	0.1700***	0.1516
	(1.4446)	(2.8891)	(0.7861)	(2.1598)	(3.3243)	(1.4164)
Growth	0.0993***	-0.0153***	0.1444***	0.0908***	-0.0174***	0.1364***
	(9.0297)	(-3.1878)	(13.8171)	(8.0000)	(-3.5658)	(12.4702)
ROA	-66.8323***	-31.3932***	-50.7905***	-74.6647***	-30.8571***	-62.8673***
	(-6.4861)	(-6.1968)	(-5.1799)	(-7.0910)	(-5.8452)	(-6.2510)
Top10	0.1450***	-0.2201***	0.4068***	0.1880***	-0.2097***	0.4546***
	(3.6988)	(-11.2461)	(10.3746)	(4.7084)	(-10.6089)	(11.3561)
CEOAge	-0.0028***	-0.0003	-0.0031***	-0.0029***	-0.0004	-0.0031***
	(-3.5853)	(-0.9304)	(-3.8948)	(-3.6401)	(-1.1514)	(-3.8694)
CEOGender	0.0073	0.0019	-0.0067	0.0075	0.0026	-0.0042

(continued)

Table 4.2 (continued)

	(1)	(2)	(3)	(4)	(5)	(6)
Variables	Total risk	Systematic risk	Idiosyncratic risk	Total risk	Systematic risk	Idiosyncratic risk
	(0.3350)	(0.1800)	(-0.3242)	(0.3366)	(0.2422)	(-0.2033)
CEOShare	0.2167***	0.1082***	0.1855***	0.2374***	0.1049***	0.2120***
	(3.3581)	(3.8749)	(2.8891)	(3.6452)	(3.6996)	(3.2380)
Duality	0.0092	-0.0064	0.0229*	0.0089	-0.0059	0.0227*
	(0.6687)	(-1.0258)	(1.6805)	(0.6397)	(-0.9332)	(1.6462)
BoardSize	-0.0045	-0.0009	-0.0055	-0.0038	-0.0009	-0.0044
	(-1.3105)	(-0.4894)	(-1.6217)	(-1.1019)	(-0.4943)	(-1.2803)
BoardIndep	0.0431	-0.0258	0.0509	0.0271	-0.0200	0.0292
	(0.4146)	(-0.5229)	(0.4940)	(0.2543)	(-0.3991)	(0.2766)
Constant	6.7349***	1.7187***	6.6417***	6.7582***	1.7445***	6.6479***
	(51.2417)	(24.2593)	(54.4598)	(50.0160)	(23.7756)	(53.2187)
Year	Yes	Yes	Yes	No	No	No
Industry	Yes	Yes	Yes	No	No	No
Year × Industry	No	No	No	Yes	Yes	Yes
Obs	19,116	19,116	19,116	19,116	19,116	19,116
R^2	0.6663	0.2593	0.4771	0.7002	0.3433	0.5288

Note This table reports the panel regression results of firm risk on BDA of Chinese listed companies during the sample period from 2003 to 2019. The standard errors are clustered at the firm level and t-statistics are shown in parentheses. *, ** and *** denote statistical significance at the 10%, 5% and 1% level, respectively

of firm risk. Firm age (FirmAge) and Intangibility (Intang) are negatively correlated with total risk and systematic risk, indicating that firms with longer establishment histories and a higher percentage of intangible assets tend to assume lower risk. Conversely, Capital Expenditure (Capex) shows a significant positive relationship with firm risk measured across all three approaches. This aligns with findings in prior studies (Brandt et al., 2010; Brown & Kapadia, 2007; Irvine & Pontiff, 2009; Jiang et al., 2009; Vozlyublennaia, 2013; Wei & Zhang, 2005). Furthermore, CEO age (CEOAge) exhibits a negative association with total and idiosyncratic risk, suggesting that firms led by older CEOs tend to embrace lower risks, consistent with Berger et al. (2014). Conversely, CEO Shareholding (CEOshare) is positively associated with firm risk at the 1% level, indicating that firms with higher CEO shareholding tend to undertake higher risks.

4.4.3 Which Firms Will Take More (or Less) Risk?

Theoretical analysis shows that firm risk reflects the propensity of firms to pay for it in pursuit of profit. It is fundamentally born in firms' preferences and attitudes toward uncertainty. The evidence to date confirms the positive effect of BDA on firm risk. However, the specific impact of BDA on firm risk may vary in different contexts. In this section, we examine whether the impact of BDA on firm risk depends on firm characteristics and, specifically, whether financing constraints and free cash flow have an impact on the relationship.

4.4.3.1 Big Data Analytics, Financing Constraints and Firm Risk

We first examine whether the impact of BDA on firm risk differs by financing constraints. When firms with presence of more financial constraints, on the one hand, an increase in financing costs may directly lead to higher firm risk. On the other hand, firms may prefer to make profits from high-risk, high-return investments, thereby alleviating the financing constraint dilemma. Therefore, we expect the positive impact of BDA on firm risk to increase in this scenario. Conversely, the relationship between BDA and firm risk may diminish when firms have easy access to capital.

To test this argument, following Fee et al. (2009), we construct a model that measures the degree of financing constraints.

$$P(FC = 1 or 0|Z_{i,t}) = \frac{e^{Z_{i,t}}}{1+e^{Z_{i,t}}} \tag{4.4}$$

$$Z_{i,t} = \alpha_0 + \alpha_1 Size_{i,t} + \alpha_2 Leverage_{i,t} + \alpha_3 \left(\frac{CashDiv}{TA}\right)_{i,t} + \alpha_4 \frac{M}{B}_{i,t} + \alpha_5 \left(\frac{NWC}{TA}\right)_{i,t} + \alpha_6 \left(\frac{EBIT}{TA}\right)_{i,t} \tag{4.5}$$

where Size is the size of the firm's assets, the natural logarithm of total assets; Leverage is the firm's financial leverage, total liabilities divided by total assets; CashDiv is the cash dividends paid by the firm in the year; M/B is the firm's market-to-book ratio, the ratio of market value to book value; NWC is net working capital, working capital net of money capital and short-term investments; EBIT is earnings before interest and taxes; and TA is total assets.

First, we standardize asset size, firm age, and cash dividend payout ratio by year, and rank listed companies in ascending order according to the mean values of the standardized variables. We group firms by whether the selected firm characteristic falls in the top or bottom tercile. For financing constraints, a dummy variable, FC. Listed companies with greater than 66% quantile are defined as less financing constraints group with FC = 0 and those with less than 33% quantile are defined as more financing constraints group with FC = 1. Then, we run a logit regression according to (5), and calculate the probability of financing constraint P for each year of the firm and define it as the financing constraint index.

We add the interaction term Bigdata × FC to the baseline regression and rerun the regression. Table 4.3 report the estimation results of financing constraints as a moderating variable. All coefficients of Bigdata × FC are positive and significant at the 10% level or above. This suggests that the relationship between BDA and firm risk is strengthened when firms with presence of financial constraints. This evidence supports our contention that the positive effect of BDA on firm risk is stronger for firms with more financing constraints.

4.4.3.2 Big Data Analytics, Cash Flow Constrains and Firm Risk

Then, to verify whether the relationship between BDA and firm risk is influenced by free cash flow, we calculate the free cash flow based on The Free Cashflow to Equity Model proposed by Aswath Damodaran. The specific formula is: Equity Free Cash Flow = (net income + non-cash expenses) − working capital additions − capital expenditures − debt principal repayment + new debt issuance. The interaction term Bigdata × Free cash flow is introduced on the basis of the baseline regression and regressed again. Table 4.4 show the estimation results of cash flow constrains as a moderating variable. All three coefficients of the interaction term Bigdata × FCF are negative and significant at the 1% level. This suggests that the positive relationship between BDA and firm risk is moderated when firms have sufficient free cash flow. This evidence validates our expectation.

Table 4.3 Moderating effects: financial constraint

	(1)	(2)	(3)
	Total risk	Systematic risk	Idiosyncratic risk
Bigdata × FC	519.7078***	413.3685***	347.3831*
	(2.7193)	(4.6594)	(1.7302)
Bigdata	319.7829***	123.3470***	337.8521***
	(5.6606)	(4.5396)	(5.7251)
FC	0.0410	0.1500***	-0.0728*
	(1.1448)	(8.6085)	(-1.9464)
FirmAge	-0.0052***	-0.0028***	-0.0045***
	(-4.7728)	(-5.2322)	(-4.0467)
Size	-0.1717***	-0.0040	-0.2095***
	(-21.3932)	(-0.9624)	(-25.5473)
Lev	0.4380***	0.0798***	0.4715***
	(12.1030)	(4.6535)	(12.4250)
Intang	-0.1382	-0.0943	-0.0156
	(-1.1204)	(-1.5604)	(-0.1364)
Capex	0.0125	0.0905*	0.0111
	(0.1223)	(1.9079)	(0.1101)
Growth	0.1306***	-0.0052	0.1697***
	(11.9778)	(-1.0944)	(15.6468)
ROA	-90.8687***	-39.1214***	-68.0414***
	(-8.7946)	(-7.9583)	(-6.5727)
Top10	0.0761**	-0.2097***	0.3213***
	(1.9923)	(-11.1660)	(8.1841)
CEOAge	-0.0022***	-0.0002	-0.0026***
	(-2.8912)	(-0.5117)	(-3.3292)
CEOGender	-0.0042	-0.0009	-0.0126
	(-0.1970)	(-0.0863)	(-0.6165)
CEOShare	0.1625***	0.0738***	0.1543**
	(2.6426)	(2.7384)	(2.4947)
Duality	0.0138	-0.0038	0.0251*
	(1.0505)	(-0.6229)	(1.8838)
BoardSize	-0.0061*	-0.0018	-0.0063*
	(-1.8097)	(-1.0436)	(-1.8772)
BoardIndep	-0.0027	-0.0395	0.0209
	(-0.0263)	(-0.8176)	(0.2023)
Constant	6.7043***	1.4085***	6.7922***
	(37.7743)	(14.9431)	(37.4659)

(continued)

Table 4.3 (continued)

	(1)	(2)	(3)
	Total risk	Systematic risk	Idiosyncratic risk
Year	Yes	Yes	Yes
Industry	Yes	Yes	Yes
Obs	18,164	18,164	18,164
R^2	0.7012	0.2797	0.4956

Note This table reports the regression results of the moderating effects. The standard errors are clustered at the firm level and t-statistics are shown in parentheses. *, ** and *** denote statistical significance at the 10%, 5% and 1% level, respectively

4.4.4 Are These Results Driven by Potential Endogeneity Issues?

All evidence to date suggests that BDA has a positive impact on total, systematic, and idiosyncratic risk. However, potential endogeneity may interfere with our baseline regression results. There are two main types of possible endogeneity problems in this study. One is the simultaneity bias. In our model, we need to focus on whether BDA is also a function of firm risk. That is, firms that take higher risks are more inclined to develop BDA and thus gain excess returns. In addition, large, profitable, and growing firms are more capable of investing in big data projects, which can also bias our estimated coefficients. Another type of problem is the omitted variable problem. There may be unobservable factors that cause the underfitting of our baseline regressions.

This study takes some measures to reasonably address the potential endogeneity problem. First, in the previous section, we introduce industry-year fixed effects to address the simultaneity bias caused by unobservable industry-specific and time-invariant variables. Second, we use instrumental variables to address the endogeneity problem due to simultaneity bias and omitted variables. Finally, we add regional characteristics to further mitigate endogeneity issues in our study.

4.4.4.1 Instrumental Variable

Previous studies have confirmed that the lack of technical talent is a significant constraint to firms' development of big data or AI technologies (Babina et al., 2020; Tambe, 2014). Following Zhang et al. (2021a, b), we construct an instrument based on the Pilot program for cultivating top students in basic disciplines (the "Everest Program"). The Everest Program is a talent training program launched in 2009 by China's Ministry of Education, together with the Ministry of Organization and the

Table 4.4 Moderating effects: cash flow constraint

	(1)	(2)	(3)
	Total risk	Systematic risk	Idiosyncratic risk
Bigdata × FCF	-929.6074***	-369.6302***	-801.8250***
	(-3.1953)	(-2.7951)	(-2.6318)
Bigdata	325.1962***	129.1614***	333.3681***
	(5.3196)	(4.4399)	(5.2852)
FCF	-0.1578***	0.0225	-0.1984***
	(-4.5719)	(1.4811)	(-5.7922)
FirmAge	-0.0083***	-0.0036***	-0.0077***
	(-6.6391)	(-5.5997)	(-6.0659)
Size	-0.2056***	-0.0356***	-0.2237***
	(-28.4403)	(-9.4111)	(-31.4418)
Lev	0.3820***	0.0324	0.4285***
	(8.5567)	(1.5237)	(9.5300)
Intang	-0.1546	-0.0862	-0.0919
	(-1.0212)	(-1.1709)	(-0.6127)
Capex	0.3284**	0.1716***	0.2910**
	(2.4131)	(2.8374)	(2.1799)
Growth	0.1334***	-0.0061	0.1802***
	(9.3429)	(-0.9107)	(13.2037)
ROA	-56.4817***	-34.5205***	-38.4942***
	(-4.4991)	(-5.7273)	(-3.0773)
Top10	0.2533***	-0.2027***	0.4750***
	(5.5112)	(-8.9180)	(10.2871)
CEOAge	-0.0028***	-0.0001	-0.0035***
	(-2.9462)	(-0.1985)	(-3.5939)
CEOGender	-0.0045	-0.0013	-0.0156
	(-0.1668)	(-0.1039)	(-0.6002)
CEOShare	0.1490**	0.0862***	0.1240*
	(2.2736)	(3.0381)	(1.8832)
Duality	0.0067	-0.0008	0.0112
	(0.4284)	(-0.1143)	(0.7096)
BoardSize	-0.0012	0.0012	-0.0050
	(-0.2755)	(0.5607)	(-1.1320)
BoardIndep	0.2006	0.0067	0.1722
	(1.5830)	(0.1115)	(1.3357)
Constant	7.2789***	2.1040***	7.0564***
	(49.2565)	(27.0566)	(48.6771)

(continued)

Table 4.4 (continued)

	(1)	(2)	(3)
	Total risk	Systematic risk	Idiosyncratic risk
Year	Yes	Yes	Yes
Industry	Yes	Yes	Yes
Obs	12,913	12,913	12,913
R^2	0.6500	0.2852	0.4677

Note This table reports the regression results of the moderating effects. The standard errors are clustered at the firm level and t-statistics are shown in parentheses. *, ** and *** denote statistical significance at the 10%, 5% and 1% level, respectively

Ministry of Finance, to cultivate top-notch innovative talents in science and technology disciplines. There are 17 universities[3] selected in the first batch. The pilot was launched in five disciplines: mathematics, physics, chemistry, biology and computer science. The program's implementation has delivered many scientific and technical talents to firms, effectively alleviating the insufficient supply of big data talents for firms.

The program launched its first pilot cohort in 2009, and universities officially implemented it in 2010. Therefore, the first batch of students affected by the program were mainly undergraduates enrolled in 2010, and this batch of students graduated in 2014. Therefore, the time when the Everest program starts to deliver talents to firms in science and engineering disciplines is 2014 and later years. The instrumental variable design model is as follows:

$$IV_{i,t} = \frac{\ln(\sum_{k=1}^{n} \frac{1}{distance_{ik}})}{N_{ct}} \times Post_t \quad (4.6)$$

where i denotes the firm, k denotes the first batch of pilot universities, c denotes the city where the office of the firm is located, and t denotes the year; $distance_{ik}$ denotes the calculated linear distance between the latitude and longitude of the office of firm i and the latitude and longitude of the main campus of college k; n denotes the number of the first batch of pilot universities ($n = 17$), N_{ct} denotes the total number of listed companies in the city c where the office of the firm is located in year t; $Post_t$ is a time dummy variable, t takes the value of 1 in 2014 and later, and 0 otherwise. From model (4.6), it can be seen that the farther the firm is from the university in a straight line, the less it is influenced by the policy, and the lower the probability that the university provides big data talents for the firm. Similarly, the more the number of listed companies in the city where the firm's office is located, the less the firm is influenced by the

[3] The first batch of 17 pilot universities include Peking University, Tsinghua University, Beijing Normal University, Nankai University, Jilin University, Fudan University, Shanghai Jiao Tong University, Nanjing University, University of Science and Technology of China, Zhejiang University, Xiamen University, Shandong University, Wuhan University, Sun Yat-sen University, Sichuan University, Xi'an Jiaotong University, Lanzhou University.

policy. That is, the lower the probability of firms obtaining big data talents. Therefore, the instrument we constructed satisfies the correlation condition. The essential requirement for the validity of an instrumental variable is that it should not affect the dependent variable while influencing the endogenous explanatory variables that may be present. Since the instrumental variables we construct are difficult to influence with firm risk through other channels. Therefore, the instrumental variable in this study satisfies the exclusivity condition.

Table 4.5 reports the regression results of the 2SLS estimators. Since the value of Bigdata is small, we multiply it by 100 to make it easier to display in the table. Column (1) indicates the regression results of the first stage, and the remaining columns indicate the regression results of the second stage. In the first stage, we estimate the relationship between the behavior of the Everest Project in providing big data talent to firms and BDA. The results show that the coefficient of the instrumental variable is positive and significant at the 1% level. This suggests that the availability of big data talent improves BDA. In the second stage, we estimate firm risk based on the fitted values of BDA obtained from the first stage regression. The results show that the estimated coefficients of BDA are all positive and significant at the 10% level or above. The additional evidence based on the instrumental variable of big data talent supply proves the consistency of our baseline regression results.

In addition, the evidence of underidentification test and weak identification test, to some extent, shows the validity of our instrument. Specifically, the Kleibergen-Paap rk LM statistic has a p-value of 0.0000, strongly rejecting the original hypothesis of unidentifiability. The Cragg-Donald Wald F-statistic is 41.940, the Kleibergen-Paap rk Wald F-statistic is 15.877, and the Stock-Yogo weak ID test 15% critical value is 8.96. i.e., for a test with a nominal size of 5%, the true size will not exceed 15%. According to Stock and Yogo (2005), we reject the original hypothesis that the instrument is uncorrelated with each of our dependent variables, indicating to some extent the validity of our instrument.

4.4.4.2 Omitted Unobserved Factors

In addition to firm characteristics, CEO and board characteristics, there may be a category of omitted variables, namely regional characteristics. Regional characteristics are external environmental factors that are independent of the firm and can have an impact on the firm, and these factors may also interfere with our regression results. For example, in cities with higher levels of economic development, firms may be more inclined to take higher risks in pursuit of higher productivity or returns. Conversely, in cities with relatively poor economic development, firms may be less inclined to take higher risks and instead pursue safer and more stable returns.

Following Bernile et al. (2018), city size and level of economic development control variables are added. We use the city's total population where the firm is registered as a proxy variable for city size and the city's GDP as a proxy variable for the level of economic development. We add these two potential omitted variables controlling for all factors and re-run the regressions. Table 4.6 reports the regression

Table 4.5 Instrumental variable

	(1)	(2)	(3)	(4)
	Bigdata/10^{-2}	Total risk	Systematic risk	Idiosyncratic risk
	1st Stage	2nd Stage		
Talent	0.0006***			
	(3.9846)			
Bigdata/10^{-2}		41.0463**	13.8211*	38.8234**
		(2.0908)	(1.7916)	(1.9678)
FirmAge	-0.0001**	-0.0009	-0.0018**	0.0004
	(-2.2467)	(-0.4795)	(-2.2034)	(0.2419)
Size	0.0005***	-0.2022***	-0.0267***	-0.2308***
	(5.2054)	(-16.8761)	(-5.1286)	(-19.5968)
Lev	-0.0008	0.3865***	-0.0383*	0.5174***
	(-1.3084)	(8.9104)	(-1.8862)	(12.5700)
Intang	-0.0027*	-0.1993	-0.1497**	-0.0097
	(-1.6457)	(-1.3665)	(-2.1908)	(-0.0715)
Capex	-0.0034**	0.4267***	0.2446***	0.3308**
	(-2.1845)	(3.1576)	(4.1612)	(2.4867)
Growth	0.0003**	0.0894***	-0.0187***	0.1354***
	(2.0785)	(7.0640)	(-3.3621)	(11.2368)
ROA	0.0677	-69.5650***	-32.1240***	-53.5371***
	(0.3527)	(-5.4176)	(-5.5057)	(-4.4915)
Top10	-0.0012*	0.2799***	-0.1682***	0.5295***
	(-1.6608)	(5.5967)	(-7.3051)	(10.8872)
CEOAge	-0.0000	-0.0029***	-0.0004	-0.0032***
	(-0.1963)	(-3.2529)	(-0.9546)	(-3.5791)
CEOGender	-0.0003	0.0155	0.0037	0.0017
	(-0.7652)	(0.5670)	(0.3155)	(0.0644)
CEOShare	0.0006	0.2835***	0.1401***	0.2425***
	(0.4108)	(3.4157)	(4.1842)	(3.0186)
Duality	0.0005*	-0.0060	-0.0115	0.0088
	(1.8293)	(-0.2944)	(-1.4071)	(0.4400)
BoardSize	-0.0001	-0.0011	0.0004	-0.0025
	(-1.5821)	(-0.2774)	(0.2137)	(-0.6035)
BoardIndep	0.0005	0.0186	-0.0357	0.0292
	(0.2859)	(0.1598)	(-0.6803)	(0.2558)
Year	Yes	Yes	Yes	Yes
Industry	Yes	Yes	Yes	Yes
Constant	-0.0048**	6.1195***	1.7469***	6.1496***

(continued)

Table 4.5 (continued)

	(1)	(2)	(3)	(4)
	$Bigdata/10^{-2}$	Total risk	Systematic risk	Idiosyncratic risk
	1st Stage	2nd Stage		
	(-2.2306)	(27.2279)	(16.6726)	(28.0057)
Obs	19,099	19,099	19,099	19,099
R^2	0.1832	0.5797	0.1476	0.3622

Note This table reports the regression results of the IV test. The standard errors are clustered at the firm level and t-statistics are shown in parentheses. *, ** and *** denote statistical significance at the 10%, 5% and 1% level, respectively

results, and the coefficients of the BDA are positive and significant at the 1% level in the regressions with total risk, systematic risk, and idiosyncratic risk as dependent variables. Thus, our regression results remain robust after controlling for regional characteristics.

4.5 Big Data Analytics and Corporate Policies

We demonstrated the positive correlation between BDA and firm risk in the previous subsections. In this section, we focus on corporate policies and try to understand the avenues through which BDA can influence firm risk. Referring to Bertrand Schoar (2003), Kini and Williams (2012), Ferris et al. (2017), and Bernile et al. (2018), we examine the relationship between corporate policies and BDA. Specifically, we investigate the impact of BDA on investment, R&D, and M&A, respectively, and demonstrate the relationship between these corporate policies and firm risk.

4.5.1 Big Data Analytics and Investment Intensity

This study separately explores the impact of BDA on the growth rate of total investment, new investment, and overinvestment. First, we measure the annual growth rate of investment using the amount of change in the ratio of total investment to total assets over two years. Of which, total investment = cash paid for the acquisition of fixed assets, intangible assets and other long-term assets + net cash paid for the acquisition of subsidiaries and other business units − net cash recovered from the disposal of fixed assets, intangible assets and other long-term assets − net cash received from the disposal of subsidiaries and other business units. Second, we estimate the new investment using two accounting-based frameworks, i.e., the logarithm of new investment and the ratio of new investment to total assets. New investment spending is the difference between total investment and maintenance investment. Of which,

Table 4.6 Addition of control variables

	(1)	(2)	(3)
	Total risk	Systematic risk	Idiosyncratic risk
Bigdata	318.9533***	119.4521***	335.9919***
	(5.1741)	(4.0352)	(5.2630)
FirmAge	-0.0087***	-0.0040***	-0.0073***
	(-7.4204)	(-6.8459)	(-6.3106)
Size	-0.1746***	-0.0175***	-0.2043***
	(-27.8121)	(-5.1295)	(-34.3426)
Lev	0.4124***	-0.0290	0.5411***
	(10.9025)	(-1.5581)	(14.8471)
Intang	-0.2953**	-0.2020***	-0.0892
	(-2.2851)	(-3.0605)	(-0.7411)
Capex	0.2811**	0.1775***	0.2014*
	(2.5367)	(3.4759)	(1.8473)
Growth	0.0997***	-0.0162***	0.1450***
	(8.5604)	(-3.1640)	(13.2965)
ROA	-65.9456***	-32.9925***	-47.8764***
	(-5.9792)	(-6.0597)	(-4.5969)
Top10	0.1108***	-0.2181***	0.3681***
	(2.6936)	(-10.6435)	(8.9466)
CEOAge	-0.0028***	-0.0003	-0.0032***
	(-3.3477)	(-0.7854)	(-3.8003)
CEOGender	-0.0001	0.0027	-0.0172
	(-0.0035)	(0.2505)	(-0.7840)
CEOShare	0.1969***	0.0934***	0.1729**
	(2.9083)	(3.1834)	(2.5605)
Duality	0.0088	-0.0080	0.0251*
	(0.6234)	(-1.2185)	(1.7959)
BoardSize	-0.0067*	-0.0010	-0.0084**
	(-1.8339)	(-0.5554)	(-2.3611)
BoardIndep	-0.0069	-0.0580	0.0065
	(-0.0633)	(-1.1250)	(0.0596)
Population	-0.0201*	-0.0121**	-0.0170
	(-1.8040)	(-2.2013)	(-1.5386)
GDP	0.0262***	0.0094**	0.0258***
	(3.2228)	(2.3819)	(3.2354)
Constant	6.7310***	1.7642***	6.5935***
	(47.6908)	(23.7679)	(49.6486)

(continued)

Table 4.6 (continued)

	(1)	(2)	(3)
	Total risk	Systematic risk	Idiosyncratic risk
Year	Yes	Yes	Yes
Industry	Yes	Yes	Yes
Obs	17,219	17,219	17,219
R^2	0.6738	0.2643	0.4859

Note This table reports the regression results for the test of the adding of control variables. The standard errors are clustered at the firm level and t-statistics are shown in parentheses. *, ** and *** denote statistical significance at the 10%, 5% and 1% level, respectively

maintenance investment = depreciation of fixed assets + amortization of intangible assets + amortization of long-term amortization costs. That is an estimate of the total necessary investment spend to maintain the regular operation of machinery, equipment and other operating assets to ensure that the company's operating capacity does not decline. Finally, following Richardson (2006), we estimate the level of corporate investment using model (4.7).

$$\begin{aligned} INV_{i,t} = {} & \alpha_0 + \alpha_1 Growth_{i,t-1} + \alpha_2 Leverage_{i,t-1} + \alpha_3 Cash_{i,t-1} \\ & + \alpha_4 Firmage_{i,t-1} + \alpha_5 Size_{i,t-1} + \alpha_6 Return_{i,t-1} \\ & + \alpha_7 INV_{i,t-1} + \sum Year + \sum Industry + \varepsilon_{i,t} \end{aligned} \tag{4.7}$$

where INV is the ratio of capital expenditure to total assets, Cash is the firm's cash holdings, Return is the firm's annual return on individual stocks, other independent variables include Growth, Leverage, Firm age, and Size, Year is the annual dummy variable, and Industry is the industry dummy variable. We estimate the investment INV for the period and use the estimated residuals to measure the firm's inefficient investment. When the residual is greater than 0 it indicates overinvestment, otherwise it is underinvestment. This study focuses on overinvestment, and overinvestment takes the residual value when the regression residual is greater than 0; and 0 otherwise.

Table 4.7 reports the results of the estimation of BDA and investment intensity. We find evidence that the coefficients on BDA are positive and statistically significant in columns (1)–(4), thus, BDA significantly increases investment growth rates, new investment, and overinvestment.

Previous empirical studies have demonstrated that expanding corporate investment may increase firm risk, especially overinvestment. Van Cauwenberge et al. (2019) found through a study of foreign direct investments (FDI) in Dutch listed firms that systemic risk significantly increases when firms engage in direct foreign investment activities. Tang and Zhang (2019) examined the portfolio choice of non-financial firms by constructing a portfolio choice model. The study shows that firms investing in fixed and financial assets will take higher risks while increasing their

Table 4.7 Testing the mediation effects of investment intensity

	(1)	(2)	(3)	(4)
	InvGrowth	Ln (NewInv)	NewInv/TA	OverInv
Bigdata	12.5837***	550.5617***	20.4756***	561.1568***
	(4.0540)	(3.2457)	(2.7772)	(3.3343)
FirmAge	0.0010***	-0.0168***	-0.0004***	0.0619***
	(15.5000)	(-4.7800)	(-3.3744)	(17.9156)
Size	-0.0017***	0.9890***	0.0001	-0.2461***
	(-4.8471)	(53.1987)	(0.1456)	(-13.3706)
Lev	-0.0078***	-0.1975*	-0.0070*	0.7808***
	(-3.6373)	(-1.8534)	(-1.7762)	(6.9592)
Intang	-0.0282***	1.4673***	0.0435**	-1.8396***
	(-3.4715)	(3.8674)	(2.3917)	(-4.1864)
Capex	0.3239***	15.8362***	0.8390***	61.5115***
	(32.9614)	(54.2397)	(73.4446)	(121.6457)
Growth	0.0019**	0.2021***	0.0137***	-0.4263***
	(2.0843)	(4.3087)	(7.1079)	(-9.3543)
ROA	0.3361	74.6065**	-0.0415	67.8906*
	(0.4884)	(2.0472)	(-0.0296)	(1.9270)
Top10	-0.0005	-0.0035	0.0102**	-0.0447
	(-0.2326)	(-0.0310)	(2.4640)	(-0.3703)
CEOAge	0.0000	-0.0025	-0.0002**	0.0033
	(0.8390)	(-1.1965)	(-2.5374)	(1.2433)
CEOGender	0.0005	0.0149	-0.0017	0.0372
	(0.3715)	(0.2454)	(-0.7493)	(0.5110)
CEOShare	-0.0116***	0.3152**	0.0056	-0.6037***
	(-3.0726)	(2.5420)	(1.1230)	(-2.7819)
Duality	-0.0004	0.0133	0.0018	-0.0144
	(-0.5036)	(0.3753)	(1.3382)	(-0.3157)
BoardSize	-0.0000	0.0030	-0.0004	-0.0018
	(-0.1580)	(0.3099)	(-1.1996)	(-0.1492)
BoardIndep	-0.0001	-0.1434	-0.0022	-0.1517
	(-0.0207)	(-0.5319)	(-0.2282)	(-0.4379)
Constant	0.0102	-4.1158***	0.0045	1.2725***
	(1.3507)	(-10.7893)	(0.3484)	(3.2689)
Year	Yes	Yes	Yes	Yes
Industry	Yes	Yes	Yes	Yes

(continued)

Table 4.7 (continued)

	(1)	(2)	(3)	(4)
	InvGrowth	Ln (NewInv)	NewInv/TA	OverInv
Obs	15,169	5279	5279	15,169
R^2	0.1407	0.7213	0.6752	0.6445

Note This table reports the regression results of the mediation effect test for investment intensity. The standard errors are clustered at the firm level and t-statistics are shown in parentheses. *, ** and *** denote statistical significance at the 10%, 5% and 1% level, respectively

profitability. Firms need to make a trade-off between risk and profit. Thus, the estimation results indicate that BDA increases investment growth rate, new investment and overinvestment, and then raises firm risk.

4.5.2 Big Data Analytics and R&D Intensity

In theory, R&D investment has two unique characteristics. First, R&D is a long-term investment with a long payback period and uncertainty (Lee & O'neill, 2003). Second, the intangible nature of R&D makes it impossible for outsiders to obtain an accurate valuation of R&D investments. So, it is difficult to use as collateral to obtain financing (Abdoh & Liu, 2021). According to Bhagat and Welch (1995), Kothari et al. (2002), Eberhart et al. (2004) and Gu (2016), the benefits of R&D expenditures have higher uncertainty compared to capital expenditures. As a result, investments in R&D expenditures may carry a higher risk than capital expenditures. Based on this hypothesis, we study R&D investment separately from firm investment to verify whether BDA affects firm risk by influencing R&D investment.

This study uses R&D expenditure and R&D personnel input to measure the R&D intensity of firms. Ln (R&D expend), the natural logarithm of R&D expend; R&D expend/OI, the ratio of R&D expenditure to operating income. Ln (R&D pers.), the natural logarithm of the number of R&D personnel; R&D pers./TE, the ratio of R&D personnel. Table 4.8 report the estimated results of the relationship between BDA and R&D intensity, with the coefficient of Bigdata being significantly positive at the 1% level. As a result, BDA boosts the intensity of R&D.

There is a widespread understanding that R&D investments are highly risky in nature. Patel and Chrisman (2014) examined the relationship between R&D investment and firm risk using the Behavioral Agency Model (BAM). The results suggest that R&D expenditures can explore higher growth opportunities accompanied by increased risk. In comparison, exploratory R&D investments carry a higher risk than development R&D investments. Ho et al. (2004) examined the relationship between firm R&D intensity and firm risk through the portfolio analysis, Monte Carlos simulation and correlation analysis. The results indicate that R&D intensity is positively related to systemic risk. In other words, R&D-intensive firms are exposed to greater

Table 4.8 Testing the mediation effects of R&D intensity

	(1)	(2)	(3)	(4)
	Ln (R&D expend)	R&D expend/OI	Ln (R&D pers.)	R&D pers./TE
Bigdata	570.7956***	30.8764***	665.8989***	165.8561***
	(4.4796)	(4.9225)	(4.9180)	(6.9762)
FirmAge	-0.0125***	-0.0006***	-0.0057	-0.0013***
	(-3.3242)	(-5.9560)	(-1.6427)	(-3.8181)
Size	0.8537***	-0.0002	0.6659***	-0.0044**
	(40.4764)	(-0.3526)	(31.4884)	(-2.1790)
Lev	-0.3296***	-0.0427***	-0.1236	-0.0617***
	(-2.8266)	(-10.8054)	(-1.0414)	(-4.7437)
Intang	-0.6383	0.0398***	-0.0253	0.0590
	(-1.3115)	(2.7714)	(-0.0547)	(1.3443)
Capex	1.0926***	0.0291***	1.8704***	-0.1088***
	(3.4363)	(2.9470)	(5.0831)	(-2.9655)
Growth	-0.0131	-0.0024***	-0.0048	0.0066**
	(-0.4876)	(-3.2905)	(-0.1731)	(2.2590)
ROA	237.5500***	-4.8889***	109.4950***	0.9320
	(8.7165)	(-4.6903)	(4.1036)	(0.3109)
Top10	-0.3667***	-0.0142***	-0.2213	-0.0515***
	(-2.6428)	(-3.3889)	(-1.6319)	(-3.5098)
CEOAge	0.0027	0.0001	0.0010	-0.0001
	(1.1261)	(1.4215)	(0.4092)	(-0.4722)
CEOGender	0.1413**	0.0030	0.1560**	0.0160**
	(2.5730)	(1.5402)	(2.4987)	(2.1294)
CEOShare	0.0676	0.0114**	0.1633	0.0524***
	(0.5090)	(2.0434)	(1.2272)	(2.6787)
Duality	-0.0101	0.0007	-0.0190	0.0005
	(-0.2626)	(0.5281)	(-0.4779)	(0.1081)
BoardSize	0.0046	0.0002	0.0289**	-0.0015
	(0.3170)	(0.5106)	(2.0818)	(-1.1335)
BoardIndep	-0.4622	0.0092	0.0419	0.0438
	(-1.2926)	(0.8591)	(0.1190)	(1.1239)
Constant	-0.8637*	0.0603***	-9.6954***	0.2804***
	(-1.8903)	(5.4033)	(-22.1923)	(6.5480)
Year	Yes	Yes	Yes	Yes
Industry	Yes	Yes	Yes	Yes

(continued)

Table 4.8 (continued)

	(1)	(2)	(3)	(4)
	Ln (R&D expend)	R&D expend/OI	Ln (R&D pers.)	R&D pers./TE
Obs	11,647	11,647	7690	7690
R^2	0.6142	0.3867	0.5697	0.3111

Note This table reports the regression results of the mediation effect test for R&D intensity. The standard errors are clustered at the firm level and t-statistics are shown in parentheses. *, ** and *** denote statistical significance at the 10%, 5% and 1% level, respectively

systemic risk. Kothari et al. (2002) estimated the relationship between R&D investment and future earnings uncertainty through a simulation approach. It was found that R&D investment may increase firm risk by reducing the predictability of future earnings. Coles et al. (2006) also found that R&D investments are inherently risky and that making R&D investments is an effective means for managers to increase firm risk. Thus, BDA has a significant positive indirect effect on firm risk, which is mediated by a positive effect on R&D.

4.5.3 *Big Data Analytics and M&A Intensity*

This study uses M&A frequency and M&A spending to measure M&A intensities, estimated as dependent variables. Ln (M&A freq + 1), the natural logarithm of the number of M&As initiated in the current year plus one; Ln (Serial M&A freq + 1), the natural logarithm of the sum of the number of M&As initiated from t-2 to t plus one. Ln (M&A expend), the natural logarithm of the firm's M&A expenditure in the current year; Ln (Serial M&A expend), the natural logarithm of the sum of a firm's M&A expenditure from t-2 to t. The estimation results in Table 4.9 shows that BDA significantly improves firm M&A intensity, which is statistically significant at the 5% level or above.

The literature has primarily confirmed the positive effect of M&A on firm risk. Lee and Caves (1998) argue that the profits sought by M&A activities are not always realized and that there is high uncertainty about the outcome of M&A activities, which may expose firms to greater risk. Furfine and Rosen (2011) studied the impact of M&A on firm risk. The findings suggest that the risks of the acquired firm may be transferred to the merging firm. Thus, on average, mergers and acquisitions significantly increase firm risk. The findings of Chari and Chang (2009), based on a sample of US firms' cross-border M&A, suggest that M&A may increase firm risk. The primary source of risk is the uncertainty arising from information asymmetry between the merging firm and the target firm. Therefore, BDA has a significant positive indirect effect on firm risk, which is mediated by a positive effect on M&A.

Table 4.9 Testing the Mediation Effects of M&A intensity

	(1)	(2)	(3)	(4)
	Ln (M&A freq + 1)	Ln (Serial M&A freq + 1)	Ln (M&A expend)	Ln (Serial M&A expend)
Bigdata	199.5660***	351.2481***	573.0072***	641.4724**
	(2.8671)	(3.2524)	(2.6200)	(1.9688)
FirmAge	-0.0022	-0.0000	-0.0040	0.0238***
	(-1.4695)	(-0.0018)	(-0.9936)	(3.8853)
Size	0.0676***	0.0724***	0.5109***	0.6914***
	(7.4785)	(5.1722)	(23.4739)	(19.5808)
Lev	0.2104***	0.0368	0.3795***	-0.3329
	(5.5057)	(0.4438)	(3.1244)	(-1.4548)
Intang	0.1860	0.3355	1.1086***	2.4525***
	(1.4802)	(1.4334)	(2.7144)	(3.8029)
Capex	0.1670	-0.4022	-0.2660	-3.7505***
	(1.4617)	(-1.5680)	(-0.7245)	(-5.8241)
Growth	0.0519***	-0.0384***	0.2269***	0.5712***
	(4.5360)	(-2.6275)	(6.0694)	(15.2212)
ROA	-31.5198***	-13.6686	-25.4163	-74.0684
	(-3.0292)	(-0.5796)	(-0.7124)	(-1.1209)
Top10	-0.2916***	-0.0800	-0.1125	1.0651***
	(-5.9000)	(-0.7196)	(-0.7796)	(4.3299)
CEOAge	-0.0028***	-0.0012	-0.0080***	-0.0061
	(-3.0143)	(-0.7155)	(-2.7800)	(-1.2502)
CEOGender	-0.0311	-0.0412	-0.1291*	0.0269
	(-1.4000)	(-0.9056)	(-1.8924)	(0.2244)
CEOShare	-0.0410	0.2264*	-0.2407	-0.4168
	(-0.7303)	(1.7839)	(-1.2346)	(-1.2793)
Duality	0.0343**	0.0214	0.1097**	0.0573
	(2.3539)	(0.7752)	(2.4337)	(0.7859)
BoardSize	-0.0107**	-0.0175**	-0.0421***	-0.0116
	(-2.5147)	(-2.0925)	(-3.5771)	(-0.4947)
BoardIndep	-0.2252*	-0.4932*	-0.3421	-0.9783
	(-1.8237)	(-1.9382)	(-0.9414)	(-1.5395)
Constant	0.2516	0.0282	8.4432***	4.2176***
	(1.5234)	(0.1088)	(19.1432)	(5.8219)
Year	Yes	Yes	Yes	Yes
Industry	Yes	Yes	Yes	Yes

(continued)

Table 4.9 (continued)

	(1)	(2)	(3)	(4)
	Ln (M&A freq + 1)	Ln (Serial M&A freq + 1)	Ln (M&A expend)	Ln (Serial M&A expend)
Obs	13,500	2919	13,500	2919
R^2	0.1058	0.1294	0.2086	0.4655

Note This table reports the regression results of the mediation effect test for M&A intensity. The standard errors are clustered at the firm level and t-statistics are shown in parentheses. *, ** and *** denote statistical significance at the 10%, 5% and 1% level, respectively

4.6 Robustness Tests

In this section, we discuss the results of several tests to check the robustness of our main results.

4.6.1 *Alternative Firm Risk*

In addition to total risk, systematic risk and idiosyncratic risk, the firm risk may also be reflected in changes in firm profitability (Choy et al., 2014; Fan et al., 2021). Following Faccio et al. (2011), Kini and Williams (2012) and Sila et al. (2016), we use the volatility of return on assets (ROA) over the observed period as alternative variables for firm risk. Therefore, the higher the ROA volatility, the higher firm risk. Specifically, we first calculate the industry-adjusted ROA by year, which is the difference between a firm's ROA and the average ROA of the firm's industry in that year. This aims to eliminate the effects of industry economic cycles beyond the control of firm insiders' actions, thereby providing a clearer measure of the risks arising from firm business decisions. Second, we calculate the standard deviation of each firm's industry-adjusted ROA over the entire sample period (2003–2019). Following John et al. (2008), we measure profitability volatility over a 5-year window from t to t + 4 and a 3-year window from t to t + 2, respectively. Finally, we calculate the extreme difference of industry-adjusted ROA to further measure the coefficient of variation of firm profitability.

$$ROA\_Adj_{i,t} = ROA_{i,t} - \frac{1}{X}\sum_{k=1}^{X} ROA_{i,t} \tag{4.8}$$

$$Sd[(ROA)\_T]_{i,t} = \sqrt{\frac{1}{T-1}\sum_{t=1}^{T}\left(ROA_{Adj_{i,t}} - \frac{1}{T}\sum_{t=1}^{T} ROA_{Adj_{i,t}}\right)^2} \tag{4.9}$$

$$R[(ROA)\_T]_{i,t} = Max\left(ROA\_Adj_{i,t}\right) - Min\left(ROA\_Adj_{i,t}\right) \tag{4.10}$$

Table 4.10 reports the estimation results of the alternative measure of firm risk as the dependent variable. The dependent variables in columns (1)-(2) are the standard deviation and extreme deviation of firm profitability constructed over the window from t to t + 4, respectively. Similarly, the dependent variables in columns (3)-(4) were constructed over the window from t to t + 2. The estimation results show that the estimated coefficients of BDA remain positive and significant at the 1% level. Therefore, we conclude that our results remain robust to using alternative variables to measure firm risk.

4.6.2 Alternative Big Data Analytics

Traditional analytics, stand-alone computing and storage can no longer help when confronting massive data. BDA must rely on powerful computing, analysis, and storage power. Therefore, big data is not isolated. It cannot be separated from the support of cloud computing, artificial intelligence and modern storage technology. In the dictionary formed by expanding the seed terms "big data" and "massive data", we have reincorporated the keywords of the above technologies into the extended set. Referring to the big data measurement in the previous section, the BDA in a broad sense Bigdata_b was constructed as a proxy variable and regressed again. Table 4.11 presents the estimation results of alternative measures. The coefficient of Bigdata_b is positive and significant at the 1% level. It indicates that our results remain robust to using alternative variables to measure big data analytics.

4.6.3 Adjustment of Sample Period

On September 05, 2015, China's State Council issued the "*Outline of Action to Promote the Development of Big Data*". It is proposed that data has become a national fundamental strategic resource, and big data is increasingly impacting global production, circulation, distribution and consumption activities as well as economic operation mechanism, social lifestyle and national governance capacity. The outline points out to comprehensively promote the development and application of big data in China, which has set off a boom of BDA in China. A potential concern is that we believe there are two possibilities for companies to develop big data after 2015. One is that firms have a need for BDA, and developing it may bring potential value to firms. Therefore, firms are actively investing in BDA. The other is that companies chase social hotspots and falsify information about big data in their annual reports to obtain financing in the capital market without investing in BDA.

To avoid the possible influence of firms falsifying big data information on the results, we intercept the subsample from 2003 to 2014 and re-run the regression. Table 4.12 reports the OLS estimation results, which show that the coefficients of the BDA remain positive and significant at the 10% level or above in the subsample

Table 4.10 Robustness test of alternative measures of firm risk

	(1)	(2)	(3)	(4)
	Sd (ROA)_5	R (ROA)_5	Sd (ROA)_3	R (ROA)_3
Bigdata	274.2537***	615.4927***	335.3122***	610.0420***
	(7.6274)	(8.3970)	(7.8474)	(8.4898)
FirmAge	0.0013	0.0031	0.0017	0.0032
	(1.0147)	(1.1756)	(1.0729)	(1.2414)
Size	-0.0091	-0.0170	-0.0097	-0.0146
	(-1.2294)	(-1.0778)	(-1.0817)	(-0.9302)
Lev	0.2197***	0.4717***	0.2563***	0.4503***
	(3.8090)	(3.8511)	(3.6922)	(3.7081)
Intang	-0.2153	-0.4732	-0.2461	-0.4086
	(-1.2597)	(-1.2853)	(-1.2023)	(-1.1386)
Capex	0.2973	0.7377	0.3654	0.7142
	(1.3959)	(1.5070)	(1.4061)	(1.4879)
Growth	-0.0269**	-0.0576**	-0.0334**	-0.0539**
	(-2.1764)	(-2.1027)	(-2.2144)	(-1.9758)
ROA	-50.3071***	-66.5402*	-55.6310**	-64.1205*
	(-2.8016)	(-1.8928)	(-2.5429)	(-1.8234)
Top10	0.0728	0.1490	0.0953	0.1433
	(1.3161)	(1.2318)	(1.4372)	(1.2126)
CEOAge	0.0008	0.0012	0.0012	0.0017
	(0.6113)	(0.3931)	(0.7038)	(0.5677)
CEOGender	-0.0379	-0.0794	-0.0457	-0.0804
	(-1.0350)	(-1.0134)	(-1.0158)	(-1.0245)
CEOShare	-0.0101	-0.0283	-0.0186	-0.0288
	(-0.1471)	(-0.1932)	(-0.2241)	(-0.1988)
Duality	0.0091	0.0131	0.0086	0.0124
	(0.3833)	(0.2568)	(0.2972)	(0.2430)
BoardSize	-0.0003	0.0008	0.0000	0.0015
	(-0.0369)	(0.0518)	(0.0011)	(0.0940)
BoardIndep	0.0663	0.2200	0.0963	0.2154
	(0.3459)	(0.5146)	(0.4115)	(0.5057)
Constant	0.1901	0.3161	0.1718	0.2237
	(1.2107)	(0.9347)	(0.9037)	(0.6668)
Year	Yes	Yes	Yes	Yes
Industry	Yes	Yes	Yes	Yes

(continued)

Table 4.10 (continued)

	(1)	(2)	(3)	(4)
	Sd (ROA)_5	R (ROA)_5	Sd (ROA)_3	R (ROA)_3
Obs	16,773	19,116	16,773	19,116
R^2	0.2769	0.2679	0.2768	0.2631

Note This table reports the regression results of alternative measures of firm risk. The standard errors are clustered at the firm level and t-statistics are shown in parentheses. *, ** and *** denote statistical significance at the 10%, 5% and 1% level, respectively

regressions. This remains consistent with our baseline regression results. Thus, external policy shocks to the country do not significantly impact the regression results, and our results remain robust.

4.7 Big Data Analytics and Firm Value

Our findings suggest that BDA increase firm risk by aggressively pursuing R&D, investments and M&A. However, BDA may be a double-edged sword and may not unconditionally lead to high value. If investing in BDA comes at the expense of shareholder value, this action is not inherently desirable. Therefore, in this section, we directly examine whether the benefits of BDA for the firm outweigh its costs. In other words, whether BDA affects firm value.

Following Daines (2001), Fang et al. (2009), Vafeas and Vlittis (2019) and Hasan et al. (2021), we use Tobin's Q as a proxy variable for firm value. Tobin's Q is measured as market value divided by total assets net of intangible assets and goodwill. We are considering the possible lag in the impact of BDA on firm value and verifying the persistence of the effect. We run regressions using Tobin's Q from period t to t + 2 as the dependent variable. Table 4.13 shows the OLS estimation results, where firm values from period t to t + 2 positively correlated with BDA and are significant at 10% or above. Thus, BDA directly increases firm value, and this impact has some persistence. In addition, the coefficient of BDA decreases year by year from period t to t + 2, which shows that the positive impact of BDA on firm value diminishes over time.

4.8 Conclusion

We use the annual reports disclosed by Chinese A-share listed companies to calculate the similar words and similarities of "big data" using deep learning. Then, we use text mining to capture the frequency of keyword occurrences to measure BDA at the firm level. Our study examines the relationship between BDA and firm risk in the Chinese

Table 4.11 Robustness test of alternative measures of big data analytics

	(1)	(2)	(3)
	Total risk	Systematic risk	Idiosyncratic risk
Bigdata_b	102.4787***	42.6314***	97.7739***
	(6.7536)	(5.5750)	(6.2357)
FirmAge	-0.0028**	-0.0023***	-0.0014
	(-2.3976)	(-3.9991)	(-1.2223)
Size	-0.1847***	-0.0212***	-0.2143***
	(-29.7251)	(-6.4200)	(-36.7425)
Lev	0.3613***	-0.0462**	0.4934***
	(10.0353)	(-2.5361)	(14.4353)
Intang	-0.3135**	-0.1873***	-0.1184
	(-2.4779)	(-2.9979)	(-1.0310)
Capex	0.3157***	0.2113***	0.2248**
	(2.9589)	(4.2559)	(2.1590)
Growth	0.0997***	-0.0152***	0.1449***
	(8.9452)	(-3.1303)	(13.6928)
ROA	-66.9411***	-31.1850***	-51.1330***
	(-6.4759)	(-6.1027)	(-5.2286)
Top10	0.2412***	-0.1804***	0.4929***
	(6.3792)	(-9.6516)	(13.0626)
CEOAge	-0.0029***	-0.0003	-0.0032***
	(-3.6879)	(-0.9261)	(-4.0092)
CEOGender	0.0017	-0.0011	-0.0113
	(0.0758)	(-0.1111)	(-0.5431)
CEOShare	0.2993***	0.1447***	0.2566***
	(4.6819)	(5.1799)	(4.0489)
Duality	0.0119	-0.0055	0.0255*
	(0.8596)	(-0.8841)	(1.8671)
BoardSize	-0.0043	-0.0007	-0.0054
	(-1.2202)	(-0.3923)	(-1.5583)
BoardIndep	0.0239	-0.0344	0.0338
	(0.2311)	(-0.7020)	(0.3277)
Constant	6.9329***	1.8374***	6.7841***
	(51.7406)	(26.0533)	(53.6049)
Year	Yes	Yes	Yes
Industry	Yes	Yes	Yes

(continued)

Table 4.11 (continued)

	(1)	(2)	(3)
	Total risk	Systematic risk	Idiosyncratic risk
Obs	19,116	19,116	19,116
R^2	0.6647	0.2560	0.4752

Note This table reports the regression results of alternative measures of BDA. The standard errors are clustered at the firm level and t-statistics are shown in parentheses. *, ** and *** denote statistical significance at the 10%, 5% and 1% level, respectively

institutional context based on the logic of "institutional environment - influence mechanism - influence channel - economic consequences". Specifically, based on a combined dataset of over 2,000 Chinese companies from 2003 to 2019, we observe a rapid growth trend in BDA capabilities starting in 2013. Our main regression results support our hypothesis that BDA significantly increases firm risk. We then demonstrate that after controlling for two sources of endogeneity - simultaneity bias and omitted variables. Our inferences do not change when we use the Pilot program for cultivating top students in basic disciplines (The Everest program) as an instrumental variable or add a control variable for regional characteristics. This evidence demonstrates the robustness of our baseline regression results.

In addition, we verify the moderating effects of two variables-financing constraints and cash flow constraints-on the relationship between BDA and firm risk. We find that the positive relationship between BDA and firm risk is increased when firms face more financing constraints. The positive relationship is weakened when the free cash flow is sufficient. We then focus on various firm policies and examine the channels through which BDA affect firm risk. We find that BDA leads to higher total, systematic, and idiosyncratic risk by encouraging firms to adopt riskier R&D, investment, and M&A strategies. Overall, our findings consistently support the view that BDA will incentivize senior executives to increase firm risk through higher-risk corporate policies.

However, BDA may be a double-edged sword for firms, and BDA may not unconditionally lead to high value. Further, we investigate the relationship between BDA and firm value. The results suggest that BDA increases firm value and that this positive relationship is somewhat persistent. Our findings support the view that, at least for public companies in non-IT industries, BDA should be encouraged where the company can afford the costs. However, our estimates reflect the average impact of BDA. Therefore, in some cases, the costs of BDA may outweigh its benefits, for example, in highly volatile markets or where there is high uncertainty in the business. Our conclusions may not be applicable.

Our conclusion may have a degree of generalizability. The impact of BDA on corporate policies like investments, R&D, and M&A is likely to be somewhat consistent across different markets. The ability of big data to provide detailed insights, improve decision-making, and potentially lead to riskier but more informed strategies is a global phenomenon. However, the perception and management of risk may vary

Table 4.12 Robustness test of adjustment of sample period

	(1)	(2)	(3)
	Total risk	Systematic risk	Idiosyncratic risk
Bigdata	767.1741***	142.3462**	818.7965***
	(4.6632)	(2.3152)	(4.7129)
FirmAge	-0.0054***	-0.0027***	-0.0030*
	(-3.2890)	(-3.5814)	(-1.9512)
Size	-0.1305***	0.0207***	-0.1754***
	(-16.8622)	(4.9376)	(-25.7079)
Lev	0.2594***	-0.0603***	0.4528***
	(5.9988)	(-2.9046)	(11.1939)
Intang	-0.2850*	-0.0771	-0.0239
	(-1.8874)	(-1.0325)	(-0.1824)
Capex	0.0108	0.0038	-0.0746
	(0.0890)	(0.0694)	(-0.6380)
Growth	0.0939***	-0.0283***	0.1378***
	(6.7006)	(-5.8041)	(9.9268)
ROA	-56.5261***	-26.7726***	-28.8623**
	(-4.0428)	(-3.8987)	(-2.2529)
Top10	0.0491	-0.2155***	0.3513***
	(1.0101)	(-8.4014)	(7.5781)
CEOAge	-0.0020**	-0.0008*	-0.0021**
	(-1.9893)	(-1.7367)	(-2.0655)
CEOGender	0.0164	0.0048	0.0015
	(0.5830)	(0.3455)	(0.0614)
CEOShare	0.2652***	0.0023	0.2938***
	(2.9699)	(0.0641)	(3.3700)
Duality	0.0143	-0.0146*	0.0334*
	(0.7841)	(-1.7989)	(1.8989)
BoardSize	-0.0075*	-0.0052**	-0.0051
	(-1.8964)	(-2.4951)	(-1.3211)
BoardIndep	-0.1210	-0.0613	-0.0807
	(-0.9788)	(-1.0879)	(-0.6708)
Constant	5.8573***	0.8974***	5.9307***
	(35.9508)	(10.5855)	(41.5738)
Year	Yes	Yes	Yes
Industry	Yes	Yes	Yes

(continued)

Table 4.12 (continued)

	(1)	(2)	(3)
	Total risk	Systematic risk	Idiosyncratic risk
Obs	10,353	10,353	10,353
R^2	0.6477	0.1749	0.4525

Note This table reports the regression results of robustness test of adjustment of sample period. The standard errors are clustered at the firm level and t-statistics are shown in parentheses. *, ** and *** denote statistical significance at the 10%, 5% and 1% level, respectively

significantly across different financial and political systems. For example, in markets with more stringent regulatory environments or conservative investment cultures, the increased risk from aggressive strategies may be less tolerated or managed differently, altering the impact of BDA on firm risk. Moreover, the regulatory framework governing data privacy, usage, and analytics can greatly influence how big data is employed by firms. In regions with strict data protection laws (like the EU with GDPR), the use of big data might be more constrained, thus potentially leading to different types of risks or risk levels. Besides, data validity and the extent of technological infrastructure available in different markets can affect the implementation and effectiveness of BDA, and consequently its impact on firm risk. In conclusion, while the core relationship between BDA and increased firm risk might have some level of generalizability across different markets, the extent and nature of this impact are likely to vary based on the specific financial, regulatory of each market.

4.9 Chapter Summary

This chapter empirically investigates the internal mechanisms through which data capability influences corporate decision-making behavior, risk-taking levels, and strategic choices by constructing a firm-level Big Data Analytics Index (BDA Index). Using a sample of Chinese A-share listed companies covering nearly 20,000 firm-year observations from 2003 to 2019, and after controlling for variables such as industry, region, and governance structure, the study systematically presents the evolutionary logic of corporate risk behavior in the context of data-driven decision-making, revealing the "double-edged sword effect" brought by big data capability: it may not only enhance firms' innovation capacity and resource allocation efficiency but also lead to expanded risk exposure due to increased strategic aggressiveness.

Theoretically, drawing on the Resource-Based View (RBV), this chapter regards BDA as a strategic resource of firms, embeds it into corporate behavior models, and explores its impact pathways on risk levels. From the perspective of literature review, although existing studies have extensively focused on the applications of BDA in marketing, supply chain, and customer management, the mechanism of its role in risk-taking decisions remains a blank area. By introducing a mediating effect

Table 4.13 Big data analytics and firm value

	(1)	(2)	(3)
	Tobin's Q_t	Tobin's Q_{t+1}	Tobin's Q_{t+2}
Bigdata	376.0815***	264.6271***	163.6807**
	(4.7658)	(3.5706)	(2.1055)
FirmAge	0.0179***	0.0133***	0.0084**
	(5.9122)	(4.0147)	(2.3304)
Size	-0.4402***	-0.4300***	-0.4443***
	(-19.6948)	(-18.8003)	(-19.2951)
Lev	0.1923*	-0.0265	-0.1376
	(1.7599)	(-0.2327)	(-1.1642)
Intang	3.8231***	3.6886***	3.4838***
	(10.4081)	(9.8539)	(8.9443)
Capex	-0.5457**	-1.0482***	-0.9858***
	(-2.3827)	(-4.4004)	(-3.8226)
Growth	0.0378*	0.0445*	-0.0279
	(1.7601)	(1.9210)	(-1.1484)
ROA	409.7449***	339.5603***	271.3656***
	(11.7725)	(8.7957)	(6.6265)
Top10	-0.0208	0.2506**	0.5682***
	(-0.2019)	(2.2085)	(4.6702)
CEOAge	0.0025	0.0036*	0.0043*
	(1.3910)	(1.8333)	(1.8938)
CEOGender	-0.0010	-0.0075	-0.0384
	(-0.0207)	(-0.1361)	(-0.5819)
CEOShare	-0.7193***	-0.7364***	-0.7411***
	(-5.2229)	(-4.7634)	(-4.0971)
Duality	0.0456	0.0621*	0.0905**
	(1.4806)	(1.7897)	(2.3109)
BoardSize	-0.0035	-0.0082	-0.0105
	(-0.4258)	(-0.9517)	(-1.1094)
BoardIndep	0.6494***	0.6634**	0.4712*
	(2.5990)	(2.5070)	(1.7543)
Year FE	Yes	Yes	Yes
Industry FE	Yes	Yes	Yes
Constant	10.9328***	10.7579***	11.1585***
	(24.7905)	(24.0927)	(24.3226)

(continued)

Table 4.13 (continued)

	(1)	(2)	(3)
	Tobin's Q_t	Tobin's Q_{t+1}	Tobin's Q_{t+2}
Observations	19,116	15,836	13,745
R-squared	0.4102	0.3932	0.3905

Note The table reports the regression results of BDA on firm value. The standard errors are clustered at the firm level and t-statistics are shown in parentheses. *, ** and *** denote statistical significance at the 10%, 5% and 1% level, respectively

framework of "Big Data Capability—Corporate Decision-Making—Risk-Taking," we find that BDA significantly enhances firms' strategic offensiveness, manifested in increased merger and acquisition frequency, strengthened R&D intensity, and more concentrated asset allocation, which in turn causes firms to face higher volatility and uncertainty in the short term.

Empirical results show that firms with stronger BDA capabilities have significantly higher levels of total risk, systematic risk, and unsystematic risk than the industry average. Among them, the increase in total risk reaches 17.3%, systematic risk rises by 10.8%, and the growth of idiosyncratic risk is more pronounced, at approximately 23.5%. Further analysis reveals that this risk increment mainly stems from the strategic aggressive behaviors adopted by firms after improving BDA capabilities, such as cross-industry mergers and acquisitions, rapid expansion, and increased use of capital leverage.

This chapter focuses on constructing and verifying three main mechanism pathways:

1. Information Transparency Pathway: BDA improves firms' responsiveness to external market changes, mitigates information asymmetry, and helps managers judge risks and opportunities more accurately. However, it may also lead to managerial overconfidence in the future, resulting in more radical expansion decisions.
2. Resource Restructuring Pathway: The improved efficiency of resource allocation driven by data makes firms more inclined to concentrate investments in high-return projects, neglecting the principle of risk diversification, which is particularly prominent in R&D expenditures and fixed asset expansion.
3. Institutional Buffering Pathway: On the premise of improving governance mechanisms and data ethics systems, firms can alleviate the risk diffusion effect brought by BDA to a certain extent. This study finds that governance variables such as board structure, the proportion of independent directors, and the proportion of executive shareholdings have significant moderating effects on the relationship between BDA and risk.

In addition, the study also finds that the higher the volatility of the industry in which a firm operates and the greater the macro policy uncertainty, the more obvious the incentive effect of BDA on corporate risk. This implies that BDA is not an "absolute positive," and its impact on corporate performance and risk has "conditional boundaries."

The research in this chapter has important reference significance for both policymakers and corporate managers. First, from an institutional perspective, the government should construct a data governance system centered on data rights confirmation, compliance with data usage, and data profit-sharing mechanisms. Only in an institutional environment of "usable but invisible" and "usable but controllable" can firms reasonably unleash data dividends and avoid the diffusion of systemic risks caused by regulatory gaps or data abuse.

Second, from the perspective of corporate management, the improvement of BDA capabilities needs to be accompanied by adjustments to management systems. For example, corporate governance should attach more importance to executive data literacy training, risk assessment mechanisms for strategic behaviors, and prudent management of excessive expansion behaviors. Only by achieving the combination of "data capability + strategic stability" can firms truly balance the tensions between efficiency and risk, and between innovation and stability.

Third, promoting the findings of this chapter globally also requires adapting to local conditions. Differences in institutional environments, cultural values, and market maturity may affect the marginal effects of BDA on corporate risk behavior. Therefore, when replicating Chinese experiences, multinational enterprises should set technical governance boundaries and strategic incentive policies in light of local conditions.

In terms of academic contributions, this chapter is mainly reflected in the following aspects: it is the first to systematically construct and verify a three-stage transmission model of "BDA Capability—Strategic Behavior—Corporate Risk," filling the gap in the interdisciplinary research of big data technology and corporate risk; it proposes a method for constructing a Big Data Capability Index based on deep learning technology, overcoming the subjectivity and unstructured problems existing in traditional questionnaire surveys or coarse-grained keyword weighting; by introducing multiple endogenous control variables, instrumental variable methods, and robustness test means, it improves the causal identification ability and explanatory power of empirical analysis; it strengthens the depth of linking theory with practice—combining academic models with data from Chinese local firms to enhance the practical guiding significance of the research.

From an overall logical perspective, the analytical framework of "Data—Corporate Behavior—Risk Structure" proposed in this chapter has provided a solid theoretical basis for understanding the behavioral changes of micro subjects in the context of the digital economy. However, the impact of data is not limited to the individual firm level, and its broader diffusion effects have emerged in regional economies. Specifically, the accumulation of data capability will not only improve the operational efficiency and strategic behavior radius of individual firms but also significantly stimulate regional entrepreneurial activity through the pathway of "Firm Clusters—Entrepreneurial Density—Ecological Environment."

Nevertheless, in the process of the continuous integration of digital governance and corporate practice, academia and industry have increasingly recognized that data is not merely a tool or capability; its deeper role is reflected in its path of shaping corporate value. Starting from the logic of this chapter, we have initially revealed the impact of data capability on corporate behavior patterns, but it is still necessary to further answer a more macro value-oriented question: can firms' accumulation of data analytics capabilities be effectively transformed into the improvement of corporate value? Especially in the context of a country in economic transition like China, the improvement of corporate value relies not only on traditional capital investment and technological progress but also on the systematic support of data resource acquisition capability, analysis capability, and application capability. This is precisely the question that the next chapter of this book—Chapter 5: "Big Data Analytics and Firm Value: Evidence from Non-IT Firms in China"—attempts to explore in depth.

From a logical path perspective, the connection between this chapter and Chapter 5 is natural and reasonable. On the one hand, corporate value, as a comprehensive indicator, reflects external investors' systematic judgments on firms' future growth potential, profitability, and risk levels. Therefore, if a firm has strong capabilities in data analytics and can optimize key elements such as internal management processes, precision marketing strategies, and innovation capability development through data empowerment, such capabilities should be reasonably reflected in market valuations. On the other hand, the improvement of corporate value is the core goal of all corporate policies and management behaviors, and it is also a key dimension to verify whether big data capabilities truly generate "economic returns." It can be said that this chapter constructs the basic framework of the mechanism through which data capability influences corporate behavior, while Chapter 5 backtracks and verifies the ultimate value orientation on this basis, with natural extensibility from theoretical logic and empirical methods to policy implications.

It is worth highlighting that Chapter 5 further refines the selection of research objects, focusing on non-IT firms in China. This strategy has important practical significance and theoretical value. In existing studies, the relationship between data capability and corporate performance has mostly taken internet firms and technology-based companies as core samples. However, in China's economic system, non-IT firms (including manufacturing, traditional service industries, resource-based enterprises, etc.) not only account for most of the market share but also face an urgent challenge of digital transformation. Therefore, examining the matching process between digital capability acquisition and value realization in non-IT firms can not only verify the spillover mechanism of data factors in traditional industries but also provide an important perspective for understanding the heterogeneous performance of Chinese firms in the overall digitalization process.

In fact, this chapter has initially demonstrated the impact mechanism of data capability on corporate risk and policies, and non-IT firms face more complex transformation challenges in this context. On the one hand, such firms have formed strong path dependence in long-term operations, with complex decision-making chains and large organizational inertia, and the introduction of data capability often faces organizational hierarchical barriers and cultural cognitive obstacles; on the other hand, non-IT firms generally lack native data processing capabilities, and links such as data collection, sorting, cleaning, and modeling often rely on external platforms and service providers, which also results in their inherent disadvantages in data usage efficiency and strategic response speed. For this reason, when certain non-IT firms can effectively establish data analytics capabilities and embed them into core business processes, their effect on improving the overall corporate value is even more research-worthy and theoretically significant. This logic also echoes the important principles of "increasing marginal returns" and "latecomer advantages" in economics: in an environment where digital capability was originally scarce, once it is constructed and activated, it can generate stronger signal effects and market returns.

From another perspective, the corporate policy choices and risk-bearing capacity discussed in this chapter can also be regarded as the intermediate pathway through which corporate data capability is transmitted to market confidence. When evaluating corporate value, investors often focus on the stability and growth potential of its future cash flows. If a firm can improve supply and demand forecasting, reduce inventory volatility, and optimize asset allocation through data analytics, it can still show strong operational stability and profitability even in a highly uncertain external environment, thereby increasing its valuation level. Especially in an institutional environment where the capital market highly relies on signal transmission mechanisms, explicit management strategies for data capability (such as active disclosure of data strategies and establishment of CDOs) have also become powerful tools for firms to attract capital and build brand reputation. Therefore, the micro mechanism of data capability influencing corporate policies depicted in this chapter and the corporate value performance discussed in Chapter 5 are not a fragmented research shift but a natural extension of a causal chain.

In addition, this chapter also discusses the correlation between data capability and corporate risk behavior, that is, firms with high data capability tend to have higher risk tolerance and dare to adopt aggressive policies, which theoretically constitutes an important basis for Chapter 5. Corporate value stems not only from current asset status but also from its risk allocation capability and future growth potential. If a firm enhances its risk identification and prediction capabilities through big data analytics, the "high risks" it undertakes are actually "controllable risks," and such firms are more likely to be given high valuations in the capital market. Against this theoretical background, Chapter 5 verifies the systematic relationship between data capability and corporate value based on micro data of Chinese non-IT firms, and conducts empirical investigations on heterogeneous factors in different industries, periods, and regions, thereby revealing the value generation path of data factors in real economic activities.

It is worth further exploring that the connection between this chapter and Chapter 5 is reflected not only in the continuation of research themes and theoretical logic but also in the upgrading of research methods and data application levels. In this chapter, we mainly reveal the micro mechanism by constructing risk tolerance indicators and analyzing the interactive relationship between corporate governance structure and data capability. In Chapter 5, the research path will focus more on the capital market feedback mechanism of corporate value, adopting market valuation models and panel data methods to depict the impact of big data capability on corporate market performance from both static and dynamic dimensions. This leap in research methods not only expands the breadth of research on data factors but also improves the predictive ability and explanatory power for actual corporate behaviors.

From the perspective of the overall research context, the transition from this chapter to Chapter 5 also represents a shift in our research paradigm from "internal management logic" to "external value feedback." In this process, data factors are not only regarded as tools for optimizing internal efficiency of firms but also endowed with strategic significance of influencing capital market behaviors and building industrial competitive advantages. This inward-outward path extension helps us establish a complete growth logic of data-driven firms, thereby providing theoretical support and empirical basis for macro policy formulation, industrial support directions, and corporate strategic deployment.

In summary, this chapter provides a solid foundation and clear logical presupposition for the development of Chapter 5—from how data capability changes corporate decisions to how corporate value reflects differences in data capability, we can systematically answer the core question of "how data factors, as a new type of production factor, intervene in and restructure the logic of corporate growth." The next chapter will continue this research main line, further through in-depth analysis of Chinese non-IT firms, reveal how data analytics capabilities release their value signals in the capital market, how they ultimately transform into the steady improvement of corporate value by enhancing operational transparency, strengthening market confidence, and guiding resource allocation. This research not only enriches the empirical basis of data economy research but also has important enlightenment significance for understanding the digital transformation path of traditional industries and constructing a corporate strategic system centered on data.

References

Abdoh, H., & Liu, Y. (2021). Does R&D intensity matter in the executive risk incentives and firm risk relationship? *Economic Modelling, 96*, 13–24.

Acharya, A., Singh, S. K., Pereira, V., & Singh, P. (2018). Big data, knowledge co-creation and decision making in the fashion industry. *International Journal of Information Management, 42*, 90–101.

Akter, S., Wamba, S. F., Gunasekaran, A., Dubey, R., & Childe, S. J. (2016). How to improve firm performance using big data analytics capability and business strategy alignment? *International Journal Prodction Economics, 182*, 113–131. https://doi.org/10.1016/j.ijpe.2016.08.018.

Albuquerque, R., Koskinen, Y., & Zhang, C. (2019). Corporate social responsibility and firm risk: Theory and empirical evidence. *Management Science, 65*(10), 4451–4469.

Awan, U., Bhatti, S. H., Shamim, S., Khan, Z., Akhtar, P., & Balta, M. E. (2021a). The role of big data analytics in manufacturing agility and performance: Moderation–mediation analysis of organizational creativity and of the involvement of customers as data analysts. *British Journal of Management, 33*(3), 1200–1220.

Awan, U., Arnold, M. G., & Gölgeci, I. (2021b). Big data analytics capability and decision-making: The role of data-driven insight on circular economy performance. *Technological Forecasting and Social Change, 168*, Article 120766.

Babina, T., Bernstein, S., & Fedyk, A. (2020). *Artificial intelligence, firm growth, and industry concentration* (NBER Working Paper No. 27847).

Batten, J., Szilagyi, P., & Warren, G. (2021). Convertible debt and asset substitution of multinational corporations. *Journal of Corporate Finance, 67*, Article 101843.

Berger, A. N., Kick, T., & Schaeck, K. (2014). Executive board composition and bank risk taking. *Journal of Corporate Finance, 28*, 48–65.

Bernile, G., Bhagwat, V., & Yonker, S. (2018). Board diversity, firm risk, and corporate policies. *Journal of Financial Economics, 127*(3), 588–612.

Bertrand, M. & Schoar, A. (2003). Managing with style: The effect of managers on firm policies. *The Quarterly Journal of Economics, 118*(4), 1169–1208.

Bhagat, S., & Welch, I. (1995). Corporate research & development investments international comparisons. *Journal of Accounting and Economics, 19*(2–3), 443–470.

Brandt, M. W., Brav, A., Graham, J. R., Kumar, A. (2010). The Idiosyncratic Volatility Puzzle: Time Trend or Speculative Episodes? *The Review of Financial Studies, 23*(2), 863–899. https://doi.org/10.1093/rfs/hhp087.

Brown, G., & Kapadia, N. (2007). Firm-specific risk and equity market development☆. *Journal of Financial Economics, 84*(2), 358–388. https://doi.org/10.1016/j.jfineco.2006.03.003.

Bruce, H. L., Wilson, H. N., Macdonald, E. K., Clarke, B. (2019). Resource integration, value creation and value destruction in collective consumption contexts. *Journal of Business Research, 103*, 173–185. https://doi.org/10.1016/j.jbusres.2019.05.007.

Chaivisuttangkun, S., & Jiraporn, P. (2021). The effect of co-opted directors on firm risk during a stressful time: Evidence from the financial crisis. *Finance Research Letters, 39*. https://doi.org/10.1016/j.frl.2020.101538.

Chari, M. D. R., & Chang, K. (2009). Determinants of the share of equity sought in cross-border acquisitions. *Journal of International Buiness Studies, 40*(8), 1277–1297. https://doi.org/10.1057/jibs.2008.103.

Chatterjee, S., Ghosh, S. K., Chaudhuri, R., & Seetharaman, P. (2023). Assessing the impact of big data analytics on decision-making processes, forecasting, and performance of a firm. *Technological Forecasting and Social Change, 196*, Article 122824.

Choy, H., Lin, J., & Officer, M. S. (2014). Does freezing a defined benefit pension plan affect firm risk? *Journal of Accounting and Economics, 57*(1), 1–21. https://doi.org/10.1016/j.jacceco.2013.11.004.

Ciampi, F., Demi, S., Magrini, A., Marzi, G., & Papa, A. (2021). Exploring the impact of big data analytics capabilities on business model innovation: The mediating role of entrepreneurial orientation. *Journal of Business Research, 123*, 1–13. https://doi.org/10.1016/j.jbusres.2020.09.023.

Coles, J., Daniel, N., & Naveen, L. (2006). Managerial incentives and risk-taking. *Journal of Financial Economics, 79*(2), 431–468. https://doi.org/10.1016/j.jfineco.2004.09.004.

Cronbach, L.J. (1951). Coefficient alpha and the internal structure of tests. *Psychometrika, 16*(3), 297–334.

Daines, R., 2001. Does Delaware law improve firm value? *Journal of Financial Economics, 62*(3), 525–558.

Eberhart, A. C., Maxwell, W. F., & Siddique, A. R. (2004). An examination of long-term abnormal stock returns and operating performance following R&D increases. *Journal of Finance, 59*(2), 623–650.

Faccio, M., Marchica, M. T., & Mura, R. (2011). Large Shareholder Diversification and Corporate Risk-Taking. *The Review of Financial Studies, 24*(11), 3601–3641. https://doi.org/10.1093/rfs/hhr065.

Fan, Y., Boateng, A., Ly, K. C., & Jiang, Y. (2021). Are bonds blind? Board-CEO social networks and firm risk. *Journal of Corporate Finance, 68*. https://doi.org/10.1016/j.jcorpfin.2021.101922.

Fang, V. W., Noe, T. H., & Tice, S. (2009). Stock market liquidity and firm value. *Journal of Financial Economics, 94*(1), 150–169. https://doi.org/10.1016/j.jfineco.2008.08.007.

Fee, C. E., Hadlock, C. J., & Pierce, J. R. (2009). Investment, Financing Constraints, and Internal Capital Markets: Evidence from the Advertising Expenditures of Multinational Firms. *The Review of Financial Studies, 22*(6), 2361–2392. https://doi.org/10.1093/rfs/hhn059.

Ferris, S. P., Javakhadze, D., & Rajkovic, T., (2017). CEO social capital, risk-taking and corporate policies. Journal of Corporate Finance, *47*, 46–71. https://doi.org/10.1016/j.jcorpfin.2017.09.003.

Furfine, C. H. & Rosen, R. J. (2011). Mergers increase default risk. *Journal of Corporate Finance, 17*(4), 832–849.

Ghasemaghaei, M., & Calic, G. (2019). Does big data enhance firm innovation competency? The mediating role of data-driven insights. *Journal of Business Research, 104*, 69–84.

Ghasemaghaei, M., & Calic, G. (2020). Assessing the impact of big data on firm innovation performance: Big data is not always better data. *Journal of Business Research*, 108, 147–162. https://doi.org/10.1016/j.jbusres.2019.09.062.

Graddy-Reed, A. (2021). Decisions of firm risk and the role of organizational identity. *Small Business Economics, 57*(1), 1–21. https://doi.org/10.1007/s11187-019-00290-2.

Gupta, S., Drave, V. A., Dwivedi, Y. K., Baabdullah, A. M., Ismagilova, E. (2020). Achieving superior organizational performance via big data predictive analytics: *A dynamic capability view. Industrial Marketing Management*, *90*, 581–592.

Harrison, J. S., Thurgood, G. R., Boivie, S., & Pfarrer, M. D. (2020). Perception Is Reality: How CEOs' Observed Personality Influences Market Perceptions of Firm Risk and Shareholder Returns. *Academy of Management Journal, 63*(4), 1166–1195. https://doi.org/10.5465/amj.2018.0626.

Hasan, M. M., Lobo, G. J., & Qiu, B. (2021). Organizational capital, corporate tax avoidance, and firm value. *Journal of Corporate Finance, 70*, https://doi.org/10.1016/j.jcorpfin.2021.102050.

Huang, J., Cao, J., Hasan, T., & Zhao, J. (2021). Low-carbon city initiatives and firm risk: A quasi-natural experiment in China. *Journal of Financial Stability, 57*. https://doi.org/10.1016/j.jfs.2021.100949.

Huang, J., Sun, P., & Zhang, Y. (2021). Does big data analytics enhance firm innovation? The role of entrepreneurial orientation. *Journal of Business Research, 128*, 647–659.

Irvine, P. J., & Pontiff, J. (2009). Idiosyncratic Return Volatility, Cash Flows, and Product Market Competition. *The Review of Financial Studies, 22*(3), 1149–1177. https://doi.org/10.1093/rfs/hhn039.

Jiang, G. J., Xu, D., & Yao, T. (2009). The Information Content of Idiosyncratic Volatility. *Journal of Financial and Quantitative Analysis, 44*(1), 1–28. https://doi.org/10.1017/s0022109009090073.

Jo, H., & Na, H. (2012). Does CSR reduce firm risk? Evidence from controversial industry sectors. *Journal of Business Ethics, 110*(4), 441–456.

John, K., Litov, L., & Yeung, B. (2008). Corporate governance and risk-taking. *The Journal of Finance, 63*(4), 1679–1728.

Jones, C. I., & Tonetti, C. (2020). Nonrivalry and the Economics of Data. *American Economic Review, 110*(9), 2819–2858. https://doi.org/10.1257/aer.20191330.

Kabir Hassan, M., Chiaramonte, L., Dreassi, A., Paltrinieri, A., & Pisera, S. (2021). The crossroads of ESG and religious screening on firm risk. *Research International Business and Finance, 58*. https://doi.org/10.1016/j.ribaf.2021.101500.

Kim, H., & Yasuda, Y. (2018). Business risk disclosure and firm risk: Evidence from Japan. *Research in International Business and Finance, 45*, 413–426. https://doi.org/10.1016/j.ribaf.2017.07.172.

Kini, O., & Williams, R. (2012). Tournament incentives, firm risk, and corporate policies. *Journal of Financial Economics, 103*(2), 350–376. https://doi.org/10.1016/j.jfineco.2011.09.005.

Kothari, S. P., Laguerre, T. E., & Leone, A. J. (2002). Capitalization versus expensing: Evidence on the uncertainty of future earnings from capital expenditures versus R&D outlays. *Review of Accounting Studies, 7*(4), 355–382.

Lee, P. M., & O'neill, H. M. (2003). Ownership structures and R&D investments of US and Japanese firms: Agency and stewardship perspectives. *Academy of Management Journal, 46*(2), 212–225. https://doi.org/10.5465/30040615.

Lee, T. J., & Caves, R. E. (1998). Uncertain outcomes of foreign investment: Determinants of the dispersion of profits after large acquisitions. *Journal of International Business Studies, 29*(3), 563–581. https://doi.org/10.1057/palgrave.jibs.8490007.

Low, C., Chen, Y.& Wu, M. (2011). Understanding the determinants of cloud computing adoption. *Industrial Management data Systems. 111(7)*, 1006–1023. https://doi.org/10.1016/j.chb.2017.07.027.

Merendino, A., Dibb, S., Meadows, M., Quinn, L., Wilson, D., Simkin, L., Canhoto, A. (2018). Big data, big decisions: The impact of big data on board level decision making. *Journal of Business Research, 93*, 67–78. https://doi.org/10.1016/j.jbusres.2018.08.029.

Merton, R. C. (1987). A simple model of capital market equilibrium with incomplete information.

Mikalef, P., Boura, M., Lekakos, G., & Krogstie, J. (2019). Big data analytics and firm performance: Findings from a mixed-method approach. *Journal of Business Research,* 98, 261–276. https://doi.org/10.1016/j.jbusres.2019.01.044.

Mikalef, P., Pappas, I. O., Krogstie, J., & Giannakos, M. (2020). Big data analytics capability: Antecedents and business value. *Information & Management, 57*(8), Article 103169.

Mikolov, T., Sutskever, I., Chen, K., Corrado, G. S., Dean, J. (2013). Distributed representations of words and phrases and their compositionality. *Advances in Neural Information Processing.Systems, 26*.

Müller, O., Fay, M., & vom Brocke, J. (2018). The Effect of Big Data and Analytics on Firm Performance: An Econometric Analysis Considering Industry Characteristics. *Journal of Management Information Systems, 35*(2), 488–509. https://doi.org/10.1080/07421222.2018.1451955.

Neyland, J. (2020). Love or money: The effect of CEO divorce on firm risk and compensation. *Journal of Corporate Finance*, 60, 101507. https://doi.org/10.1016/j.jcorpfin.2019.101507.

Patel, P. C., & Chrisman, J. J. (2014). Risk abatement as a strategy for R&D investments in family firms. *Strategic Management Journal, 35*(4), 617–627. https://doi.org/10.1002/smj.2119.

Perryman, A. A., Fernando, G. D., & Tripathy, A. (2016). Do gender differences persist? An examination of gender diversity on firm performance, risk, and executive compensation. *Journal of Business Research, 69*(2), 579–586. https://doi.org/10.1016/j.jbusres.2015.05.013.

Peters, L. D. (2016). Heteropathic versus homopathic resource integration and value co-creation in service ecosystems. Journal of Business Research, 69(8), 2999–3007. https://doi.org/10.1016/j.jbusres.2016.02.033.

Rego, L. L., Billett, M. T., & Morgan, N. A. (2009). Consumer-based brand equity and firm risk. *Journal of Marketing, 73*(6), 47–60. https://doi.org/10.1509/jmkg.73.6.47.

Rossi, F., & A, H. M. (2020). Corporate non-financial disclosure, firm value, risk, and agency costs: Evidence from Italian listed companies. *Review of Managerial Science, 14*(5), 1149–1181. https://doi.org/10.1007/s11846-019-00358-z.

Richardson, S. (2006). Over-investment of free cash flow. *Review of Accounting Studies, 11*(2–3), 159–189. https://doi.org/10.1007/s11142-006-9012-1.

Sharpe, W. F. (1964). Capital asset prices: A theory of market equilibrium under conditions of risk. *The Journal of Finance, 19*(3), 425–442.

Shamim, S., Zeng, J., Shariq, S. M., & Khan, Z. (2019). Role of big data management in enhancing big data decision-making capability and quality among Chinese firms: A dynamic capabilities view. *Information and Management*, *56*(6). https://doi.org/10.1016/j.im.2018.12.003.

Sila, V., Gonzalez, A., & Hagendorff, J. (2016). Women on board: Does boardroom gender diversity affect firm risk? *Journal of Corporate Finance, 36*, 26–53. https://doi.org/10.1016/j.jcorpfin.2015.10.003.

Simon, H. A. (1996). Models of my life. MIT press.

Singh, N. (2022). Developing business risk resilience through risk management infrastructure: The moderating role of big data analytics. *Information System Management, 39*(1), 34–52.

Sivarajah, U., Kamal, M. M., Irani, Z., & Weerakkody, V. (2017). Critical analysis of Big Data challenges and analytical methods. *Journal of Business Research, 70*, 263–286.
Stock, J., & Yogo, M. (2005). Asymptotic distributions of instrumental variables statistics with many instruments. *Identification and inference for econometric models: Essays in honor of Thomas Rothenberg 6*, 109–120.
Tambe, P. (2014). Big Data Investment, Skills, and Firm Value. *Management Science 60*(6), 1452–1469. https://doi.org/10.1287/mnsc.2014.1899.
Tang, H., & Zhang, C. (2019). Investment risk, return gap, and financialization of non-listed non-financial firms in China. *Pacific-Basin Finance Journal, 58*, https://doi.org/10.1016/j.pacfin.2019.101213.
Tseng, H. T., Aghaali, N., & Hajli, N. (2022). Customer agility and big data analytics in new product context. *Technological Forecasting and Social Change, 180*, 121690. https://doi.org/10.1016/j.techfore.2022.121690.
Vafeas, N., & Vlittis, A. (2019). Board executive committees, board decisions, and firm value. *Journal of Corporate Finance, 58*, 43–63. https://doi.org/10.1016/j.jcorpfin.2019.04.010.
Van Cauwenberge, A., Vancauteren, M., Braekers, R., & Vandemaele, S. (2019). International trade, foreign direct investments, and firms' systemic risk: Evidence from the Netherlands. *Economic Modelling, 81*, 361–386. https://doi.org/10.1016/j.econmod.2019.07.001.
Van der Voort, H., van Bulderen, S., Cunningham, S., & Janssen, M. (2021). Data science as knowledge creation a framework for synergies between data analysts and domain professionals. *Technological Forecasting and Social Change, 173*, 121160. https://doi.org/10.1016/j.techfore.2021.121160.
Vozlyublennaia, N. (2013). Do firm characteristics matter for the dynamics of idiosyncratic risk? *Journal of International Financial Markets, Institutions and Money 27*, 35–46. https://doi.org/10.1016/j.intfin.2013.07.006.
Wamba, S. F., Gunasekaran, A., Akter, S., Ren, S.J. F., Dubey, R., & Childe, S. J. (2017). Big data analytics and firm performance: Effects of dynamic capabilities. Journal of Business Research. *70*, 356–365. https://doi.org/10.1016/j.jbusres.2016.08.009.
Wei, S. X., & Zhang, C. 2005. Idiosyncratic risk does not matter: A re-examination of the relationship between average returns and average volatilities. *Journal of Banking & Finance, 29*(3), 603–621. https://doi.org/10.1016/j.jbankfin.2004.05.021.
Wei, Y., Zhang, J., Wang, F., & Cheng, M. (2022). Research of data assets disclosure and analyst forecasts: Evidence from text analysis. *Journal of Industrial Engineering and Engineering Management*, 1–12.
Yasmin, M., Tatoglu, E., Kilic, H. S., Zaim, S., & Delen, D. (2020). Big data analytics capabilities and firm performance: An integrated MCDM approach. *Journal of Business Research, 114*, 1–15. https://doi.org/10.1016/j.jbusres.2020.03.028.
Zhang, Z., Wang, X., & Jia, M. (2021a). Poverty as a Double-Edged Sword: How CEOs' Childhood Poverty Experience Affect Firms' Risk Taking. *British Journal of Management*. https://doi.org/10.1111/1467-8551.12515.
Zhang, Y., Lu, Y., & Li, L. (2021b). Effects of Big Data on Firm Value in China: Evidence from Textual Analysis of Chinese Listed Firms' Annual Reports. *Economic Research Journal, 56*(12), 42–59.

Chapter 5
Data Analysis and Corporate Value: Based on the Performance of Big Data in the Capital Market

5.1 Introduction

Big data analytics (BDA) has become an essential strategic resource in modern business environments for its capacity to optimize decision-making and enhance performance (Mikalef et al., 2018; Jones & Tonetti, 2020). Yet, the value creation of BDA is not guaranteed, as many firms still face managerial and technical challenges that prevent them from realizing expected returns (Brinch et al., 2021; Tarafdar et al., 2013). Against this backdrop, whether and how BDA adoption truly enhances firm value remains an important and unresolved question. This chapter addresses this gap by providing empirical evidence on the relationship between BDA adoption and firm value.

Drawing on annual reports of Chinese listed non-IT firms from 2003 to 2020, this chapter employs a pre-trained model to expand keywords related to "big data" and applies text-mining techniques to capture their frequency. By assigning weights based on semantic similarity, we construct a comprehensive firm-level indicator of BDA utilization. Empirical analyses demonstrate that BDA adoption significantly improves firm value. Robustness checks and endogeneity tests confirm the validity of these findings. Moreover, the chapter investigates underlying mechanisms and shows that BDA contributes to firm value primarily by enhancing efficiency and stimulating innovation. In addition, governance plays a moderating role: the positive effect of BDA on firm value is stronger when firms face more stringent external governance or possess stronger internal governance mechanisms.

This chapter makes three key contributions. First, while prior research has examined the role of BDA in performance, decision-making, and innovation (e.g., Mikalef et al., 2019a; Sena et al., 2019), the extent to which these benefits translate into firm value remains underexplored. We add to this literature by providing direct evidence of value creation. Second, unlike questionnaire-based measures (Raguseo & Vitari, 2018; Upadhyay & Kumar, 2020), our unstructured text-based approach covers nearly all A-share listed firms and provides a more dynamic and objective measure of

X. Li et al., *Data as a New Factor of Production*, Applied Economics and Policy Studies, https://doi.org/10.1007/978-981-95-9985-1_5

BDA capability. Third, we identify and empirically validate the mechanisms—efficiency and innovation—through which BDA affects firm value, offering insights for managers considering BDA adoption strategies.

The remainder of this chapter is structured as follows. Section 5.2 develops the hypotheses. Section 5.3 presents the data, variables, and regression model. Section 5.4 discusses the empirical results, robustness checks, and mechanism tests. Section 5.5 concludes.

5.2 Hypothesis Development

Our study presents two competing hypotheses to explain the relationship between BDA and firm value. On the one hand, we hypothesize that the implementation of BDA by firms may positively impact their overall firm value. Extensive prior research has consistently demonstrated that a robust utilization of BDA leads to improved firm performance (Mikalef et al., 2019a; Olabode et al., 2022). BDA has emerged as a replacement for traditional statistical tools, providing value to firms in various financial and non-financial dimensions (Yasmin et al., 2020). This study analyzes the positive impact of big data analytics on firm value with the help of resource-based view (RBV) (Barney, 1991), dynamic capability view (DCV) (Teece et al., 1997) and knowledge-based view (KBV) (Maroufkhani et al., 2019).

First, BDA as an in-house VRIN resource within a firm has the potential to enhance efficiency, aligning with the principles of RBV. This strategic approach posits that possessing such resources can lead to competitive success by contributing to the firm's overall competitiveness. Companies can leverage BDA insights into customer behavior to optimize business operations, efficiently allocate resources, and reduce production costs (Mikalef et al., 2018). Similarly, BDA facilitates a deeper understanding of employee situations, allowing companies to identify skill and knowledge gaps accurately. This insight aids in designing targeted training and development programs, thereby improving employee productivity and overall company productivity. Furthermore, BDA assists in identifying inefficiencies in processes and operations, enabling optimization of supply chain management, logistics management, and inventory management, thereby enhancing overall management efficiency (Maheshwari et al., 2021).

Second, BDA fosters firm innovation, empowering an organization to cultivate dynamic capabilities to seize external opportunities. This enables them to reconfigure themselves and gain competitive advantages in the dynamic and volatile marketplace, aligning with the essence of DCV. Through the analysis of vast and intricate data, companies can identify unnoticed market trends, explore new business opportunities, and develop innovative products, services, and business models (Ciampi et al., 2021). Simultaneously, BDA helps optimize innovation processes and enhance innovation efficiency (Ghasemaghaei & Calic, 2020). Additionally, BDA offers real-time feedback on the effectiveness of innovation, enabling swift adjustments to the innovation approach. This enhances a company's agility in innovation and enables rapid responses to evolving market conditions and customer needs, thereby sustaining a competitive edge and contributing to long-term value creation (Mikalef et al., 2019b). Accordingly, we propose the following hypothesis.

Third, the adoption of BDA tools by organizations to translate vast amounts of data into actionable insights in dynamic market scenarios can facilitate accurate predictions and enhance decision-making processes. This aligns with the principles of KBV. By leveraging BDA, companies can identify patterns and relationships within extensive datasets, uncover novel insights, and predict future trends. This empowers decision-makers with comprehensive information and valuable insights to make informed choices (Ghasemaghaei & Calic, 2019). Moreover, BDA provides real-time information, enabling companies to make prompt and effective decisions, promptly adapt to market dynamics, and meet customer demands (Ghasemaghaei & Calic, 2019). By monitoring key performance indicators through BDA, businesses can swiftly identify areas requiring attention and take measures to enhance overall performance.

Hypothesis 1a: All else being equal, firms that effectively utilize BDA tend to have higher value.

On the contrary, we propose an alternative hypothesis suggesting that the implementation of BDA may have a negative impact on firm value. A survey conducted by Gartner Consulting in the U.S. in 2016 revealed that although companies continue to increase their investments in BDA, the growth rate is slowing down, and several organizations are encountering unsatisfactory outcomes from their BDA initiatives. It is worth noting that not all efforts in BDA yield the anticipated returns, and more than 50% of big data projects fail to achieve their strategic objectives (Mithas et al., 2013). Despite the substantial number of companies investing in BDA, a significant portion has struggled to extract tangible benefits from it (Popovič et al., 2018; Wamba et al., 2017). In fact, there are arguments suggesting that BDA might even have a detrimental effect on company value rather than being beneficial (Kiron, 2017).

First, the implementation and maintenance costs associated with BDA are substantial. BDA encompasses a combination of arithmetic, algorithms, and mathematics, necessitating not only high-quality data but also well-developed information systems, analytical tools, and a skilled workforce proficient in handling big data. Each of these requirements entails significant investments. Research by Grover et al. (2018) indicates that many companies allocate more than 10% of their IT budgets solely to data-related expenses. In the face of such high costs, if the benefits derived from BDA implementation fail to outweigh the expenses, companies may experience investment losses, potentially leading to financial strain.

Second, BDA has the potential to result in poor decision-making within companies. The capacity to collect and analyze large volumes of data takes considerable time to develop and cultivate, and extracting value from such vast datasets can be challenging. On one hand, insufficient data collection capabilities within a company may introduce excessive data noise or biases, directly impacting the formation of accurate knowledge and insights. On the other hand, the extraction of meaningful information necessitates the development of appropriate analytical methods or algorithms tailored to the company's specific needs. However, the biased nature of these methods may lead to erroneous conclusions, subsequently influencing decision-making within company management.

Lastly, the collection and utilization of big data raise concerns regarding privacy and security. Inadequate data management practices can expose companies to risks such as data breaches and other security incidents. Such incidents can result in reputational damage and a decrease in company value. For instance, following the Facebook user privacy data breach in 2018, the company's stock price plummeted by approximately 19% within a few days. Facebook also faced heightened regulatory scrutiny, incurring additional costs in the form of legal fees, privacy enhancements, and potential fines. The scandal eroded trust among Facebook users, potentially exerting a long-term negative impact on the company's value and reputation. Accordingly, we propose the following hypothesis.

Hypothesis 1b: All else being equal, firms that have limited utilization of BDA tend to have lower value.

5.3 Research Design

5.3.1 Sample and Data

We select all A-share listed companies from 2003 to 2020 as the initial research sample and exclude the data as follows: (I) the observations of ST, *ST and delisted firms; (II) the observations with missing values of variables; and (III) the observations of listed companies in the IT industry. Because the BDA belongs to the IT industry, the impact of BDA on them may be different from that of other industries, so we exclude them. In the robustness test, we re-include the IT industry in our sample. Ultimately, our sample comprises 32,376 observations from 3,078 listed companies. The BDA measures are based on the analysis of annual reports of listed companies. We obtain annual reports from the Shanghai Stock Exchange, the Shenzhen Stock Exchange and the Cninfo database. We use the market index from China Market Index Database, and the financial data from the China Stock Market Accounting Research (CSMAR) database. All continuous variables are winsorized at their 1% and 99% values. Standard errors of all regression results are adjusted for firm-level clustering.

5.3.2 Measuring Firm Value

Consistent with the scholarly contributions of Shen (2021) and Ravid and Sekerci (2020), our study adopts Tobin's Q as a measure of firm value. Tobin's Q is calculated by the sum of the market value of equity and the book value of total liabilities, and then divided by the book value of assets. We choose Tobin's Q as a measure of firm value rather than accounting yield metrics for two main reasons. Firstly, Tobin's Q accounts for the potential time lag in the influence of big data analytics on firm value. By capturing the expected future earnings of the company, Tobin's Q adequately considers the temporal delay associated with the incremental value attributed to big data analytics. Secondly, Tobin's Q reflects the firm's risk profile and is less susceptible to managerial manipulation compared to accounting return indicators. Furthermore, we employ the market value as a proxy variable for Tobin's Q, thereby reinforcing the robustness of the findings and mitigating potential indicator selection bias.

5.3.3 Measuring BDA

The measure of BDA has been paid increasing attention in academia and industry. Since BDA is an abstract concept, it is challenging to find an indicator to measure it accurately in reality. To date, most studies have used questionnaires to measure BDA. (Ghasemaghaei, 2021; Mikalef et al., 2020). However, the 5-point or 7-point Likert scale has some limitations and cannot accurately describe the differences between firms with close capabilities of BDA. The annual report disclosed by the listed company is an objective summary and statement based on the firm's actual operation. Accordingly, we consider that the frequency of big data-related terms in annual reports reflects firms' BDA capabilities (Zhang et al., 2021). Based on the above basic assumptions, we think it is scientifically feasible to use the frequency statistics of the words related to "big data" in firms' annual reports to measure BDA. However, in contrast to previous studies such as Zhang et al. (2021), we do not think it is entirely reasonable to use the same weights for different "big data" keywords.

Following Loughran and McDonald (2011) and Sun et al. (2024), we provide a comprehensive measure of BDA adoption based on a Word2vec model trained on unstructured text corpus disclosed by listed companies. The term "big data" originated in the 1980s, and according to Gartner, Inc., it is characterized as "massive data." In light of this, the present study selects these two expressions as the seed words for the dictionary. Utilizing the Continuous Bag of Words (CBOW) model within Word2Vec, the seed word set is expanded to identify similar terms along with their respective degrees of similarity. The frequency of key terms and the overall count of words in the distinct annual report word vector datasets are then determined, based on both the original seed word set and the newly expanded set of words. Following Wei et al. (2022), we calculate BDA adoption by the following model:

$$Bigdata_{it} = \frac{\sum Freq_{itn} \times Sim_n}{Totalwords_{it}} \tag{5.1}$$

where $Bigdata_{it}$ is the BDA adoption. $Freq_{itn}$ is the exact word frequency of the nth word in the dictionary in the annual report of firm i in year t. Sim_n is the similarity between the nth word in the dictionary and the seed word. We assign the similarity of the seed word to 1. $Totalwords_{it}$ is the total number of words in the annual report of firm i in year t after excluding English and numbers.

5.3.4 Control Variables

Consistent with prior literature (Amin et al., 2021; Hatch et al., 2021; Shen, 2021), our regression model includes a vector of control variables. We include firm size (Size) and firm age (Age) to account for market competitiveness and stability of firms. Companies with higher revenue growth and greater profitability tend to be more valuable, we include firm growth (Growth) and return on assets (ROA). Considering that operational capacity and solvency affect firm value, we include financial leverage (Lev) and tangible asset ratio (Tang). We also include capital expenditures (Capex) and operating cash flow (Cashflow) to illustrate the payments position of firms.

5.3.5 Regression Analysis

We estimate the following baseline regression model to analyze the firm value implication of big data analytics:

$$Tobin'sQ_{i,j,p,t} = \alpha_0 + \alpha_1 Bigdata_{i,j,p,t} + \alpha_2 Controls_{i,j,p,t} + \delta_{j,t} + \phi_{p,t} + \mu_i + \sigma_t + \varepsilon_{i,j,p,t} \quad (5.2)$$

where Tobin's $Q_{i,j,p,t}$ is the firm value of firm i in industry j province p_t in year t, and $Bigdata_{i,j,p,t}$ is the BDA adoption. $Controls_{i,j,p,t}$ are control variables that may affect the firm value, $\delta_{j,t}$ is the industry-year fixed effect. $\varphi_{p,t}$ is the province-year fixed effect. μ_i is the firm fixed effect, σ_t is period fixed effect, $\varepsilon_{i,j,p,t}$ is random error. The standard errors of all regressions are clustered at the firm-level to control for the autocorrelation between different years of the same firm.

5.4 Empirical Results

5.4.1 Descriptive Statistics

We find that the level of BDA has increased year by year since 2013, which is comparable with the numerous media disclosures that 2013 is the first year of big data ear in the world. In general, the firm value is also showing an increasing trend. Panel B reports the distribution of observations by industry. The industry categories are based on the 2012 industry classification standards implemented by the China

Securities Regulatory Commission. For instance, we observe that the manufacturing industry represents the most significant percentage of our sample (67.64%), while the education industry represents the smallest percentage (0.08%). We also find that, on average, the industry of health and social work shows higher levels of BDA (0.1328), whereas residential services, repairs and other services has the lowest BDA (0.0023).

Table 5.1 presents the descriptive statistics for the final sample. We find that the mean value of firm value measured by Tobin's Q for the sample firms is 2.0838 and the statistics are consistent with the data from previous studies in the literature. For example, Hatch et al. (2021) and Shen (2021) report mean values of 1.955 and 1.965 for firm value measured by Tobin's Q, respectively. On average, our sample covers larger (Size = 22.0602), more leveraged (Lev = 0.4587) firms, and they have higher growth opportunities (Growth = 0.1872). On average, the sample firms exhibit a proportion of tangible assets (Tang) at 24.6%, net cash flow from operations (Cashflow) at 4.85%, and capital expenditures (Capex) at 5.29%. These findings align with the values reported by Amin et al. (2021). In addition, the mean value of return on assets (ROA) is 0.0343, which is consistent with the value reported by Xie et al. (2022). The firm value measured by Tobin's Q is positively correlated with Bigdata, and the correlations of firm value with control variables are broadly consistent with previous literature.

5.4.2 Baseline Regression Results

Table 5.2 presents the regression results for the effect of BDA on firm value. We use the ordinary least squares (OLS) regression model, with standard errors adjusted for within-firm clustering. Our main firm value measure is Tobin's Q, and the explanatory variable is BDA (Bigdata). Column (1) show the regression results with year and firm fixed effects. The coefficient estimate on BDA is 428.1434 for firm value, and is significant at the 1% level. The results suggest that firms with better BDA are associated with higher firm value. For economic significance, on average, a one standard deviation increases in BDA results in 2.05% (= 428.1434 × 0.0001/2.0838) increase in Tobin's Q. In addition, to exclude the interference of industry and region on the regression results, we include firm and year-industry fixed effects in Column (2) and firm year-province fixed effects in Column (3). The results show that the coefficients on the variable Bigdata remain significantly positive.

In addition, we find that the signs and statistical significance of the control variables are comparable with past studies. For example, Lev, Growth, ROA, Capex, Cashflow are positively correlated with firm value, suggesting that firms with higher financial leverage, growth, return on assets, capital expenditure and Operating cash flow are more likely to have higher firm value (e.g., Amin et al., 2021; Shen, 2021) We observed that the firm size and proportion of tangible assets ratio is negatively associated with Tobin's Q, which is similar to related past studies (e.g., Hatch et al., 2021 and Nam & Uchida, 2019). Finally, we observe that firm age (Age) is positively related to firm value.

Table 5.1 Summary statistics

Variables	N	Mean	SD	Min	Median	Max
Variables used in the main analysis						
Tobin's Q	32,376	2.0838	1.3825	0.9140	1.6193	9.2445
MarketValue	32,376	22.5747	1.1879	20.2475	22.4361	26.1445
Bigdata	32,376	0.0000	0.0001	0.0000	0.0000	0.0011
Bigdata_b	32,376	0.0002	0.0004	0.0000	0.0001	0.0037
Size	32,376	22.0602	1.3263	19.3048	21.8807	27.0107
Lev	32,376	0.4587	0.2087	0.0535	0.4586	0.9790
Tang	32,376	0.2460	0.1726	0.0020	0.2141	0.7364
Age	32,376	2.1708	0.7451	0.0000	2.3026	3.2958
Growth	32,376	0.1872	0.4713	-0.6195	0.1121	3.2017
ROA	32,376	0.0343	0.0631	-0.2855	0.0341	0.1970
Capex	32,376	0.0529	0.0509	0.0002	0.0376	0.2492
Cashflow	32,376	0.0485	0.0732	-0.1910	0.0478	0.2578
Variables used in channel and cross-sectional analyses						
R&D pers	21,658	8.4912	10.7698	0.0000	4.9600	64.0900
R&D spend	22,488	3.3363	3.6298	0.0000	3.0100	24.1800
IN	23,598	0.0036	0.0097	0.0000	0.0006	0.0688
IE	23,598	1.5374	4.1359	0.0000	0.0000	29.0201
TFP_OP	32,341	14.0979	1.0577	7.8726	14.0656	18.7983
TFP_LP	32,341	14.6697	1.0974	8.7738	14.5927	19.4436
ME	31,922	-0.1541	0.8564	-6.3119	-0.0395	0.5718
OE	32,138	11.3322	37.6893	0.1361	3.7141	343.46
INS	32,327	48.1554	23.4690	0.0001	51.1000	101.1401
Analyst	32,376	1.3253	1.1793	0.0000	1.0986	4.3307
Big4	32,375	0.0630	0.2429	0.0000	0.0000	1.0000
Top10	32,376	58.3133	15.2474	1.3200	59.3500	101.1600
SEP	30,858	5.0088	7.9072	-7.6400	0.0000	70.8016
Disacc	31,878	0.0752	0.0637	0.0054	0.0587	0.4045

Overall, our findings support Hypothesis 1: that is, firms with higher levels of BDA have higher firm value.

5.4.3 Robustness Checks

Existing evidence indicates a positive correlation between BDA and firm value. However, it is important to consider potential endogeneity issues that may affect the

Table 5.2 BDA and firm value

	(1)	(2)	(3)
	Tobin's Q	Tobin's Q	Tobin's Q
Bigdata	428.1434***	347.7889***	405.4656***
	(3.9398)	(3.1889)	(3.7302)
Size	-0.7491***	-0.7505***	-0.7537***
	(-22.4986)	(-22.5500)	(-23.4057)
Lev	0.5831***	0.6011***	0.5442***
	(4.8219)	(5.1400)	(4.6363)
Tang	-0.6249***	-0.6710***	-0.6261***
	(-4.9115)	(-5.0906)	(-4.8602)
Age	0.7721***	0.7847***	0.7809***
	(22.2686)	(21.7112)	(21.7603)
Growth	0.0312*	0.0295*	0.0359**
	(1.9135)	(1.8393)	(2.2641)
ROA	2.2363***	2.0746***	2.1543***
	(10.0539)	(9.6326)	(9.9873)
Capex	0.7198***	0.6132***	0.6545***
	(3.7883)	(3.2787)	(3.4759)
Cashflow	0.5555***	0.5182***	0.5322***
	(4.7097)	(4.4771)	(4.5821)
Constant	16.6580***	16.6809***	16.7658***
	(23.4255)	(23.5178)	(24.2450)
Year	Yes	No	No
Firm	Yes	Yes	Yes
Year-Industry	No	Yes	No
Year-Province	No	No	Yes
Obs	32,376	32,376	32,376
R^2	0.6329	0.6501	0.6450

Note The standard errors are clustered at the firm-level and t-statistics are reported in parentheses. *, ** and *** denote statistical significance at the 10%, 5% and 1% levels, respectively

results of our baseline regression. To address these endogeneity concerns, our study conducts several tests to assess the robustness of the regression results and ensure the validity of our findings.

5.4.3.1 Instrumental Variable Estimation

Following Huang et al. (2019), we employ historical post and telecommunications data from various cities in 1984 as the IV of the BDA. On the one hand, communication technology is the critical source of big data, as it collects data from a variety of sources such as email, social media, and messaging platforms. Post offices and fixed-line telephones, as traditional and modern communication technologies, can influence the future development of BDA in terms of usage habits and investment capacity. Therefore, the number of historical post offices in cities and fixed-line telephones as IVs satisfy the relevance requirement. On the other hand, the number of post offices and fixed-line telephones are not directly related to the firm value, satisfying the exogenous condition of the IV. However, the city-level post offices and fixed-line telephones data from 1984 only constitute cross-sectional data, which means they do not provide enough variation over time. Referring to Nunn and Qian (2014), our study constructs an interaction term for the number of post offices per million people at the city level in 1984 (correlated with individuals) and national Internet penetration rate (correlated with time) as an IV for BDA. Moreover, we also construct an interaction term for the number of fixed-line telephones per hundred people at the city level in 1984 (correlated with individuals) and national Internet penetration rate (correlated with time) as an IV for BDA. Since the value of Bigdata is small, we multiply it by 106 to make it easier to display in the list.

Table 5.3 presents the results of the IV regressions. Column (1) presents the results of the first-stage regression. The coefficient on the variable POST is 0.0067, which is significant at the 1% level. This indicates a significant positive correlation between our instrument and BDA. The F-test statistic in the first-stage regression is 115.473, exceeding the critical value of 8.96 suggested by Stock-Yogo (2005), which confirms that weak instrument concerns are not present. Columns (2) presents the results of the second-stage regressions. The coefficients on Bigdata are significantly positive for Tobin's Q. Column (3) presents the first-stage regression results with Post and Tel as instrumental variables. The coefficients on the instrumental variables, Post and Tel, are 0.0045 and 0.3415, respectively, and both are significant at the 10% level or higher. The p-value of the unidentifiable test is 0.0003, indicating that instrumental variables are not under-identified. The F-test statistic in the first-stage regression is 76.490, suggesting that weak instruments do not affect the regression results in our study. Furthermore, the p-value of the over-identification test is 0.6463, which is greater than 0.1, indicating that all instrumental variables are exogenous. Moving to column (2), the second-stage regression results demonstrate that the coefficient of Bigdata remains significantly positive. These findings support the conclusion that BDA enhances firm value. Consequently, the results are consistent with our baseline regressions when we use IV regression to address endogeneity concerns.

Table 5.3 Instrumental variable estimation

	(1)	(2)	(3)	(4)
	Bigdata/10–6	Tobinb's Q	Bigdata/10–6	Tobinb's Q
Post	0.0067***		0.0045*	
	(2.8518)		(1.8438)	
Tel			0.3415***	
			(4.2004)	
Bigdata/10–6		0.0037*		0.0033*
		(1.7888)		(1.7958)
Size	16.8953***	-0.7850***	16.5852***	-0.7788***
	(5.8845)	(-17.7319)	(5.8368)	(-18.2233)
Lev	-0.0749	0.5691***	-0.8209	0.5693***
	(-0.0067)	(4.4481)	(-0.0736)	(4.4748)
Tang	-35.8377***	-0.5405***	-34.1044***	-0.5538***
	(-3.8883)	(-3.6035)	(-3.7048)	(-3.7578)
Age	30.1516***	0.7285***	31.3451***	0.7367***
	(5.7017)	(13.8337)	(5.9527)	(15.1023)
Growth	0.8805	0.0262	0.9637	0.0268
	(0.5621)	(1.4672)	(0.6149)	(1.5059)
ROA	4.1575	2.2333***	7.2249	2.2366***
	(0.2312)	(9.4862)	(0.4031)	(9.5581)
Capex	63.5282***	0.4879**	61.0022***	0.5103**
	(3.8558)	(2.1498)	(3.7098)	(2.3191)
Cashflow	-22.4114**	0.5817***	-21.0057**	0.5750***
	(-2.2157)	(4.5699)	(-2.0713)	(4.6049)
Constant	-399.6194***		-412.2420***	
	(-6.4384)		(-6.6061)	
Year	Yes	Yes	Yes	Yes
Firm	Yes	Yes	Yes	Yes
Obs	33,098	30,331	33,098	30,331
R^2	0.6885	0.1118	0.6900	0.1278

Note The standard errors are clustered at the firm-level and t-statistics are reported in parentheses. *, ** and *** denote statistical significance at the 10%, 5% and 1% levels, respectively

5.4.3.2 Alternative Measures of Firm Value

To investigate the potential influence of endogeneity on our baseline regression results, we conducted an additional analysis using market value as a proxy variable for firm value. The estimation results of the proxy variables are presented in Table 5.4. Notably, the coefficient of BDA is found to be positive and significant at the 1% level. Consistent with our baseline regression, we include firm and year-industry fixed effects in Column (2) and firm year-province fixed effects in Column (3). This finding suggests a positive relationship between BDA and market value. Consequently, the inclusion of the proxy variable in our analysis further strengthens and validates our baseline regression results, underscoring the significant impact of BDA in increasing firm value.

Table 5.4 Alternative Measures of firm value

	(1)	(2)	(3)
	MarketValue	MarketValue	MarketValue
Bigdata	134.1413***	114.6427***	120.7431***
	(4.2192)	(3.6526)	(3.7405)
Size	0.7149***	0.7143***	0.7118***
	(79.1740)	(80.9600)	(82.7436)
Lev	0.1555***	0.1699***	0.1454***
	(4.9903)	(5.6743)	(4.7680)
Tang	-0.0850***	-0.1019***	-0.0851***
	(-2.7324)	(-3.2671)	(-2.7234)
Age	0.2783***	0.2756***	0.2785***
	(24.5817)	(23.9809)	(23.9819)
Growth	0.0028	-0.0003	0.0034
	(0.6570)	(-0.0716)	(0.8150)
ROA	0.9511***	0.8995***	0.9272***
	(16.3441)	(16.0883)	(16.2196)
Capex	0.4114***	0.3587***	0.3772***
	(7.4965)	(6.7685)	(6.9899)
Cashflow	0.2168***	0.1889***	0.2127***
	(6.6377)	(6.0908)	(6.6731)
Constant	6.0846***	6.1079***	6.1601***
	(31.4921)	(32.3456)	(33.1337)
Year	Yes	No	No
Firm	Yes	Yes	Yes
Year × Industry	No	Yes	No
Year × Province	No	No	Yes
Obs	32,376	32,376	32,376
R^2	0.9598	0.9622	0.9613

Note The standard errors are clustered at the firm-level and t-statistics are reported in parentheses. *, ** and *** denote statistical significance at the 10%, 5% and 1% levels, respectively

5.4.3.3 Alternative Measures of BDA

In the presence of vast amounts of data, traditional analysis, standalone computing, and storage capabilities are no longer sufficient. BDA relies on powerful computing power, analytical capabilities, and storage capacity. Consequently, big data cannot be viewed in isolation; it is inseparable from the support of cloud computing, artificial intelligence, and modern storage technologies.

To capture the comprehensive scope of BDA, our research expands upon the seed words "big data" and "massive data" by incorporating keywords related to the aforementioned technologies into an expanded vocabulary. This approach allows us to construct a broader measure of BDA, represented by the proxy variable Bigdata_b. By re-running the regression using this alternative measure of BDA, we assess its impact on the explanatory variables.

Table 5.5 presents the estimation results of the proxy variables, revealing that the coefficient of Bigdata_b is significantly positive at the 1% level. This finding indicates a positive relationship between the broadly defined BDA and firm value. Consequently, the utilization of this alternative measure of BDA provides further validation for our baseline regression results, reinforcing the conclusion that BDA significantly enhances firm value.

5.4.3.4 Additional Control Variables

Our baseline regression model incorporates essential control variables to address potential confounding factors that may influence firm value. In addition to the explanatory variables, our model includes several other variables that have been identified in prior research as relevant to firm value.

Prior research has indicated that stock market metrics could potentially have an impact on firm value (Hatch al., 2021; Nguyen et al., 2020). In column (1) of Table 5.6, we control for stock market factors, such as stock return (Return), stock liquidity (Turnover), number of shares outstanding (Tradableshare), cash dividends (Dividen), and cash holdings (Cash). The results demonstrate that even after accounting for these factors, the positive relationship between BDA and firm value remains significant.

Furthermore, considering the influence of CEO characteristics on firm value, as highlighted by Brochet et al. (2021), we incorporate a set of CEO-related variables in column (2) of the table. These variables include CEO age (CEOAge), CEO gender (CEOGender), CEO shareholding (CEOShare), whether the CEO also serves as the chairman of the board (CEODuality), and CEO education (CEODegree). Notably, the coefficient of BDA remains significantly positive at the 1% level, indicating its robust impact on firm value.

Lastly, recognizing the significance of board of directors' attributes in relation to firm value (Xie et al., 2022), we introduce additional controls in column (3) of our analysis. These controls encompass board size (Board Size), board independence (Board Indep), average board age (Board Age), percentage of female directors (Board Gender), and board shareholding (Board Share). Importantly, our regression results

Table 5.5 Alternative Measures of BDA

	(1)	(2)	(3)
	Tobin's Q	Tobin's Q	Tobin's Q
Bigdata_b	146.7976***	118.0230***	134.2763***
	(4.5630)	(3.6348)	(4.1395)
Size	-0.7525***	-0.7532***	-0.7569***
	(-22.5394)	(-22.5850)	(-23.4338)
Lev	0.5873***	0.6036***	0.5484***
	(4.8659)	(5.1700)	(4.6765)
Tang	-0.6161***	-0.6665***	-0.6204***
	(-4.8459)	(-5.0590)	(-4.8161)
Age	0.7683***	0.7820***	0.7783***
	(22.1556)	(21.6613)	(21.6556)
Growth	0.0312*	0.0295*	0.0360**
	(1.9200)	(1.8429)	(2.2745)
ROA	2.2291***	2.0708***	2.1473***
	(10.0174)	(9.6063)	(9.9488)
Capex	0.7165***	0.6128***	0.6530***
	(3.7777)	(3.2806)	(3.4749)
Cashflow	0.5547***	0.5179***	0.5324***
	(4.7054)	(4.4728)	(4.5855)
Constant	16.7180***	16.7276***	16.8197***
	(23.4569)	(23.5485)	(24.2635)
Year	Yes	No	No
Firm	Yes	Yes	Yes
Year × Industry	No	Yes	No
Year × Province	No	No	Yes
Obs	32,376	32,376	32,376
R^2	0.6332	0.6503	0.6452

Note The standard errors are clustered at the firm-level and t-statistics are reported in parentheses. *, ** and *** denote statistical significance at the 10%, 5% and 1% levels, respectively

continue to exhibit robustness, reinforcing the positive association between BDA and firm value.

5.4.3.5 Subsample Analysis

In September 2015, China's State Council issued the Outline of Action for Promoting the Development of Big Data, which underscored the strategic importance of big

Table 5.6 Additional control variables

	(1)	(2)	(3)
	Tobin's Q	Tobin's Q	Tobin's Q
Bigdata_n	253.5665***	375.6865***	392.6174***
	(2.8105)	(3.4005)	(3.8752)
Size	-0.8997***	-0.7541***	-0.7316***
	(-25.7255)	(-21.5636)	(-22.1485)
Lev	0.7167***	0.5850***	0.6219***
	(6.3663)	(4.4224)	(4.9650)
Tang	-0.7028***	-0.6478***	-0.6459***
	(-5.9017)	(-4.7035)	(-4.9887)
Age	0.0264	0.8015***	0.7229***
	(0.6488)	(21.7465)	(17.7024)
Growth	0.0239	0.0283	0.0458***
	(1.5229)	(1.6332)	(2.8446)
ROA	1.4047***	2.4377***	2.4053***
	(6.7474)	(9.9666)	(10.5422)
Capex	0.8923***	0.5975***	0.7836***
	(5.1683)	(2.8993)	(4.0902)
Cashflow	0.2435**	0.5772***	0.6562***
	(2.3953)	(4.5772)	(5.5205)
Return	0.6485***		
	(32.7868)		
Turnover	-0.0002***		
	(-7.3996)		
Tradableshare	0.5821***		
	(24.0011)		
Dividen	4.3206***		
	(5.5995)		
Sigma	3.4749***		
	(3.2777)		
CEOAget		0.0026	
		(1.4538)	
CEOGendert		0.0471	
		(0.9647)	
CEOSharet		-0.0066***	
		(-3.0622)	
CEODualityt		0.0450	
		(1.3003)	
CEODegreet		-0.0073	

(continued)

Table 5.6 (continued)

	(1) Tobin's Q	(2) Tobin's Q	(3) Tobin's Q
		(-0.5381)	
BoardSizet			0.0104
			(1.2128)
BoardIndept			0.2297
			(1.1727)
BoardAget			0.0029
			(0.7201)
BoardGendert			-0.1146
			(-1.1290)
BoardSharet			-0.7997***
			(-4.4054)
Constant	9.9321***	16.6221***	16.0944***
	(15.9051)	(22.1577)	(21.6882)
Year	Yes	Yes	Yes
Firm	Yes	Yes	Yes
Obs	31,523	28,222	30,164
R^2	0.7015	0.6455	0.6362

Note The standard errors are clustered at the firm-level and t-statistics are reported in parentheses. *, ** and *** denote statistical significance at the 10%, 5% and 1% levels, respectively

data in China's modernization efforts. This policy initiative triggered a surge in BDA development within China. However, it is important to address potential concerns regarding the authenticity of companies' claims regarding BDA implementation following the policy announcement.

Two possibilities arise regarding companies' engagement in big data development after 2015. Firstly, companies may genuinely recognize the need for big data development and acknowledge the potential value it can bring to their operations. Consequently, they actively pursue BDA initiatives aligned with their business objectives. Secondly, in order to enhance their fundraising prospects in the capital market, companies may capitalize on the social hype surrounding big data and falsely present BDA-related information in their annual reports without actually implementing BDA.

To mitigate the potential impact of firms' misleading BDA information on our study results, we conducted a sub-sample analysis by excluding data from 2015 onwards. By restricting our analysis to the period from 2003 to 2014, we re-ran the regression analysis. Table 5.7 presents the Ordinary Least Squares (OLS) estimation results for this sub-sample, revealing that the coefficient of BDA remains positive and significant at the 1% level or higher. These findings align closely with the results obtained from the baseline regressions, indicating the robustness of our findings.

Table 5.7 Subsample analysis

	(1)	(2)	(3)
	Tobin's Q	Tobin's Q	Tobin's Q
Bigdata	1359.3404***	1243.4776***	1321.3418***
	(5.1371)	(4.7252)	(4.8420)
Size	-0.8577***	-0.8454***	-0.8708***
	(-20.1553)	(-19.7075)	(-20.3425)
Lev	0.6442***	0.6990***	0.6078***
	(4.7967)	(5.2997)	(4.4837)
Tang	-0.2538	-0.3292**	-0.2510
	(-1.6290)	(-2.0451)	(-1.5920)
Age	0.6113***	0.5976***	0.6262***
	(13.0950)	(12.3960)	(12.4272)
Growth	0.0222	0.0220	0.0230
	(1.1034)	(1.1300)	(1.1514)
ROA	1.6993***	1.5728***	1.6546***
	(5.9401)	(5.5741)	(5.7122)
Capex	0.9916***	0.9044***	0.9392***
	(4.5052)	(4.1594)	(4.3475)
Cashflow	0.3339**	0.3279**	0.3378**
	(2.3513)	(2.3366)	(2.3620)
Constant	18.9090***	18.6733***	19.1834***
	(20.7397)	(20.2544)	(20.9029)
Year	Yes	No	No
Firm	Yes	Yes	Yes
Year-Industry	No	Yes	No
Year-Province	No	No	Yes
Obs	16,799	16,799	16,799
R^2	0.6714	0.6874	0.6841

Note The standard errors are clustered at the firm-level and t-statistics are reported in parentheses. *, ** and *** denote statistical significance at the 10%, 5% and 1% levels, respectively

Thus, the inclusion of this sub-sample analysis helps to address the influence of national external policy shocks on the regression results, confirming that our findings regarding the positive relationship between BDA and firm value remain robust.

5.4.4 Mechanism Tests

So far, we established the significant contribution of BDA to firm value. However, an essential aspect that remains to be explored is the underlying mechanism through which BDA influences firm value. In this section, we attempt to provide more direct evidence on the impact channels of our main finding that BDA improves firm value by enhancing productive efficiency and management efficiency, increasing innovation inputs and outputs.

5.4.4.1 Productive Efficiency and Management Efficiency

Our study investigates the influence of BDA on firm value through the lens of two distinct perspectives: productive efficiency and managerial efficiency. To measure productive efficiency, we adopt total factor productivity as a proxy variable. The calculation of total factor productivity is based on the Cobb–Douglas production function:

$$Y_{it} = A_{it} K_{it}^{\alpha} L_{it}^{\beta} M_{it}^{\gamma} \tag{5.3}$$

To derive an expression for total factor productivity, we apply a logarithmic transformation to the Cobb–Douglas production function. This transformation allows us to capture the relationship between inputs and outputs in a linear form. By taking the logarithm of the Cobb–Douglas production function, we can express total factor productivity as follows:

$$TFP_{it} = \ln Y_{it} - \alpha \ln K_{it} - \beta \ln L_{it} - \gamma \ln M_{it} \tag{5.4}$$

To address the potential issue of endogeneity in calculating firm-level total factor productivity, this study adopts the generalized OP semi-parametric method and LP semi-parametric method, as commonly utilized in existing studies. The variables used in the estimation are defined as follows:

Y represents gross output, measured by the firm's operating revenue.
K denotes fixed capital input, measured by the net fixed assets of the firm.
L represents labor input, measured by the number of employees working in the firm.
M corresponds to intermediate input, which is calculated as the difference between sales revenue and value added. The value added is computed using the "allocation method," which involves summing up depreciation, compensation of workers, net production tax, and operating surplus.

To be more specific, this study follows the approach outlined in Liu et al. (2018) by utilizing the four accounts of depreciation of fixed assets, cash paid to and for employees, operating taxes and surcharges, and operating surplus. Moreover, due to the limited availability of investment data at the firm level, the OP method employed in estimating total factor productivity replaces investment with intermediate inputs as suggested by Lu and Lian (2012), allowing for the measurement of observable productivity.

In addition to productive efficiency, this study also considers corporate management efficiency using two proxy variables: excess overhead (ME) and inventory turnover (OE). Following Yang and Yang (2015), ME is calculated as the ratio of the sum of overhead and selling expenses, adjusted for industry averages, to total operating revenues. A higher value of ME suggests lower management efficiency, as it indicates a relatively higher proportion of expenses in relation to operating revenues. Building on Li et al. (2021), OE is defined as the ratio of operating costs to the closing balance of inventories. A higher value of OE reflects more efficient management, as it signifies a greater frequency of inventory turnover and effective utilization of inventory resources.

Table 5.8 presents the estimation results of the impact of BDA on productivity and managerial efficiency. The findings in columns (1) and (2) indicate a significant and positive relationship between BDA and firms' total factor productivity. The total factor productivity coefficients calculated using both the OP and LP methods are positive and statistically significant. Moreover, the results in columns (3) and (4) demonstrate that BDA has a significant effect on reducing excess overhead and improving operational efficiency. The coefficients for excess overhead and operational efficiency are statistically significant at the 1% and 5% levels respectively. In economic terms, for every one standard deviation increase in BDA, excess overhead decreases by 12.21% (= -188.1784 × 0.0001/-0.1541) and operational efficiency improves by 7.59% (= 8606.649 × 0.0001/11.3322). In summary, the findings support the notion that BDA plays a crucial role in enhancing firm productivity and management efficiency.

Indeed, management efficiency reflects the rational organization, coordination, and operation of a company's resources, as highlighted by Sun et al. (2018). Li et al. (2018) also found that efficient management efficiency is an effective means to enhance a company's quality capability through their study of data from the "China Enterprise-Labor Matching Survey." Similarly, Pan et al. (2018) demonstrated that higher management efficiency of existing resources corresponds to higher firm value. From a productivity perspective, total factor productivity represents a firm's ability to maximize output given a certain level of inputs. According to Farrell's (1957) efficiency theory, improvements in both production efficiency and management efficiency reflect a firm's growth in economic efficiency, and both contribute to the increase in firm value. In summary, production efficiency and management efficiency act as mediating variables through which BDA enhances firm value. BDA contributes to the creation of firm value by improving production efficiency and management efficiency, thereby playing a crucial role in firm value creation.

Table 5.8 Channel tests: Productive efficiency and management efficiency

	(1)	(2)	(3)	(4)
	TFP_OP	TFP_LP	ME	OE
Bigdata_n	96.9138**	94.1220*	-188.1784***	8606.6490**
	(1.9943)	(1.8602)	(-4.1255)	(2.0853)
Size	0.5400***	0.5361***	-0.0220*	0.1342
	(35.8091)	(34.9442)	(-1.7459)	(0.1229)
Lev	0.1853***	0.1819***	-0.0917*	-3.2683
	(3.1558)	(3.1320)	(-1.6570)	(-1.0323)
Tang	-0.9555***	-1.0038***	0.1016	5.0598
	(-15.5464)	(-16.0775)	(1.6284)	(0.8135)
Age	-0.0051	0.0021	0.0554**	-0.7787
	(-0.3055)	(0.1265)	(2.1926)	(-0.6842)
Growth	0.1822***	0.1825***	-0.0220**	1.6934***
	(23.2693)	(23.5395)	(-2.5143)	(2.8202)
ROA	1.3981***	1.3649***	-0.1731	6.9729
	(14.2376)	(14.0992)	(-1.5546)	(1.3319)
Capex	-0.7680***	-0.7492***	-0.3290**	18.9051**
	(-8.3670)	(-8.1874)	(-2.3493)	(2.3188)
Cashflow	0.8454***	0.8465***	-0.0644	10.0927**
	(15.2802)	(15.2994)	(-0.8568)	(2.4911)
Constant	2.2597***	2.9163***	0.2641	7.9954
	(7.0286)	(8.9309)	(0.9684)	(0.3301)
Year	Yes	Yes	Yes	Yes
Firm	Yes	Yes	Yes	Yes
Obs	32,341	32,341	31,922	32,138
R^2	0.8952	0.9043	0.3214	0.6438

Note The standard errors are clustered at the firm-level and t-statistics are reported in parentheses. *, ** and *** denote statistical significance at the 10%, 5% and 1% levels, respectively

5.4.4.2 Innovation Inputs and Innovation Outputs

Our study explores the impact of BDA on firm value by examining two perspectives: innovation inputs and outputs. We utilize R&D personnel (R&D pers.) and R&D expenditure (R&D spend) to measure firms' innovation inputs. R&D pers. represents the proportion of R&D staff relative to the total number of employees within the firm, while R&D spend is calculated as the ratio of R&D expenditure to operating revenue. We employ innovation quantity (IN) and innovation efficiency (IE) to measure firms' innovation. IN is defined as the count of patent applications filed by the firm during the current year. Following Hirshleifer et al. (2013), we calculate IE as the ratio of the number of patent applications to the natural logarithm of R&D investment plus one. Given the tendency for listed companies to have more missing values in the disclosure of R&D data, as observed in Liu et al. (2020), we handle missing values differently depending on the time period. We establish a threshold at 2011, a year when the proportion of firms disclosing R&D data experienced a significant increase. Consequently, missing values of R&D data for firms after 2011 are replaced with 0, while missing values for observations in 2011 and earlier are retained. Similarly, we encounter missing values in the patent data of listed companies spanning from 2003 to 2017, and we apply the same treatment by filling in these missing values with 0. The specific calculation formula is as follows:

$$IE = \frac{IN}{\ln(1 + R\&D)} \tag{5.5}$$

Table 5.9 presents the regression results for the effect of BDA on innovation inputs and outputs. The results presented in columns (1) and (2) demonstrate that the coefficients of BDA on R&D personnel and R&D expenditure exhibit a significant positive relationship, with statistical significance. In terms of economic significance, a one standard deviation increase in BDA corresponds to a 10.58% (= 8987.0679 × 0.0001/8.4912) increase in R&D personnel and a 1.72% (= 573.9661 × 0.0001/3.3363) increase in R&D expenditure. The results in columns (3) and (4) reveal a significant and positive association between BDA and innovation quantity and innovation efficiency. In economic terms, a one standard deviation increase in BDA corresponds to an 11.20% (= 4.0308 × 0.0001/0.0036) increase in innovation quantity and a 15.03% (= 2310.6493 × 0.0001/1.5374) improvement in innovation efficiency.

Previous research has consistently highlighted the significant role of innovation in creating firm value. For instance, Vithessonthi and Racela (2016) confirm a positive correlation between R&D intensity and firm value by examining a dataset of non-financial firms listed on the American Stock Exchange. Building on this, Leung and Sharma (2021) uncover that although R&D intensity may initially have a negative impact on firms' short-term profitability, it ultimately fosters long-term firm value. Furthermore, Ehie and Olibe (2010) as well as Tsao et al. (2015) provide detailed evidence showcasing the positive contribution of R&D investment to firm value, focusing respectively on the aftermath of the 9/11 attacks and family firms. Regarding innovation, the literature provides compelling evidence for its direct or indirect contribution to firm value creation. Rubera and Kirca (2012) employ a meta-analytic approach to showcase the positive impact of innovation on firm value. Bena et al. (2022) further demonstrate that innovation plays a crucial role in mitigating the loss of firm value when market factors undergo changes. Additionally, Sorescu and Spanjol (2008) categorize innovation into breakthrough and incremental innovations, and establish the positive effects of both types on firm value creation.

In summary, firms that allocate more resources to R&D and achieve higher levels of innovation tend to exhibit stronger market performance and consequently generate higher enterprise value (Tang et al., 2021). Moreover, the findings presented in Table 5.9 suggest that BDA has a positive impact on both innovation inputs and outputs, indicating that innovation inputs and outputs serve as mediating variables

Table 5.9 Channel tests: Innovation inputs and innovation outputs

	(1)	(2)	(3)	(4)
	R&D pers	R&D spend	IN	IE
Bigdata	8987.0679***	573.9661*	4.0308**	2310.6493***
	(6.6270)	(1.8226)	(2.2341)	(2.6708)
Size	0.1648	0.1556**	0.0020***	0.8680***
	(0.7070)	(2.1205)	(8.9470)	(8.2222)
Lev	0.4032	-1.7829***	0.0004	0.2691
	(0.4837)	(-7.3469)	(0.5650)	(0.7851)
Tang	-2.1909**	0.4866	0.0014**	0.6857**
	(-2.0260)	(1.5574)	(2.2077)	(2.2003)
Age	4.4115***	-0.0503	0.0003	0.0335
	(11.5244)	(-0.5261)	(0.8543)	(0.1921)
Growth	-0.0742	-0.3373***	-0.0005***	-0.2179***
	(-0.6294)	(-9.4501)	(-5.4775)	(-4.9896)
ROA	-3.0931**	-4.8481***	-0.0008	-0.2418
	(-2.5352)	(-10.4188)	(-0.7928)	(-0.4978)
Capex	0.3480	2.6690***	0.0001	-0.1227
	(0.2228)	(5.4135)	(0.0954)	(-0.1914)
Cashflow	-1.3127	-0.5456**	-0.0005	-0.3101
	(-1.5337)	(-2.2677)	(-0.7509)	(-0.9839)
Constant	-4.8956	0.7465	-0.0422***	-17.8435***
	(-0.9719)	(0.4760)	(-8.8397)	(-8.0587)
Year	Yes	Yes	Yes	Yes
Firm	Yes	Yes	Yes	Yes
Obs	21,658	22,488	23,598	23,598
R^2	0.7773	0.8397	0.7458	0.6200

Note The standard errors are clustered at the firm-level and t-statistics are reported in parentheses. *, ** and *** denote statistical significance at the 10%, 5% and 1% levels, respectively

through which BDA enhances firm value. In other words, BDA contributes to firm value creation by bolstering innovation inputs and outputs, thereby underscoring its significance in driving firm value.

5.4.5 Heterogeneity Analyses

In this section, our study aims to explore the economic mechanisms underlying the observed relationship between BDA and firm value. Specifically, it investigates how this relationship is influenced by external and internal governance mechanisms. By examining these factors, the study seeks to provide additional evidence and insights into the drivers of firm value enhancement through BDA.

5.4.5.1 External Governance Mechanisms

Our study employs three variables as proxies for external governance mechanisms: institutional ownership (INS), analyst attention (Analyst), and external audit quality (Big4). Prior research by Kim and Lu (2011), Balachandran et al. (2020), Obaydin et al. (2021), and Teng et al. (2021) has established the influential role of institutional investors in shaping firms' external governance. Institutional ownership is measured as the percentage of shares held by institutional investors, including funds, brokerage firms, insurance companies, trusts, and banks. Analysts fulfill an external governance role within the corporate governance mechanism through direct monitoring, involving regular tracking and analysis of a company's financial statements and participation in surplus announcement meetings to directly engage with the company's management. They also provide indirect monitoring by disseminating information to institutional and individual investors via media channels and research reports (Miller, 2006). Drawing from Shi et al. (2018), our study employs analyst attention as a measure of firms' external governance mechanisms, specifically capturing the number of analysts or analyst teams that actively cover firms on an annual basis. Furthermore, we consider external audit quality as an essential aspect of external governance. To proxy for external audit quality, we examine whether the auditor works for a Big 4 accounting firm in China. We construct a dummy variable called Big4, which takes a value of one if the auditor is from a Big 4 accounting firm within China, and zero otherwise.

Table 5.10 presents the heterogeneous association between BDA and firm value. In column (1), the coefficient of the interaction term between BDA and institutional ownership (Bigdata × INS) is highly significant at the 1% level and positive. These findings indicate that the involvement of institutional investors has a positive moderating effect on the relationship between BDA and firm value. In other words, the impact of BDA in enhancing firm value is strengthened when institutional investors are present. Moving to column (2), the coefficient of the interaction term between BDA and analyst attention (Bigdata × Analyst) is also significantly positive. This suggests that analyst attention acts as a positive moderator between BDA and firm value. In essence, the effect of BDA in enhancing firm value is more pronounced when there is greater analyst attention. In column (3), the coefficient of the interaction term between BDA and external audit quality (Bigdata × Big4) is significantly positive. This finding indicates that external audit quality serves as a positive moderator between BDA and firm value. Specifically, higher external audit quality strengthens the impact of BDA in enhancing firm value. To summarize, the positive effect of BDA on firm value becomes more prominent when firms operate under robust external governance mechanisms.

Table 5.10 Cross-sectional analyses: External governance mechanisms

	(1)	(2)	(3)
	Tobin's Q	Tobin's Q	Tobin's Q
Bigdata	516.4624***	299.9967***	386.2038***
	(4.7838)	(2.9800)	(3.5642)
Bigdata × INS	11.9959***		
	(3.2388)		
INS	0.0096***		
	(8.7409)		
Bigdata × Analyst		141.5132**	
		(1.9832)	
Analyst		0.2933***	
		(23.7569)	
Bigdata × Big4			1088.4354**
			(2.0500)
Big4			0.0948
			(1.5056)
Size	-0.8125***	-0.8865***	-0.7526***
	(-24.0082)	(-25.8362)	(-22.5254)
Lev	0.6627***	0.6940***	0.5857***
	(5.4741)	(5.8789)	(4.8376)
Tang	-0.5849***	-0.5736***	-0.6228***
	(-4.5717)	(-4.5790)	(-4.9043)
Age	0.8337***	0.8080***	0.7743***
	(23.7017)	(23.8675)	(22.3575)
Growth	0.0125	0.0334**	0.0311*
	(0.7677)	(2.1098)	(1.9157)
ROA	2.1376***	1.4585***	2.2354***
	(9.6446)	(7.0479)	(10.0674)
Capex	0.6676***	0.2517	0.7178***
	(3.5211)	(1.3580)	(3.7796)
Cashflow	0.5465***	0.4593***	0.5559***
	(4.6706)	(4.0680)	(4.7122)
Constant	17.8644***	19.6043***	16.7222***
	(24.8386)	(26.8672)	(23.4675)
Year	Yes	Yes	Yes
Firm	Yes	Yes	Yes

(continued)

Table 5.10 (continued)

	(1)	(2)	(3)
	Tobin's Q	Tobin's Q	Tobin's Q
Obs	32,327	32,376	32,375
R^2	0.6375	0.6517	0.6332

Note The standard errors are clustered at the firm-level and t-statistics are reported in parentheses. *, ** and *** denote statistical significance at the 10%, 5% and 1% levels, respectively

5.4.5.2 Internal Governance Mechanisms

Our study incorporates three measures of internal governance mechanisms: equity concentration (Top10), separation of powers (SEP), and financial reporting opacity (Disacc). To proxy for equity concentration, we utilize the percentage of shares held by a firm's top ten shareholders. This measure captures the extent to which ownership is concentrated among a select group of shareholders. Mikkelson and Ruback (1991) demonstrate that large shareholders provide support for corporate decision-making, which in turn increases firm value by deterring opportunistic managerial behavior. For the separation of powers, we employ a proxy that quantifies the degree of separation between the two powers within a firm. This measure is calculated by comparing the firm's ultimate control ratio with its ownership ratio. The calculations for control and ownership are based on the methodologies proposed by La Porta et al. (1999) and Claessens et al. (2000). The separation of powers measure captures the level of division between control and ownership within the firm's governance structure. Regarding financial reporting opacity, we adopt a measure based on surplus management, as outlined by Dechow et al. (1995). Specifically, we calculate a three-year rolling average of the absolute value of manipulable accrued profits using the modified Jones model. This measure provides an indication of the level of opacity in a firm's financial reporting practices.

Table 5.11 presents the heterogeneous association between BDA and firm value, considering the influence of internal governance mechanisms. In column (1), the coefficient of the interaction term between BDA and equity concentration (Bigdata × Top10) is significantly positive at the 1% level. This indicates that equity concentration has a positive moderating effect on the relationship between BDA and firm value. In other words, the impact of BDA in enhancing firm value is strengthened when equity concentration is more pronounced. Moving to column (2), the coefficient of the interaction term between BDA and the degree of separation of powers (Bigdata × SEP) is also significantly positive at the 1% level. This suggests that the degree of separation of powers within a firm's governance structure acts as a positive moderator between BDA and firm value. Specifically, the effect of BDA in enhancing firm value is more pronounced when there is a higher degree of separation between the two powers. In column (3), the coefficient of the interaction term between BDA and financial reporting opacity (Bigdata × Disacc) is significantly negative at the 5% level. These results indicate that financial reporting opacity has a negative moderating effect on the relationship between BDA and firm value. Thus, the impact of BDA in enhancing firm value is weakened when financial reporting opacity is higher. In conclusion, the positive effect of BDA on firm value becomes more significant when firms operate under robust internal governance mechanisms.

5.5 Conclusion

In this study, we develop a measure of BDA by utilizing a pre-trained language model in the field of deep learning and natural language processing. We apply this measure to Chinese Shanghai and Shenzhen A-share listed companies operating in non-IT industries as our research sample spanning the period from 2003 to 2020. Our objective is to investigate the causal impact of BDA on firm value. The empirical results provide compelling evidence that the implementation of BDA significantly enhances firm value. To ensure the robustness of our findings, we conduct a series of endogeneity and robustness tests. These tests support the reliability of our results.

In addition, our study explores the moderating role of external and internal governance mechanisms in the relationship between BDA and firm value. The findings confirm that the positive impact of BDA on firm value is more pronounced when firms face stronger external governance mechanisms and internal governance mechanisms. Furthermore, we examine and validate the channels through which BDA influences firm value, specifically focusing on productivity, and managerial efficiency, innovation inputs and outputs. The empirical findings from this study provide support for the notion that BDA enhances firm value by positively impacting these factors.

This study significantly contributes to the comprehension of BDA's impact on firm value, offering valuable insights into the influence of external and internal governance mechanisms during this process. Moreover, our findings provide actionable guidance for organizations considering the adoption of BDA.

5.6 Chapter Summary

While such restructuring is taking place, we have also observed the emergence of a phenomenon with more pronounced spillover effects: the accumulation and diffusion of data capabilities are reshaping the entrepreneurial vitality of regional economies. As nodes in the market system, enterprises' enhanced data capabilities often trigger chain reactions. In particular, when enterprises in traditional industries successfully transform through data technologies, they not only boost their own valuation levels but also inadvertently become "igniters" of emerging entrepreneurial activities within the region. This is especially evident in the context of the digital economy. In Chapter 5, we used non-IT enterprises as research samples to verify the impact of data analytics on enterprise value. On the surface, this conclusion focuses on the enterprise level, but it implicitly reflects a deeper structural change: when

Table 5.11 Cross-sectional analyses: Internal governance mechanisms

	(1)	(2)	(3)
	Tobin's Q	Tobin's Q	Tobin's Q
Bigdata	470.8105***	470.4863***	388.8882***
	(4.3286)	(4.2414)	(3.6010)
Bigdata × Top10	14.5770**		
	(2.2022)		
Top10	-0.0012		
	(-1.0154)		
Bigdata × SEP		35.3109***	
		(2.6561)	
SEP		-0.0040*	
		(-1.8809)	
Bigdata × Disacc			-2227.7681**
			(-2.0630)
Disacc			1.0557***
			(6.3055)
Size	-0.7460***	-0.7350***	-0.7250***
	(-22.2895)	(-22.6236)	(-22.0531)
Lev	0.5814***	0.5616***	0.5080***
	(4.8331)	(4.8312)	(4.3011)
Tang	-0.6241***	-0.5992***	-0.6248***
	(-4.9006)	(-4.7171)	(-4.8318)
Age	0.7574***	0.7839***	0.7723***
	(20.7706)	(22.7221)	(22.3157)
Growth	0.0328**	0.0333**	0.0238
	(2.0470)	(2.0739)	(1.4729)
ROA	2.2418***	2.2709***	2.2282***
	(10.0221)	(10.4867)	(9.9840)
Capex	0.7226***	0.6167***	0.7388***
	(3.8007)	(3.1840)	(3.9036)
Cashflow	0.5540***	0.5607***	0.6155***
	(4.6973)	(4.6184)	(5.1542)
Constant	16.6193***	16.3334***	16.1597***
	(23.3131)	(23.5032)	(22.9419)
Year FE	Yes	Yes	Yes
Firm FE	Yes	Yes	Yes

(continued)

Table 5.11 (continued)

	(1)	(2)	(3)
	Tobin's Q	Tobin's Q	Tobin's Q
Obs	32,376	30,858	31,878
R^2	0.6331	0.6345	0.6344

Note The standard errors are clustered at the firm-level and t-statistics are reported in parentheses. *, ** and *** denote statistical significance at the 10%, 5% and 1% levels, respectively

non-digital native enterprises begin to demonstrate the ability to reconstruct value using data, the entire market's confidence and expectations regarding data capabilities rise in tandem. Once captured by the market, this confidence quickly transmits to the broader entrepreneurial landscape. New entrants become more willing to build their ventures around data elements, and entrepreneurial resources actively converge toward data-intensive industries and business models, thereby driving partial leaps in entrepreneurial activities and even an overall increase in vitality.

More importantly, in the process of digital upgrading by traditional enterprises, substantial "institutional space," "market space," and "service space" are often released, providing entry points for entrepreneurs to enter specific vertical fields. The growth of enterprise value—especially value growth driven by data capabilities—does not imply closed-door development; instead, it means these enterprises begin to act as platform-based and ecosystem-oriented organizations. To better acquire external innovation capabilities and compensate for their own technological shortcomings, such enterprises often engage in multi-dimensional cooperation with external small start-ups, innovation teams, or independent service providers. This cooperation mechanism not only provides entrepreneurs with clear demand directions but also reduces entrepreneurial costs and uncertainties, thereby indirectly fostering the growth of regional entrepreneurial ecosystems.

At the same time, as enterprise value and market structure evolve in tandem, the policy system adjusts its direction accordingly. After observing the success of specific non-IT enterprises through big data analytics, local governments tend to use these enterprises' development paths as reference samples for formulating digital economy policies. This "follow-up" behavior of policies further reinforces the leading role of data capabilities in entrepreneurial orientation. For example, some local governments, drawing on the experience of successful enterprises, have introduced entrepreneurship support policies centered on data elements, promoted the construction of basic data platforms, established data transaction systems, and even regarded data infrastructure construction as a strategic priority for regional development. These measures have implicitly lowered the institutional threshold for data-oriented entrepreneurship and created a more favorable policy environment for digital entrepreneurs.

Therefore, we can see that there is no disjointed boundary between value creation at the enterprise level and entrepreneurial vitality at the regional level; instead, a clear logical progressive relationship has formed. The research in Chapter 5 has revealed from a micro perspective how data analytics capabilities enhance enterprises' comprehensive value, while Chapter 6 will build on this foundation to further explore how data elements catalyze innovation behaviors and economic structural transformation at a larger scale and within more complex systems. Furthermore, the transformation process from improved enterprise value to enhanced entrepreneurial vitality reflects the deep-seated mechanism of "structural redistribution" in the digital economy. In traditional economies, value was primarily realized through the reallocation of capital, land, and labor. In the era where data has become a new production factor, the path of value creation has shifted to the integration of information, cognition, technology, and connectivity capabilities. This change has gradually transformed entrepreneurial behavior from the "heavy-asset model" dependent on offline resources to the "data entrepreneurship model" characterized by light assets, technology-driven operations, and platform embedding. This means entrepreneurs are no longer passive responders who "discover market gaps" but active "source builders" who can tap into data value based on existing enterprise experiences, market signals, and platform mechanisms.

The development of Chapter 6 aims to answer the following questions within this logical framework: How does data drive the leap in entrepreneurial vitality? How do data platforms lower entry barriers for entrepreneurs? Have data elements already acquired the characteristics of "public infrastructure" in the entrepreneurial environment? How should entrepreneurial policies design institutions around data elements? More importantly, do the mechanisms of data-driven entrepreneurial vitality differ across regions? How do the underlying institutional logic, governance capabilities, and technological levels interact with each other?

These series of questions stem from the summary of non-IT enterprises' data practice experiences in Chapter 5 and will be systematically addressed in Chapter 6. If the construction of data capabilities in Chapter 5 represents experimental and practical achievements at the individual enterprise level, Chapter 6 focuses on how these achievements diffuse and transform in collective innovation behaviors. We will observe that data capabilities are no longer an exclusive label for large enterprises or high-tech companies but are gradually permeating every corner of regional economies, becoming an important indicator for measuring regional competitiveness and the quality of entrepreneurial ecosystems.

In terms of chapter structure, Chapter 6 will start with the regional distribution of data infrastructure to evaluate its impact on entrepreneurial costs, entry barriers, and resource accessibility. Subsequently, it will conduct an in-depth analysis of the spatial–temporal heterogeneity of entrepreneurial vitality, explaining why some regions with abundant data resources lack entrepreneurial dynamism while others with relatively scarce data boast robust entrepreneurial vitality. Finally, it will explore the institutional logic and performance evaluation of digital entrepreneurship policies, attempting to establish a complete "data-institution-entrepreneurship" mechanism model, which will lay a solid foundation for subsequent research on the relationships between data elements, employment structures, and innovation governance.

In summary, the transition from Chapter 5 to Chapter 6 represents not only a progression of research objects (from enterprises to regions) and an expansion of theoretical perspectives but also a structural upgrade of the embedding path of data elements. This transition not only enhances the systematicness and explanatory power of research on the data economy but also provides an important theoretical perspective and empirical basis for understanding how contemporary China's digital economy builds bridges between traditional industries and regional development, stimulates new driving forces, and reconstructs economic logic.

References

Amin, M. R., Kim, I., & Lee, S. (2021). Local religiosity, workplace safety, and firm value. *Journal of Corporate Finance, 70*, 102093.

Balachandran, B., Duong, H. N., Luong, H., & Nguyen, L. (2020). Does takeover activity affect stock price crash risk? Evidence from international M&A laws. *Journal of Corporate Finance, 64*, 101697.

Barney, J. (1991). Firm resources and sustained competitive advantage. *Journal of Management, 17*(1), 99–120.

Bena, J., Ortiz-Molina, H., & Simintzi, E. (2022). Shielding firm value: Employment protection and process innovation. *Journal of Financial Economics, 146*(2), 637–664.

Brinch, M., Gunasekaran, A., & Wamba, S. F. (2021). Firm-level capabilities towards big data value creation. *Journal of Business Research, 131*, 539–548.

Brochet, F., Limbach, P., Schmid, M., & Scholz-Daneshgari, M. (2021). CEO tenure and firm value. *The Accounting Review, 96*(6), 47–71.

Claessens, S., Djankov, S., & Lang, L. H. (2000). The separation of ownership and control in East Asian corporations. *Journal of Financial Economics, 58*(1–2), 81–112.

Ciampi, F., Demi, S., Magrini, A., Marzi, G., Papa, A. (2021). Exploring the impact of big data analytics capabilities on business model innovation: The mediating role of entrepreneurial orientation. *Journal of Business Research, 123*, 1–13.

Dechow, P. M., Sloan, R. G., & Sweeney, A. P. (1995). Detecting earnings management. *Accounting Review*, 193–225.

Ehie, I. C., & Olibe, K. (2010). The effect of R&D investment on firm value: An examination of US manufacturing and service industries. *International Journal of Production Economics, 128*(1), 127–135.

Farrell, M. J. (1957). The measurement of productive efficiency. *Journal of the royal statistical society: series A (General), 120*(3), 253–281.

Ghasemaghaei, M. (2021). Understanding the impact of big data on firm performance: The necessity of conceptually differentiating among big data characteristics. *International Journal of Information Management, 57*, 102055.

Ghasemaghaei, M., & Calic, G. (2019). Does big data enhance firm innovation competency? The mediating role of data-driven insights. *Journal of Business Research, 104*, 69–84.

Ghasemaghaei, M., & Calic, G. (2020). Assessing the impact of big data on firm innovation performance: Big data is not always better data. *Journal of Business Research, 108*, 147–162.

Grover, V., Chiang, R. H., Liang, T. P., & Zhang, D. (2018). Creating strategic business value from big data analytics: A research framework. *Journal of management information systems, 35*(2), 388–423.

Hatch, B. C., Johnson, S. A., Wang, Q. E., & Zhang, J. (2021). Algorithmic trading and firm value. *Journal of Banking & Finance, 125*, 106090.

Hirshleifer, D., Hsu, P. H., & Li, D. (2013). Innovative efficiency and stock returns. *Journal of financial Economics, 107*(3), 632–654.
Huang, Q., Yu, Y., & Zhang, S. (2019). Internet development and productivity growth in manufacturing industry: Internal mechanism and China experiences. *China Industrial Economics, 8*, 5–23.
Jones, C. I., & Tonetti, C. (2020). Nonrivalry and the economics of data. *American Economic Review, 110*(9), 2819–2858.
Kim, E. H., & Lu, Y. (2011). CEO ownership, external governance, and risk-taking. *Journal of Financial Economics, 102*(2), 272–292.
Kiron, D. (2017). Lessons from becoming a data-driven organization. *MIT Sloan Management Review, 58*(2).
La Porta, R., Lopez-de-Silanes, F., & Shleifer, A. (1999). Corporate ownership around the world. *The Journal of Finance, 54*(2), 471–517.
Leung, T. Y., & Sharma, P. (2021). Differences in the impact of R&D intensity and R&D internationalization on firm performance–Mediating role of innovation performance. *Journal of Business Research, 131*, 81–91.
Li, D. D., Li, C., & Cai, H. (2018). Big data in financial risk management: Evidence from China's banking sector. *China Economic Review, 49*, 182–194.
Li, X. L., Zhang, F., & Wu, F. (2021). Data factors, generative artificial intelligence and residents' employment. *Journal of Labor Economics, 9*(5), 101–118.
Liu, S., Lin, Z., & Leng, Z. (2020). Whether tax incentives stimulate corporate innovation: empirical evidence based on corporate life cycle theory. *Economic Research Journal, 55*(6), 105–121.
Liu, Y., Jin, Z., He, Y., Zhu, X., & Li, M. (2018). Production efficiency driven M&As-An empirical research based on the micro perspective of Chinese listed companies. *China Economic Quarterly, 17*(04), 1329–1360.
Loughran, T., & McDonald, B. (2011). When is a liability not a liability? Textual analysis, dictionaries, and 10-Ks. *The Journal of Finance, 66*(1), 35–65.
Lu, X., & Lian, Y. (2012). Estimation of total factor productivity of industrial enterprises in China: 1999–2007. *China Economic Quarterly, 11*(02), 541–558.
Maheshwari, S., Gautam, P., & Jaggi, C. K. (2021). Role of Big Data Analytics in supply chain management: Current trends and future perspectives. *International Journal of Production Research, 59*(6), 1875–1900.
Maroufkhani, P., Wagner, R., Wan Ismail, W. K., Baroto, M. B., & Nourani, M. (2019). Big data analytics and firm performance: A systematic review. *Information, 10*(7), 226.
Mikalef, P., Pappas, I. O., Krogstie, J., & Giannakos, M. (2018). Big data analytics capabilities: A systematic literature review and research agenda. *Information Systems and E-Business Management, 16*, 547–578.
Mikalef, P., Boura, M., Lekakos, G., & Krogstie, J. (2019a). Big data analytics and firm performance: Findings from a mixed-method approach. *Journal of Business Research, 98*, 261–276.
Mikalef, P., Boura, M., Lekakos, G., Krogstie, J. (2019b). Big data analytics capabilities and innovation: The mediating role of dynamic capabilities and moderating effect of the environment. *British Journal of Management, 30*(2), 272–298.
Mikalef, P., Pappas, I. O., Krogstie, J., & Giannakos, M. (2020). Big data analytics capability: Antecedents and business value. *Information & Management, 57*(8), Article 103169.
Mikkelson, W. H., & Ruback, R. S. (1991). Targeted repurchases and common stock returns. *The RAND Journal of Economics*, 544–561.
Miller, G. S. (2006). The press as a watchdog for accounting fraud. *Journal of accounting research, 44*(5), 1001–1033.
Mithas, S., Lee, M. R., Earley, S., Murugesan, S., & Djavanshir, R. (2013). Leveraging big data and business analytics. *IT professional, 15*(6), 18–20
Nam, H., & Uchida, K. (2019). Accounts payable and firm value: International evidence. *Journal of Banking & Finance, 102*, 116–137.

Nguyen, H., Calantone, R., & Krishnan, R. (2020). Influence of social media emotional word of mouth on institutional investors' decisions and firm value. *Management Science, 66*(2), 887–910.
Nunn, N., & Qian, N. (2014). US food aid and civil conflict. *American Economic Review, 104*(6), 1630–1666.
Obaydin, I., Zurbruegg, R., Hossain, M. N., Adhikari, B. K., & Elnahas, A. (2021). Shareholder litigation rights and stock price crash risk. *Journal of Corporate Finance, 66*, 101826.
Olabode, O. E., Boso, N., Hultman, M., & Leonidou, C. N. (2022). Big data analytics capability and market performance: The roles of disruptive business models and competitive intensity. *Journal of Business Research, 139*, 1218–1230.
Pan, Y., Zhu, K., & Chen, X. (2018). *Decision Right Allocation and Firm Value: Evidence from Chinese Business Groups, 34*(12), 111–119.
Popovič, A., Hackney, R., Tassabehji, R., & Castelli, M. (2018). The impact of big data analytics on firms' high value business performance. *Information Systems Frontiers, 20*, 209–222.
Raguseo, E., & Vitari, C. (2018). Investments in big data analytics and firm performance: An empirical investigation of direct and mediating effects. *International Journal of Production Research, 56*(15), 5206–5221.
Ravid, S. A., Sekerci, N. (2020). Large investors' portfolio composition and firms value. *Journal of Corporate Finance, 61*, 101404.
Rubera, G., & Kirca, A. H. (2012). Firm innovativeness and its performance outcomes: A meta-analytic review and theoretical integration. *Journal of Marketing, 76*(3), 130–147.
Sena, V., Bhaumik, S., Sengupta, A., & Demirbag, M. (2019). Big data and performance: what can management research tell us? *British Journal of Management, 30*(2), 219–228.
Shen, M. (2021). Skilled labor mobility and firm value: Evidence from green card allocations. *The Review of Financial Studies, 34*(10), 4663–4700.
Sorescu, A. B., & Spanjol, J. (2008). Innovation's effect on firm value and risk: Insights from consumer-packaged goods. *Journal of Marketing, 72*(2), 114–132.
Stock, J. H., & Yogo, M. (2005). Testing for weak instruments in linear iv regression. *Nber Technical Working Papers, 14*(1), 80–108.
Sun, P., Hou, X., & Sheng, B. (2018). Service opening, managerial efficiency and firm export. *Economic Research Journal, 53*(7), 136–151.
Sun, P., Yuan, C., Li, X., & Di, J. (2024). Big data analytics, firm risk and corporate policies: Evidence from China. *Research in International Business and Finance, 70*, 102371.
Tang, T. Y., Zhang, S. K., & Peng, J. (2021). The value of marketing innovation: Market-driven versus market-driving. *Journal of Business Research, 126*, 88–98.
Tarafdar, M., Gupta, A., & Turel, O. (2013). The dark side of information technology use. *Information Systems Journal, 23*(3), 269–275.
Teece, D. J., Pisano, G., & Shuen, A. (1997). Dynamic capabilities and strategic management. *Strategic Management Journal, 18*(7), 509–533.
Teng, C. C., Li, S., & Yang, J. J. (2021). Family control, external governance mechanisms, and dividend payouts. *The Quarterly Review of Economics and Finance, 79*, 198–209.
Tsao, S. M., Lin, C. H., & Chen, V. Y. (2015). Family ownership as a moderator between R&D investments and CEO compensation. *Journal of Business Research, 68*(3), 599–606.
Upadhyay, P., & Kumar, A. (2020). The intermediating role of organizational culture and internal analytical knowledge between the capability of big data analytics and a firm's performance. *International Journal of Information Management, 52*, 102100.
Vithessonthi, C., & Racela, O. C. (2016). Short-and long-run effects of internationalization and R&D intensity on firm performance. *Journal of Multinational Financial Management, 34*, 28–45.
Wamba, S. F., Gunasekaran, A., Akter, S., Ren, S. J. F., Dubey, R., & Childe, S. J. (2017). Big data analytics and firm performance: Effects of dynamic capabilities. *Journal of Business Research, 70*, 356–365.
Wei, Y., Zhang, J., Wang, F., & Cheng, M. (2022). Research of data assets disclosure and analyst forecasts: Evidence from text analysis. *Journal of Industrial Engineering and Engineering Management*, 1–12.

Xie, S., Lin, B., & Li, J. (2022). Political control, corporate governance and firm value: The case of China. *Journal of Corporate Finance, 72*, 102161.
Yang, J., & Yang, J. (2015). Chinese-style tax-sharing system, tax collection centralization and tax competition. *Economic Research Journal, 50*(04), 50–61, 106.
Yasmin, M., Tatoglu, E., Kilic, H. S., Zaim, S., & Delen, D. (2020). Big data analytics capabilities and firm performance: An integrated MCDM approach. *Journal of Business Research, 114*, 1–15.
Zhang, Y., Lu, Y., Li, L. (2021). Effects of big data on firm value in China: Evidence from textual analysis of Chinese listed firms' annual reports. *Economic Research Journal, 56*(12), 42–59.

Chapter 6
Data-Driven Entrepreneurship: Structural Capital Flow and Industrial Opportunity Generation

6.1 Digital Transformation and Regional Entrepreneurial Dynamism

Entrepreneurship has long been recognized as a vital driver of sustaining economic vitality and expanding employment opportunities (Guzman & Stern, 2020). Existing studies have predominantly emphasized factors such as individual traits, institutional quality, and financing environments, yet they have paid insufficient attention to the structural role of the digital economy as a driving force for entrepreneurship. In particular, big data is reshaping the entrepreneurial ecosystem by enhancing information circulation efficiency, increasing institutional transparency, and reducing uncertainties (Buer et al., 2021; Myovella et al., 2020). However, systematic research remains scarce on revealing how data-driven digital transformation stimulates entrepreneurial activity.

To fill this gap, this chapter examines whether and how the development of the digital economy promotes entrepreneurial behavior in China. Employing the national big data comprehensive pilot zone policy as a quasi-natural experiment, combined with the full-scale "city-industry-year" dataset of nationwide industrial and commercial registrations from 2010 to 2020, this study adopts a multi-period Difference-in-Differences (DID) approach to systematically evaluate the causal effect of the policy on entrepreneurial dynamism. The results indicate that the policy has significantly increased the number of new ventures in relevant industries within pilot cities, with an average growth rate of 13.6%, accounting for approximately 4.77% of local entrepreneurial growth.

A series of robustness tests—including the parallel trends test, placebo test, Goodman-Bacon decomposition, and different DID estimation methods—all corroborate the aforementioned conclusions. Further mechanism analysis reveals that the digital economy drives entrepreneurship through two primary pathways: first, expanding entrepreneurial opportunities by facilitating information dissemination

X. Li et al., *Data as a New Factor of Production*, Applied Economics and Policy Studies, https://doi.org/10.1007/978-981-95-9985-1_6

and technology spillover, thereby providing more diversified cross-domain opportunities; second, reducing entrepreneurial costs via digital financial innovation, institutional transparency, and talent agglomeration, thus lowering capital, institutional, and technological barriers to entry.

In the heterogeneity analysis, this chapter finds that the policy effect is mainly concentrated in micro, small, and medium-sized enterprises (MSMEs), indicating that the digital economy is more effective in stimulating the vitality of start-ups. At the industry level, the policy exerts a stronger impact on the digital upgrading of non-digital industries, particularly manifesting prominently in the high-tech subsectors of manufacturing. Regarding industry entry barriers, the policy yields more significant effects in industries characterized by low market concentration, a smaller proportion of state-owned enterprises, and high skill intensity.

The contributions of this chapter are reflected in three aspects: First, by treating the "National Big Data Comprehensive Pilot Zone" as an exogenous shock, it expands the research perspective on the impact of the digital economy on entrepreneurship and highlights the driving effect of policy-oriented digital economy development. Second, starting from the two mechanism pathways of expanding entrepreneurial opportunities and reducing entrepreneurial costs, it explains how big data shapes the entrepreneurial ecosystem and examines the moderating effects of firm and industry characteristics. Third, it constructs a three-dimensional "city-industry-year" panel using full-scale nationwide industrial and commercial registration data, enhancing the representativeness and explanatory power of the research and making up for the deficiencies in sample size and coverage of previous studies.

6.2 Policy Background and Mechanism Analysis

6.2.1 Policy Background

Globally, leveraging big data to boost economic development, improve social governance, and enhance government service and regulatory capabilities has become a major trend. To address the problems existing in the development of big data at the local level in China, such as insufficient openness and sharing of government data, weak industrial foundations, and limited innovative applications, the State Council issued the Action Plan for Promoting the Development of Big Data (Document No. 50 [2015] of the State Council) on August 31, 2015. This plan defined the goals for promoting big data development over the next 5–10 years, covering areas such as social governance, economic operation, people's livelihood services, innovation and entrepreneurship, and industrial ecology, and deployed a number of key tasks around these goals. To implement the Action Plan for Promoting the Development of Big Data, Guizhou Province took the lead in launching the construction of a big data comprehensive pilot zone on September 18 of the same year. On February 25, 2016, the National Development and Reform Commission, the Ministry of Industry and

Information Technology, and the Cyberspace Administration of China jointly issued an official reply approving Guizhou to build the country's first national big data comprehensive pilot zone. Subsequently, on October 8, 2016, the list of the second batch of national big data comprehensive pilot zones was announced, including two cross-regional pilot zones (Beijing-Tianjin-Hebei, Pearl River Delta), four regional demonstration pilot zones (Shanghai, Henan, Chongqing, Shenyang), and one pilot zone for the coordinated development of big data infrastructure (Inner Mongolia).

Since the establishment of the national big data comprehensive pilot zones, each pilot zone has formulated detailed development plans in accordance with the Action Plan for Promoting the Development of Big Data, combining its own positioning and the local characteristics of each city. These plans mainly focus on big data institutional innovation, public data openness and sharing, big data innovative applications, big data industrial agglomeration, big data factor circulation, data center integration and utilization, as well as international exchanges and cooperation in big data, actively promoting the innovative development of China's big data sector. At the specific implementation level, to support the construction of big data comprehensive pilot zones, governments at the central and local levels have established special funds and major special projects for big data development. For example, Guizhou Province, Hebei Province, and Shanghai Municipality have successively issued measures for the management of special big data funds. Local governments have also leveraged social capital participation through investment and financing platforms and industrial investment platforms to support big data enterprises in conducting multi-channel and multi-level financing. According to the National Big Data Comprehensive Pilot Zone Development Report (2018 Edition), more than 1000 big data venture capital projects in the eight comprehensive pilot zones secured financing between 2016 and 2017, with over 8000 new patent applications for big data-related technologies filed during the same period. Taking Guizhou as an example, after being approved as a national big data comprehensive pilot zone, the province promoted the construction of major projects such as the government data sharing and exchange platform, the Guizhou Big Data Exchange, the remote medical big data supervision platform, and "Cloud Guizhou". Meanwhile, cities such as Guiyang, Zunyi, and Anshun have actively improved digital infrastructure and built a big data industrial ecosystem to support innovation and entrepreneurship.

6.2.2 *Mechanisms of Action and Research Hypotheses*

The development of big data broadens entrepreneurial opportunities. The establishment of national big data comprehensive pilot zones is expected to create more entrepreneurial opportunities for potential entrepreneurs. On the one hand, from the supply side of entrepreneurial opportunities, the in-depth deployment of big data has enhanced regional innovation dynamism, providing potential entrepreneurs with more new entrepreneurial opportunities. The research by Ghasemaghaei and Calic (2019) confirms that the characteristics of big data, such as rapid iteration, diversity, and high accuracy, significantly improve enterprises' analytical insight capabilities, thereby enhancing their technological innovation capabilities. This implies that the development of big data can spawn new technological achievements and innovative products, bringing more supply-side entrepreneurial opportunities to entrepreneurs. On the other hand, from the demand side of entrepreneurial opportunities, emerging business models driven by big data have also created a large number of new market demands. For instance, online retail, as one of the most prominent business model innovations in the digital economy era, has driven cross-industry market transformation. To capture this effect, drawing on the approach of Fang and Xing (2015), this paper constructs an interaction term between "the ratio of national online retail sales to provincial postal business volume" and "the postal business volume of each city" as a proxy variable for regional business model innovation, to examine the new market opportunity supply effect of big data in promoting entrepreneurship.

Hypothesis 1: The development of big data broadens the channels for potential entrepreneurs to discover entrepreneurial opportunities from both the supply and demand sides by promoting digital technological innovation and fostering new business models, thereby enhancing the level of entrepreneurial activities.

To test the role of big data comprehensive pilot zones in expanding entrepreneurial opportunities, we select the annual total number of digital technology patent applications (in logarithmic form) at the prefecture-level city as the proxy variable for the degree of digital technological innovation (1) and use the constructed online retail interaction term as the proxy variable for business model innovation to conduct a mediating effect analysis. Table 6.2 reports the regression results of the entrepreneurial opportunity channel. Column (1) of Table 6.2 shows that the pilot zone policy has significantly increased the number of digital technology patent applications, an indicator of innovation; Column (2) shows that the policy has significantly promoted the expansion of regional online retail scale. The above results verify to a certain extent the hypothesis that the development of big data creates more "blue ocean" market opportunities for potential entrepreneurs, supporting the arguments about the technological innovation and business model innovation pathways in Hypothesis 1.

The development of big data reduces entrepreneurial costs. Potential entrepreneurs' decision to engage in entrepreneurship largely depends on the comparison between expected returns and entrepreneurial costs. Lower entrepreneurial costs imply relatively higher net returns; therefore, entrepreneurial costs may be an important mediating factor affecting entrepreneurial decisions.

Hypothesis 2: The changes brought about by the development of big data in the financial market, government governance, and human capital fields can reduce the financing costs, institutional costs, and talent acquisition costs of potential entrepreneurs, thereby incentivizing their entrepreneurial decisions.

6.3 Estimation Strategy, Variable Definition, and Data Sources

6.3.1 Estimation Strategy

This paper adopts a multi-period Difference-in-Differences (DID) model to identify the impact of the national big data comprehensive pilot zone policy on regional entrepreneurial activities. Considering that entrepreneurial activities have both industrial and regional attributes, this paper selects a three-dimensional "industry-city-year" panel dataset for empirical analysis. It should be noted that there may be systematic differences in the average entrepreneurial level between policy pilot cities and non-pilot cities before the implementation of the policy, indicating that the selection of big data comprehensive pilot zones may have taken into account certain criteria, which also affect the trends of entrepreneurial activities. To avoid the above selection bias, this paper further controls for the pre-treatment characteristic variables that affect whether a city is selected as a big data comprehensive pilot zone in the baseline regression, thereby ensuring that the treatment group and the control group satisfy the pre-treatment parallel trends assumption. Based on the above considerations, we construct the following baseline regression model:

$$Y_{ict} = \alpha + \beta Policy_{ct} + \gamma_1 X_{ct} + [S \times f(t)]'\theta + \gamma_2 Z_{ct} + \mu_{ic} + \mu_{it} + \varepsilon_{ict} \quad (6.1)$$

where Y_{ict} denotes the entrepreneurial level indicator of industry i, city c in year t; $Policy_{ct}$ is the core policy variable of interest in this paper, which takes the value of 1 if city c is affected by the national big data comprehensive pilot zone policy in year t, and 0 otherwise, with its coefficient β capturing the average impact of the policy on entrepreneurial activities; X_{ct}, $S \times f(t)$ and Z_{ct} represent the first set of city characteristic control variables, the second set of interaction terms between pre-treatment characteristic variables of policy selection and time function, and the third set of other concurrent events and policy variables, respectively. The model also controls for industry-city fixed effects Z_{ct} and industry-year fixed effects μ_{it}, α is the intercept term, and ε_{ict} is the random error term.

6.3.2 Variable Definition

Entrepreneurial Dynamism Indicator: This paper selects the number of newly registered enterprises at the city-industry-year level to measure entrepreneurial dynamism. Since the number of enterprise registrations provided by the original data includes both stock and incremental information, we use the number of newly registered enterprises in each industry of each city every year as the measure of entrepreneurial activities, and take the logarithm to smooth fluctuations. The annual number of newly registered enterprises can reflect the actual occurrence of entrepreneurship and better capture changes in entrepreneurial dynamism. In addition, to avoid the problem that the logarithm cannot be taken due to zero registrations in a very small number of industries, we perform a minor translation (adding 1) on zero values. As a robustness test, we also consider the "net entrepreneurial number" indicator, i.e., the number of newly registered enterprises minus the number of concurrently canceled and revoked enterprises at the city-industry-year level, to eliminate the interference of possible opportunistic entrepreneurial behaviors induced by policy incentives on the indicator. The results calculated using the net number of registered enterprises are consistent with the main indicator, indicating that the short-term enterprise exits induced by policy incentives have no substantial impact on the conclusions.

Policy Variable: The core explanatory variable is the "national big data comprehensive pilot zone policy", which is defined as a dummy variable: $\text{Policy}_{ct} = 1$ if city c is within the scope of the national big data comprehensive pilot zone in year t, otherwise 0. For cross-provincial regional pilot zones (such as Beijing-Tianjin-Hebei and Pearl River Delta), all prefecture-level cities within the region are regarded as the treatment group. After the first batch of Guizhou pilots in 2016, other cities were successively included in the pilot zone scope in 2017. This paper uses a multi-period DID model to fully consider the differences in policy implementation time across different cities; for the years before entering the pilot zone, these cities are equivalent to the control group, thus comprehensively utilizing both temporal and spatial information to improve estimation efficiency. It should be noted that if the missing rate of city-level entrepreneurial data exceeds a certain proportion in a given year, we exclude the observation of that city in that year from the panel to reduce estimation bias caused by missing values. Finally, a balanced sample of 289 cities from 2010 to 2020 is retained (including 4 municipalities directly under the Central Government, 280 prefecture-level cities, and 5 sub-provincial cities; among them, 54 are pilot zone cities and 235 are control group cities), with balanced data covering most areas of the country.

Control Variables: To ensure that the treatment group and the control group have similar development trends before policy implementation, we introduce three types of control variables: (1) **City characteristic variables**: a series of city-level macroeconomic variables that may affect entrepreneurial activities, including per capita GDP, the proportion of the tertiary industry, urbanization rate, education level, per capita scientific research expenditure, and marketization index; (2) **Pre-treatment characteristic variables**: factors that may influence the selection of pilot zones, such as the big data-related industrial foundation, internet development level, and fiscal expenditure level of each city before 2015, which are included in the model by constructing interaction terms with time functions; (3) **Other concurrent events and policy variables**: other major policies or events that may affect entrepreneurship during the sample period, such as the business tax to value-added tax (VAT) reform pilot and the policy of establishing new free trade zones, which are controlled using dummy variables. Overall, after introducing the above control variables, the treatment group and the control group are more likely to satisfy the pre-treatment parallel trends assumption, and the DID estimation results are more robust.

6.3.3 Data Sources

The entrepreneurship data is derived from the industrial and commercial registration database of the State Administration for Market Regulation, which contains information on newly registered enterprises in various regions over the years. Considering the industrial dimension, we classify and summarize newly registered enterprises according to the National Economic Industry Classification, forming a three-level "city-industry-year" panel dataset. Macroeconomic data are mainly obtained from the China Statistical Yearbook, China City Statistical Yearbook, as well as databases such as CSMAR, EPS, and China Research Data Services Platform (CNRDS). Data on digital economy-related indicators are sourced from statistical reports and databases released by relevant competent authorities; for example, the digital financial inclusion index adopts data from the Digital Finance Research Center of Peking University, and digital infrastructure data are derived from indicators such as broadband penetration rate published by the Ministry of Industry and Information Technology. Information on big data-related policies is compiled and sorted out based on official documents. In data processing, we exclude city samples with more than 7 years of missing city-level data from 2010 to 2020, and finally obtain a balanced panel dataset of 289 cities from 2010 to 2020 (including 54 treatment group cities and 235 control group cities). Overall, there are no significant differences in key characteristics between the treatment group and the control group before policy implementation, supporting the validity of the subsequent DID design.

6.4 Analysis of Empirical Results

6.4.1 Baseline Regression

Table 6.1 reports the baseline regression results regarding the impact of the national big data comprehensive pilot zone policy on entrepreneurial activities at the city-industry level. Column (1) only controls for city-industry fixed effects and year-industry fixed effects; Column (2) further incorporates the first set of city characteristic control variables on this basis; Columns (3) and (4) respectively add interaction terms between pre-treatment characteristic variables and third-order time polynomial functions, as well as interaction terms between pre-treatment characteristic variables and time dummy variables before and after the policy implementation; Column (5) includes other concurrent events and policy characteristic variables on the basis of Column (4), presenting the complete regression results. It can be observed that across all specifications, the coefficients of the policy variable are positive and mostly statistically significant. This indicates that the establishment of national big data comprehensive pilot zones has exerted a significant facilitating effect on entrepreneurial activities at the local city-industry level. As the set of control variables becomes increasingly comprehensive, the coefficient of the policy effect experiences a slight decline but remains significant at the 5% level or higher. For instance, in Column (5), which incorporates the most comprehensive set of controls, the policy coefficient is still positive and passes the 1% significance test. Based on the estimation results in Column (5), after the implementation of the policy, the level of entrepreneurial activity in pilot zone cities is approximately 13.6% higher than that in non-pilot zone cities, with this effect being significant at the 1% level; on average, the policy implementation accounts for about 4.77% of the entrepreneurial growth at the city-industry level.

6.4.2 Pre-Treatment Parallel Trends Test

To verify the dynamic relationship between the establishment of big data comprehensive pilot zones and entrepreneurship, this paper adopts the event study approach by incorporating a series of dummy variables into the baseline regression. The results show that there are no significant differences in entrepreneurial activity across cities before the policy implementation, satisfying the pre-treatment parallel trends assumption; after the policy implementation, the average effect of the pilot zones on entrepreneurial activities exhibits an increasing trend. However, due to limitations in the observation period, the steady-state and long-term trend effects of the policy impact cannot be fully reflected.

$$\begin{aligned} InEntre_{ict} = & \alpha + \beta_1 D_{ct}^{-4} + \beta_2 D_{ct}^{-3} + \ldots + \beta_7 D_{ct}^{+3} + \gamma_1 X_{ct} \\ & + [S \times f(t)]' \theta + \gamma_2 Z_{ct} + \mu_{ic} + \mu_{it} + \varepsilon_{ict} \end{aligned} \tag{6.2}$$

To ensure the applicability of the DID method, we first test the heterogeneity of entrepreneurial trends between pilot zone cities and non-pilot zone cities before the policy implementation. Using the event study approach, we define a series of time dummy variables around the policy implementation (denoted as $D_{ct}^{-j}$for the j period before policy implementation and D_{ct}^{+j} for the period after policy implementation, excluding the year of policy implementation as the baseline period), to estimate the dynamic evolution of the policy effect across different time horizons. As shown in Fig. 6.1, the dynamic DID effect of urban entrepreneurial activities and its 95% confidence interval plotted based on Model (2) indicate that: prior to the policy implementation, there are no significant differences in the level of entrepreneurial activity between the treatment group and the control group across cities, which supports the parallel trends assumption; after the policy implementation, the entrepreneurial rate in pilot zone cities is significantly higher than that in the control group, and the policy effect shows a gradually strengthening trend.

Table 6.1 The impact of big data on entrepreneurship

Variable	(1) Entrepreneurship	(2) Entrepreneurship	(3) Entrepreneurship	(4) Entrepreneurship	(5) Entrepreneurship
Policy	0.147*** (0.052)	0.151*** (0.054)	0.119** (0.048)	0.130*** (0.048)	0.136*** (0.045)
City characteristic variables	No	Yes	Yes	Yes	Yes
Ex-ante characteristic variables × T	No	No	Yes	No	No
Ex-ante characteristic variables × T^2	No	No	Yes	No	No
Ex-ante characteristic variables × T^3	No	No	Yes	No	No
Ex-ante characteristic variables × Time dummy variables	No	No	No	Yes	Yes
Other event and policy characteristic variables	No	No	No	No	Yes
City-industry fixed effects	Yes	Yes	Yes	Yes	Yes
Year-industry fixed effects	Yes	Yes	Yes	Yes	Yes
Sample size	234,560	234,560	234,560	234,560	234,560
R^2 value	0.941	0.941	0.941	0.941	0.942

Note *, **, *** indicate significance at the 10%, 5%, and 1% levels, respectively. Robust standard errors clustered at the city level are reported in parentheses

Table 6.2 Channel analysis: regression results of entrepreneurial opportunities

Variable	(1) Digital technology innovation	(2) Business model innovation
Policy	0.193*** (0.059)	0.136* (0.074)
Control variables	Yes	Yes
City fixed effects	Yes	Yes
Year fixed effects	Yes	Yes
Sample size	3024	1883
R^2 value	0.967	0.779

Note: Regional-level data are sourced from the EPS Database and statistical yearbooks of various cities; patent data are obtained from the National Intellectual Property Administration. Other notes are the same as in Table 6.1

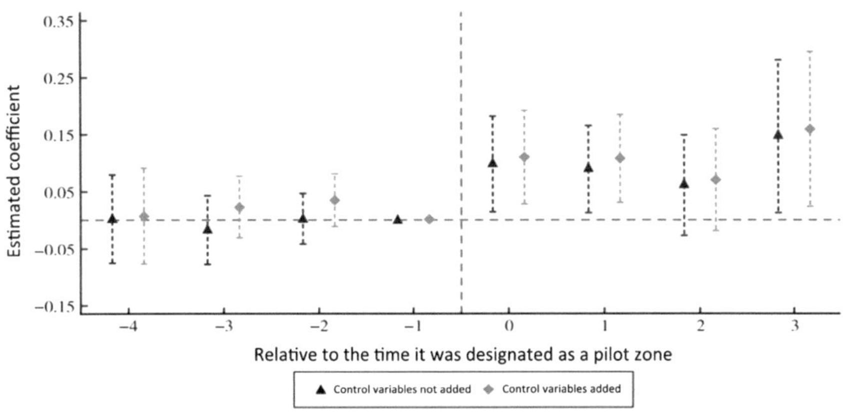

Fig. 6.1 Pre-treatment parallel trends test

6.4.3 *Placebo Test*

To rule out the interference of random factors on the policy effect, this paper randomly assigns the designation time of national big data comprehensive pilot zones to each city within the sample period and conducts 500 repeated placebo tests. The results show that the estimated coefficients are concentrated around 0 with large p-values; in contrast, the actual estimated coefficient of 0.136 is clearly an outlier, indicating that the establishment of national big data comprehensive pilot zones yields a genuine policy effect.

6.4.4 Bacon Decomposition

Given the variations in the timing of policy implementation across different regions, this paper adopts the Goodman-Bacon decomposition method to identify the weights and coefficients of each group. The results show that the weight of "bad control groups" accounts for only 0.7%, with a contribution rate of merely 0.498% to the regression coefficient, which demonstrates the robustness of the regression results.

6.4.5 CSDID

To further verify the robustness of the multi-period DID estimation results, this paper re-estimates the model using the CSDID method. The results show that the estimated coefficient is 0.070, which is significant at the 10% confidence level, consistent with the baseline regression results.

6.4.6 Instrumental Variable Method

Although this paper has adopted various methods to mitigate the potential endogeneity issues arising from the big data comprehensive pilot zone policy, it should be noted that the approval of big data comprehensive pilot zones is not based on cities as the unit of designation, making it difficult to fully account for all observable and unobservable factors. To ensure the robustness of the research results, drawing on the approach of Tian and Zhang (2022), this paper selects the interaction term between the spherical distance from each city to the nearest "eight vertical and eight horizontal" optical cable backbone network node city and the time dummy variable indicating whether the city is designated as a big data comprehensive pilot zone as the instrumental variable for the Policy term.

6.4.7 PSM-DID

Considering that the designation of national big data comprehensive pilot zones may not be completely random but rather correlated with other factors, this could lead to a correlation between the explanatory variable and the error term, resulting in endogeneity issues caused by self-selection bias, which may be the reason for partial differences in entrepreneurial activities between the treatment group and the control group before the treatment. Although this paper has taken this issue into account when selecting control variables, to further mitigate the existing endogeneity problems, referring to existing literature, this paper adopts the Propensity Score Matching

(PSM) method to match the samples. Specifically, using the control variables in this paper, we employ the nearest neighbor 1:2 matching method for the sample of national big data comprehensive pilot zone cities. Meanwhile, given that PSM is suitable for cross-sectional data while DID is applicable to time-series cross-sectional panel data, this paper respectively adopts cross-sectional PSM and annual PSM methods to obtain matched samples, and then conducts DID regression on the matched samples to further verify the robustness of the PSM-DID regression results.

6.4.8 Measuring Net Entrepreneurial Quantity

With the advancement of the construction of national big data comprehensive pilot zones, local governments have introduced subsidy incentive policies related to the big data industry, such as tax incentives, land construction support, and household registration rewards, which may induce opportunistic behaviors among some potential entrepreneurs. Given that the entrepreneurial opportunistic behavior of potential entrepreneurs is positively correlated with enterprise failure risk (Jiang et al., 2018), this paper incorporates the number of enterprise exits in the short term to exclude the potential entrepreneurial opportunistic behaviors that may occur during the policy period. This paper considers the net entrepreneurial quantity at the city-industry-year level, which is defined as the difference between the number of newly registered enterprises and the number of canceled/revoked enterprises at the city-industry level during the same period.

6.4.9 Alternative Measures of Net Entrepreneurial Quantity

In addition to the above methods, this paper also adopts a series of other approaches to verify the robustness of the research results, including changing the measurement method of the explained variable, adjusting the clustered robust standard errors, controlling for pre-treatment trends, and excluding the interference of other policies.

6.5 Mechanism Analysis of the Impact of Big Data Development on Entrepreneurship

To deeply explore the internal mechanisms through which the big data comprehensive pilot zone policy promotes entrepreneurship, this paper conducts an analysis from two key dimensions: entrepreneurial opportunities and entrepreneurial costs. Through empirical tests, this paper finds that the development of big data stimulates entrepreneurial activities mainly through the following two channels: first, promoting technological innovation and business model innovation to bring more opportunities for entrepreneurs; second, reducing financing costs, institutional costs, and labor costs to optimize the entrepreneurial environment. The detailed analysis from these two aspects, along with the corresponding tables and figures, is presented below.

6.5.1 Entrepreneurial Opportunities

The development of big data provides more entrepreneurial opportunities for potential entrepreneurs by promoting digital technological innovation and fostering new business models.

Digital Technological Innovation: The in-depth deployment of big data has significantly enhanced regional innovation dynamism, thereby driving the innovation of digital technologies. This paper selects the logarithm of the total number of annual digital technology patent applications at the prefecture-level city as the proxy variable. The empirical results show that the big data comprehensive pilot zone policy has significantly improved the level of regional digital technological innovation. This indicates that the establishment of pilot zones has stimulated more digital technological innovation, providing potential entrepreneurs with abundant technical resources and innovative ideas. As shown in Column (1) of Table 6.2, the coefficient of the Policy variable is 0.193, which is significant at the 5% level.

Business Model Innovation: Big data has boosted urban innovation dynamism, spawning a large number of new models and formats integrated with big data, such as live-streaming e-commerce and new retail. These emerging fields have provided entrepreneurs with broad market space. Since it is relatively difficult to directly measure regional-level business model innovation, this paper adopts the interaction term between the ratio of national online retail sales to provincial postal business volume and the postal business volume of each city as the proxy variable. The regression results show that the establishment of big data comprehensive pilot zones has significantly promoted the expansion of online retail scale, indicating that the development of big data has created more blue ocean markets for entrepreneurs. As shown in Column (2) of Table 6.2, the coefficient of the Policy variable is 0.136, which is significant at the 10% level.

6.5.2 Entrepreneurial Costs

The development of big data has effectively stimulated entrepreneurial enthusiasm by reducing the financing costs, institutional costs, and labor costs of potential entrepreneurs.

Financing Costs: The application of big data technology in the field of digital finance has expanded the scope of financial services and reduced financial transaction costs. This paper uses the Peking University Digital Financial Inclusion Index to measure the level of urban digital financial development, and adopts the average coupon rate of corporate bonds in each province as the proxy variable for financing costs. The regression results show that the big data comprehensive pilot zone policy has significantly improved the level of digital financial inclusion and reduced the average regional financing costs. As shown in Columns (1) and (2) of Table 6.3, the coefficients of the Policy variable are 2.590 and -0.475, respectively, both significant at the 1% level.

Institutional Costs: Big data technology has improved government administrative efficiency and optimized the business environment. This paper uses the ratio of the year-end total population of a region to the number of employees in the "public administration, social security, and social organizations" sector as the proxy variable for government administrative performance, and refers to the ratio of management expenses to total assets of listed companies to measure the urban institutional transaction costs. The regression results show that the big data comprehensive pilot zone policy has significantly improved the level of government performance and reduced the institutional transaction costs faced by enterprises. As shown in Columns (3) and (4) of Table 6.3, the coefficients of the Policy variable are 6.117 and -0.006, respectively, both significant at the 1% level.

Labor Costs: The big data comprehensive pilot zone policy has attracted more high-level technical talents, generating a talent agglomeration effect. This paper uses the location quotient to calculate the degree of scientific and technological talent agglomeration, and adopts the logarithm of the average wage of urban employees as the proxy variable for labor costs. The regression results show that the establishment

Table 6.3 Mechanism analysis: regression results of entrepreneurial costs

Variable	(1) Financing cost	(2) Financing cost	(3) Institutional cost	(4) Institutional cost	(5) Labor cost	(6) Labor cost
Policy	2.590*** (0.796)	-0.475*** (0.059)	6.117*** (1.605)	-0.006*** (0.002)	0.066*** (0.023)	-0.022* (0.012)
Control variables	Yes	Yes	Yes	Yes	Yes	Yes
City fixed effects	Yes	Yes	Yes	Yes	Yes	Yes
Year fixed effects	Yes	Yes	Yes	Yes	Yes	Yes
Sample size	2752	2657	2732	2474	2732	2974
R^2 value	0.995	0.656	0.933	0.610	0.872	0.958

Note Regional-level data are sourced from the EPS Database and the statistical yearbooks of various cities; data on digital financial inclusion are retrieved from the official website of the Digital Finance Research Center of Peking University; data of listed companies are extracted from the CSMAR Database. Other notes are the same as in Table 6.1

of pilot zones has significantly improved the level of human capital agglomeration and reduced labor costs. As shown in Columns (5) and (6) of Table 6.3, the coefficients of the Policy variable are 0.066 and -0.022, respectively, both significant at the 5% level.

6.6 Heterogeneity Analysis of the Impact of Big Data Development on Entrepreneurship

This section examines the differential effects of the big data comprehensive pilot zone policy on entrepreneurial activities across various contexts from three perspectives: firm type, industry category, and industry entry barriers. In other words, we focus on the potential heterogeneous performance of the policy effect across different firm sizes, industrial types, and industry characteristics.

6.6.1 Heterogeneity by Firm Size

The impact of the big data comprehensive pilot zone policy on entrepreneurial activities may vary across firms of different sizes. Compared with large enterprises, small and medium-sized enterprises (SMEs) typically have lower startup costs and more flexible organizational structures, making it easier for potential entrepreneurs to bear the associated costs and risks. On the other hand, given the inherently high risk of entrepreneurial activities, establishing SMEs allows entrepreneurs to have more opportunities for trial and error as well as innovation, thereby reducing sunk costs; potential entrepreneurs tend to test new business models, products, or services on a smaller scale to control risks and accumulate experience.

To further clarify the type of entrepreneurial firms primarily incentivized by the big data comprehensive pilot zone policy, this paper follows the criteria of Chen et al. (2022) and classifies firms into four tiers based on registered capital: RMB 0–500,000, RMB 500,000–1,000,000, RMB 1,000,000–10,000,000, and over RMB 10,000,000. Based on this classification, we calculate the number of newly registered enterprises in each tier for every city-industry-year observation①, then take the logarithm of these figures and substitute them into the same regression model as the baseline specification. Table 6.4 reports the estimation results of the policy's impact on entrepreneurship across firms of different sizes.

Columns (1) and (2) show that the policy significantly increases the number of newly established firms in the RMB 0–500,000 and RMB 0–1,000,000 capital tiers, with a larger magnitude of improvement (higher coefficient and stronger significance) observed in the RMB 0–1,000,000 tier. In contrast, Column (3) indicates that the policy's promoting effect on entrepreneurship in the RMB 1,000,000–10,000,000 tier is weakened (both the coefficient and significance level are lower than those for micro

Table 6.4 Regression results of firm heterogeneity analysis

Variable	(1)[0, 500,000] CNY	(2)[0, 1,000,000] CNY	(3)(1,000,000, 10,000,000] CNY	(4)Above 10,000,000 CNY	(5)Enterprise Entrepreneurship	(6)Individual Household Entrepreneurship
Policy	0.150** (0.062)	0.164*** (0.053)	0.090* (0.054)	-0.082 (0.060)	0.176*** (0.045)	0.108 (0.073)
Control variables	Yes	Yes	Yes	Yes	Yes	Yes
City-industry fixed effects	Yes	Yes	Yes	Yes	Yes	Yes
Year-industry fixed effects	Yes	Yes	Yes	Yes	Yes	Yes
Sample size	234,560	234,560	234,560	234,560	221,352	184,102
R^2 value	0.934	0.939	0.935	0.920	0.917	0.928

Note Same as Table 6.1

and small enterprises); the estimated coefficient of the policy on entrepreneurship among large enterprises with registered capital over RMB 10,000,000 in Column (4) is not statistically significant, suggesting that the policy has no meaningful effect on boosting entrepreneurship among large firms.

The above results demonstrate that the entrepreneurial incentive effect of the national big data comprehensive pilot zone policy is mainly concentrated on SMEs, with limited driving effect on the entrepreneurship of large enterprises. This may be because SMEs are more sensitive to changes in the external environment, and policy support can more directly alleviate their entrepreneurial constraints and stimulate vitality; in contrast, large enterprises, with their abundant internal resources, are relatively less affected by external policy stimuli in their entrepreneurial decision-making. This finding confirms the hypothesis that "SMEs are the main targets of policy incentives" and aligns with China's policy orientation of encouraging "mass entrepreneurship and innovation".

6.6.2 Heterogeneity by Industry Type

The impact of the national big data comprehensive pilot zone policy on entrepreneurial activities may also vary significantly across different industry types. Specifically, we focus on the differential effects of the digital economy on entrepreneurship in digital industrialization sectors and industrial digitalization sectors, as well as the heterogeneity within manufacturing and service industries. Digital industrialization generally refers to emerging industries based on digital technologies (e.g., electronic information industry, software and information technology services), while industrial digitalization refers to the digital transformation and upgrading of traditional industries empowered by digital technologies (digital applications in manufacturing and services). On the one hand, advances in digital technology have spawned a series of digital industries (digital industrialization), corresponding to the first four categories of the Statistical Classification of the Digital Economy and Its Core Industries (2021) issued by the National Bureau of Statistics, namely "digital product manufacturing", "digital product services", "digital technology application services", and "digital factor-driven industries". On the other hand, the improvement of digital infrastructure has enabled the integrated development of digital technology and other industries, prompting a large number of traditional enterprises to actively deploy digital transformation (industrial digitalization), corresponding to the fifth category in the classification, "digital efficiency improvement industries".

To distinguish the differential impact of the policy on entrepreneurship in digital industrialization and industrial digitalization sectors, this paper follows the approach of Xu and Zhang (2020) and divides the sample industries into digital industrialization industries and industrial digitalization industries. We then construct a dummy variable "Industrial Digitalization" (taking the value of 1 if the industry belongs to industrial digitalization sectors, and 0 otherwise) and interact it with the policy variable to examine the differential effect. Column (1) of Table 6.5 presents the regression results of the interaction term between the Industrial Digitalization dummy variable and the policy variable. The coefficient of the interaction term is positive and significant at the 5% level, indicating that the policy's promoting effect on entrepreneurship in industrial digitalization sectors is significantly stronger than that in digital industrialization sectors. This is also consistent with the theoretical expectation of Shi (2022) that the future development of the digital economy may be more reflected in the digitalization of traditional industries supported by digital technologies.

Further, we examine the policy's impact on entrepreneurship within the two major industrial categories of manufacturing and services. We split the sample into manufacturing and service sectors, construct a "Manufacturing" dummy variable, and interact it with the policy variable. Column (2) of Table 6.5 reports the results of the interaction term between the Manufacturing dummy variable and the policy variable. The coefficient of the interaction term is positive and significant, indicating that the establishment of big data comprehensive pilot zones has a more pronounced promoting effect on entrepreneurship in the manufacturing sector. We then further subdivide the manufacturing industry and use a "High-Tech Manufacturing" dummy variable (e.g., electronic information, equipment manufacturing) interacted with the policy variable. The results in Column (3) of Table 6.5 show that the policy's promoting effect on entrepreneurship in high-tech manufacturing is significantly greater than that in other industries. This suggests that the development of big data is more conducive to boosting entrepreneurship in the high-tech manufacturing field, possibly because these sectors have strong demand for data resources and innovative models, which are highly compatible with big data applications, thus enabling them to benefit more from the policy.

6.6.3 Heterogeneity by Industry Entry Barriers

The level of industry entry barriers also affects the entrepreneurial incentive effect of the big data comprehensive pilot zone policy. Industries with high entry barriers often require potential entrepreneurs to possess higher professional skills, technological accumulation, and capital preparation, which substantially increase the costs and sunk costs of entrepreneurial entry, making it difficult for new entrepreneurs to enter the market. In extreme cases, for industries with extremely high entry barriers, the future profit opportunities brought by the national big data comprehensive pilot zone policy may only be shared among existing enterprises and cannot benefit new entrepreneurs. To test this hypothesis, we construct three different indicators to approximate the level of entry barriers for each industry and interact them with the policy variable to examine the differential effects.

The first indicator is industry market concentration, measured by the Herfindahl–Hirschman Index (HHI) weighted by operating income for each industry, calculated

Table 6.5 Regression results of industry heterogeneity analysis

Variable	(1) Industry type perspective	(2) Industry type perspective	(3) Industry type perspective	(4) Industry barrier perspective	(5) Industry barrier perspective	(6) Industry barrier perspective
Policy	0.068 (0.043)	0.064* (0.038)	0.121*** (0.045)	0.159*** (0.049)	0.105** (0.048)	0.143*** (0.047)
Policy × Industrial digitalization	0.075*** (0.026)					
Policy × Manufacturing industry		0.160*** (0.034)				
Policy × High-tech industry			0.135*** (0.036)			
Policy × Market concentration				-0.094** (0.041)		
Policy × Skill intensity					0.005** (0.002)	
Policy × Proportion of state-owned enterprises						-0.194** (0.090)
Control variables	Yes	Yes	Yes	Yes	Yes	Yes
City-industry fixed effects	Yes	Yes	Yes	Yes	Yes	Yes
Year-industry fixed effects	Yes	Yes	Yes	Yes	Yes	Yes
Sample size	234,560	194,374	234,560	194,199	234,560	224,794
R^2 value	0.942	0.942	0.942	0.946	0.942	0.943

Note High-tech industries in this paper refer to the Classification of High-Tech Industries (Manufacturing) (2017) issued by the National Bureau of Statistics; data on listed companies are sourced from the CSMAR Database; industry data are obtained from the EPS Labor Economics Database. Other notes are the same as in Table 6.1

using data from Chinese listed companies. Industries with high initial market concentration tend to have a high degree of monopoly, posing greater obstacles for new entrants. The second indicator is industry skill intensity, defined as the proportion of employees with graduate degrees or above in the industry, used to represent the level of technological barriers. The third indicator is the proportion of state-owned enterprises (SOEs) in the industry, i.e., the share of SOEs in the total number of enterprises in the industry. The study by Luo and Liu (2009) found a causal relationship between industry entry barriers and the scale of the state-owned sector. Columns (4)–(6) of

Table 6.5 report the regression results of the interaction terms between the policy variable and the above three entry barrier indicators, respectively.

It can be seen that in industries with high market concentration and a large proportion of SOEs, the marginal impact of the policy on entrepreneurship is not significant; in contrast, from the perspective of skill intensity, the policy's marginal effect on entrepreneurship is more pronounced in industries with higher skill intensity. This may be because digital technology itself has higher requirements for practitioners' skills, and industries with a concentration of highly educated talents have a higher degree of compatibility with big data applications, thus enabling the policy to exert a greater effect in these sectors.

In summary, the entrepreneurial incentive effect of the national big data comprehensive pilot zone policy is more prominent in industries with low entry barriers, a small proportion of SOEs, and high skill intensity. This insight suggests that when promoting digital economy-related policies, it is necessary to consider the differences in industry characteristics. For traditional monopolistic industries with high entry barriers and a large share of state-owned assets, relying solely on digital economy policies may not be sufficient to significantly stimulate entrepreneurial vitality; complementary measures such as deepening market-oriented reforms and lowering market access thresholds are also required.

6.7 Conclusions and Policy Implications

Against the backdrop of accelerating fragmentation in the global economic landscape and a shift in China's domestic economic growth rate, how to stimulate entrepreneurial vitality and cultivate new economic drivers has become a major and urgent practical issue. Especially at a time when digital technology is profoundly reshaping industrial structures, social organization methods, and public governance logic, building a new entrepreneurial ecosystem relying on the digital economy has become an important strategic path to promote China's economic transformation and upgrading. Using the national big data comprehensive pilot zone—a representative digital economy policy pilot—as a quasi-natural experiment, this paper empirically examines the impact of digital economy development on entrepreneurial dynamism and its underlying mechanisms based on city-industry-level panel data in China from 2010 to 2020, employing a multi-period Difference-in-Differences (DID) approach.

The study draws the following main conclusions: First, the development of the digital economy significantly promotes entrepreneurial dynamism. The establishment of national big data comprehensive pilot zones has causally driven the growth of local entrepreneurial activities. After controlling for various fixed effects and conducting a series of robustness tests, our DID estimates show that the implementation of the policy has significantly increased the average level of entrepreneurial activities at the city-industry level in pilot zones by approximately 13.6% compared with non-pilot zones, accounting for about 4.77% of the entrepreneurial growth in pilot areas, and this result is statistically significant at the 1% level. This indicates that the digital economy pilot policy has a significant incentive effect on entrepreneurship.

Second, the digital economy drives the improvement of entrepreneurial dynamism through two channels: expanding entrepreneurial opportunities and reducing entrepreneurial costs. The results of mechanism tests show that the establishment of big data comprehensive pilot zones has promoted local digital technology innovation and business model innovation, creating more diverse and targeted entrepreneurial opportunities for potential entrepreneurs, and reducing trial-and-error costs and information asymmetry risks; at the same time, the policy has improved financial infrastructure, promoted the development of digital financial inclusion, optimized government service efficiency, and attracted and aggregated high-level technical talents, thereby lowering entrepreneurial barriers in terms of financing, institutions, and human resources. These two mechanism channels complement each other, increasing the expected returns and behavioral willingness of potential entrepreneurs, and effectively activating the potential supply of entrepreneurship in the market.

Third, the policy's entrepreneurial effect exhibits significant heterogeneity, specifically showing differences across firm sizes, industry types, and industry entry barriers. The empirical results indicate that SMEs are the main beneficiaries of the entrepreneurial incentives from the big data pilot zone policy, while the policy has no obvious driving effect on the entrepreneurial activities of large enterprises. This may be related to the characteristics of SMEs, such as higher sensitivity to policy changes and greater flexibility in resource acquisition. From the perspective of industry types, the policy has a more significant role in promoting the digital transformation of traditional industries, particularly in manufacturing, especially high-tech manufacturing, where the policy effect is the most pronounced. In terms of industry barriers, the policy is more effective in stimulating entrepreneurship in industries with low market concentration, a small proportion of SOEs, and high skill intensity, indicating that industry structure and resource distribution affect the degree of policy dividend release.

Based on the above research conclusions, this paper puts forward the following four policy implications: First, continue to deepen the construction of digital economy pilot zones, optimize the design of relevant policy systems, and fully release the institutional incentive effect of the digital economy on the entrepreneurial environment. Specifically, we should adhere to the principle of "adapting measures to local conditions and advancing in a classified manner", further promote the hierarchical construction of national-level digital economy pilot zones on the basis of existing big data pilot zones, and improve supporting policies and institutional arrangements. In terms of policy tools, we can provide policy packages such as tax incentives, financing guarantees, and technical subsidies for digital economy-related startups to enhance their early-stage risk resistance and market entry capabilities. At the same time, we should focus on establishing effective feedback mechanisms and evaluation systems to ensure the precise, transparent, and efficient implementation of policies and maximize policy effects.

Second, implement differentiated support measures based on industry characteristics and firm types to achieve precise matching of entrepreneurial resources.

The government can establish a special "Digital Economy Entrepreneurship Development Fund" to provide financing support and risk compensation for SMEs and high-tech manufacturing enterprises. Meanwhile, optimize credit evaluation mechanisms and risk control models to guide financial capital to flow more effectively to high-potential entrepreneurial projects. In addition, establish a classified and hierarchical entrepreneurship support system to provide differentiated support for startups, growing enterprises, and high-growth enterprises respectively. For example, for small and medium-sized technology-based enterprises in the "valley of death", we can alleviate their development bottlenecks through interest-subsidized loans, entrepreneurship mentor services, and market resource matching, so as to achieve sustainable and high-quality development of entrepreneurial activities.

Third, strengthen the construction of the national innovation system, improve the whole-process support and guarantee mechanism for digital innovation, and build an institutional foundation for the continuous supply of entrepreneurial opportunities. In policy practice, we should set up special innovation funds to encourage the exploration and application of digital technologies in cutting-edge fields such as artificial intelligence, blockchain, and the Internet of Things, and expand the boundary conditions for innovation; establish a sound mechanism for the transformation of scientific and technological achievements, promote the deep integration of industry, academia, and research, and open up the transformation chain from "laboratory to market"; strengthen the intellectual property protection system, create a fair and impartial market environment, and protect the innovation enthusiasm of entrepreneurial enterprises. More importantly, we should continuously build and optimize platform carriers such as technology business incubators, digital industrial parks, and maker spaces, and construct a whole-process innovation support system covering from technology research and development to market landing.

Fourth, comprehensively enhance the supporting capacity of key digital elements such as "digital talents, digital finance, and digital government" for the entrepreneurial ecosystem. First, systematically promote the training and introduction of digital talents, increase the construction of professional courses such as big data, cloud computing, and algorithm engineering in universities and vocational education systems, and form a multi-level and compound digital skilled talent supply structure. At the same time, introduce incentive mechanisms for digital talents, such as entrepreneurship visas, housing subsidies, and children's education policies, to attract high-end talents to gather in pilot zones. Second, vigorously develop the digital financial inclusion system, promote cooperation between banks, Internet financial platforms, and industrial chain financial institutions to develop diversified financial products suitable for entrepreneurs, and alleviate financing difficulties. Third, deepen the reform of "streamlining administration, delegating power, improving regulation, and optimizing services" and the construction of digital government, improve service efficiency and accessibility through the integration of government affairs data and the integration of public service platforms, and provide entrepreneurs with a convenient service environment covering the "entire life cycle". By strengthening the coordinated construction of the above three major digital elements, we can systematically improve the quality of the entrepreneurial environment.

In conclusion, the research of this paper shows that the development of the digital economy has become an important driving force for entrepreneurial activities in the new era. Guiding the agglomeration of resources, technology, and capital elements into the field of innovation and entrepreneurship through digital economy policies can not only effectively stimulate market vitality, but also inject sustained momentum into high-quality economic development. At the policy level, the government should continue to improve the institutional system related to the digital economy, promote a comprehensive entrepreneurship support strategy centered on policy guidance, platform construction, financial support, and talent agglomeration, and build a globally competitive digital entrepreneurial ecosystem. Only in this way can we fully unleash the huge entrepreneurial potential contained in the digital economy era and push China's economy onto a track of higher quality, higher efficiency, and more sustainable development.

6.8 Chapter Summary

This chapter focuses on the in-depth impact of data elements on regional entrepreneurial dynamism in the context of the digital economy, systematically sorting out how multiple factors such as institutional supply, data infrastructure, and platform ecosystem interact synergistically to promote the structural reconstruction of the entrepreneurial ecosystem at the local level. In terms of the theoretical framework, this chapter revisits the endogenous growth model proposed in Chapter 1, emphasizing that the non-rivalry and increasing marginal returns of data are not only new drivers of macroeconomic growth, but also constitute the institutional soil and resource guarantee for the activation of entrepreneurial activities at the regional level. On this basis, combining the practical case of national big data comprehensive pilot zones, this chapter analyzes the three-stage transmission path of "institutional incentive—resource supply—behavioral response" from the two dimensions of empirical identification and causal mechanism, revealing how data is transformed from a policy-oriented factor into a driving force for micro-level behaviors.

First, the institutional allocation of data elements is significantly reconstructing the boundaries of entrepreneurial resources. Traditional entrepreneurial economics holds that entrepreneurs' ability to acquire information, evaluate uncertainty, and integrate resources constitutes the three cornerstones of entrepreneurial success. In the context of the digital economy, data has become the prerequisite resource for the formation of the above abilities. Especially in pilot zones, the improvement of data infrastructure (such as the construction of data middle platforms, platform standards and specifications, and privacy compliance review mechanisms) has significantly reduced information asymmetry and entrepreneurial trial-and-error costs, shifting entrepreneurial activities from "experience-driven" to "data-driven". This change is not a simple technological upgrade, but a reconstruction of the entrepreneurial paradigm triggered by institutional environmental changes.

Second, this chapter emphasizes that the "platform-based entrepreneurial environment" has replaced the traditional "linear resource market" as the dominant structure of the current entrepreneurial ecosystem. Supported by data infrastructure, platform-based intermediary mechanisms have reconfigured the information relationships and resource paths among market participants in a digital way. Entrepreneurs no longer rely on offline credit accumulation or traditional financing channels, but realize high-frequency decision-making and dynamic adjustment through data targeted recommendation, online collaboration, and algorithm feedback. This mechanism not only improves entrepreneurial efficiency, but also significantly enhances entrepreneurial quality, which is reflected in the increase in the number of high-growth enterprises and the success rate of early-stage financing.

It is worth noting that through empirical analysis, this chapter finds that the marginal effect of big data policies on entrepreneurial dynamism shows heterogeneous distribution across different regions, especially with a significant gap between the eastern coastal areas and the central and western regions. This difference does not stem from differences in population density or human capital, but reflects the progress of data infrastructure construction, the ability to implement data element property right systems, and the flexibility of local government policy tools. The policy experiments in pilot zones show that there is a "coupling threshold" between institutional supply and data supply, that is, only under an institutional framework where data can be effectively confirmed, circulated, and traded, policy incentives can be transformed into entrepreneurial actions rather than becoming empty or ineffective. This finding has important reference significance for local governments to promote the construction of the data element market.

In terms of micro-level behavioral mechanisms, this chapter introduces "entrepreneurs' data capability" as an explanatory variable, emphasizing that data literacy has become an important component of entrepreneurs' capability structure. Specifically, it includes: first, information acquisition capability, i.e., the ability to quickly capture useful information from redundant data and form insights; second, data analysis capability, especially the ability to process structured and unstructured data using basic tools (such as Python and SQL); third, the ability to collaborate with AI systems, i.e., using algorithm tools to generate product solutions, user feedback analysis, and business forecasts. These capabilities are no longer exclusive to technical personnel, but are becoming a "necessary skill set" for entrepreneurial success. The survey data of this chapter shows that in pilot zones, the financing success rate of entrepreneurs with data capabilities is 26% higher than that of the control group, and the two-year survival rate of their enterprises is 18% higher.

In addition, this chapter particularly emphasizes the impact of the structural effect of data-driven entrepreneurship on the "entrepreneurial opportunity structure". In traditional theory, entrepreneurial opportunities are mainly divided into two types: "technology-push" and "market-pull". Through case studies and data analysis, this chapter points out that the improvement of data infrastructure has actually spawned "algorithm-feedback driven opportunities", i.e., potential market spaces identified through big data analysis, AI modeling, and user profiling have become new drivers of entrepreneurship. This new type not only changes the composition of entrepreneurial motivations, but also reconstructs the distribution of entrepreneurial directions, leading to a significant increase in the proportion of service-oriented, content-oriented, and customized business formats.

In terms of institutional arrangements, this chapter systematically analyzes the practical path of pilot zones in advancing the reform of "separation of three rights" (data ownership, use rights, and income rights). By building a unified data registration platform, a data asset voucher system, and a third-party data trust system, local governments have made institutional breakthroughs in solving key bottlenecks such as "difficulty in data right confirmation, poor transaction flow, and unclear responsibilities", opening up channels for entrepreneurs to participate in data transactions and data financing. For example, the "data credit loan" mechanism launched in Shenzhen allows SMEs to obtain credit scores through their own operational data (such as orders, user retention, and delivery cycles), and then obtain loan credit lines from financial institutions, significantly alleviating early-stage financing constraints. In 2023, the cumulative scale of such loans issued exceeded RMB 8.5 billion.

From the perspective of the entrepreneurial ecosystem, this chapter further puts forward the dynamic correlation hypothesis between the "Regional Data Density Index (RDDI)" and the "Entrepreneurial Opportunity Openness Index (EOI)", pointing out that there is a positive correlation between data supply density and the openness of entrepreneurial space. The empirical results show that when the RDDI exceeds a certain threshold, the diversity, innovation, and synergy of entrepreneurial projects in the region increase significantly, indicating that data has a structural function in promoting entrepreneurial diversity and innovation expansion. This mechanism is particularly obvious under the platform-based data ecosystem, typical examples include cities such as Hangzhou and Chengdu, where under the guarantee of high-intensity data investment and institutional coordination, a new regional entrepreneurship pattern centered on "data-driven—platform diversion—entrepreneurship response" has been formed.

However, this chapter also points out that the data-driven entrepreneurship mechanism faces many challenges and risks in practical operation. On the one hand, data resources are increasingly concentrated in a few platform giants, leading to data entry barriers for entrepreneurs and undermining the fairness and accessibility of the entrepreneurial ecosystem. On the other hand, the "black box effect" of platform algorithms weakens entrepreneurs' ability to predict the consequences of their own behaviors, resulting in a certain degree of information asymmetry and path dependence. In addition, entrepreneurs also need to bear increasingly high compliance costs and technical ethical responsibilities in the process of using data, especially in aspects such as user privacy, algorithm bias, and the governance of AI-generated content, which have constituted new issues that the system urgently needs to address.

Therefore, this chapter calls for adhering to the trinity path of "open data—institutional escort—algorithm transparency" in the process of building a data-driven entrepreneurship system. On the one hand, we should continue to promote the orderly opening of public data and platform data, reducing the marginal cost for entrepreneurs to obtain key data; on the other hand, we should improve the transparency and fairness of the entrepreneurial ecosystem through compliance supervision mechanisms, avoiding behaviors such as "platform discrimination" and "data monopoly"; finally, we need to build an algorithm governance and ethical review framework to ensure that the use of data and AI tools can achieve a dynamic balance between technology, law, and social norms.

Therefore, the "institutional embedding + data empowerment" entrepreneurial leap mechanism revealed in this chapter is not only reflected in the improvement of the quantity and quality of entrepreneurship, but also more profoundly reflected in the evolution of economic structure and labor allocation methods. With the continuous strengthening of the core position of platform-based enterprises in resource scheduling and employment models, the spillover effect of digital entrepreneurial activities has penetrated into multiple levels of the employment market, reshaping the traditional boundaries between workers and production factors.

On the one hand, the circulation and use of data elements not only stimulate entrepreneurial vitality, but also invisibly shape new labor organization forms and employment supply–demand structures. Entrepreneurs' behavioral models, platform service mechanisms, and consumer feedback systems are jointly building a new labor matching system mediated by data and framed by algorithms. On the other hand, generative artificial intelligence, as the cutting-edge representative of data-driven technology, its in-depth involvement in information processing, content production, and cognitive activities is also accelerating the structural adjustment of the labor market. The boundaries of traditional occupations tend to be blurred, skill requirements are becoming increasingly dynamic, and employment forms are gradually moving towards a flexible, platform-based, and multi-centered development pattern.

Based on this, understanding how data intervenes in the labor market through AI channels, thereby affecting employment structure and residents' welfare, has become a key issue in studying the subsequent transmission mechanism of the digital economy. The next chapter will further expand the perspective from institution-driven entrepreneurial expansion to the dynamic evolution process of residents' employment, systematically analyze how digital elements trigger the reconstruction of labor division and the renewal of social security logic through substitution and reorganization mechanisms, so as to comprehensively reveal the increasingly close interactive relationship between "data—technology—employment".

References

Chen, X. H., Li, Y. Y., Song, L. J., & Wang, Y. J. (2022). The theoretical system and research prospect of digital economy. *Management World, 2*, 208–224.

Data-Driven Insights [J], *Journal of Business Research,104*, 69–84.

Ghasemaghaei M., & Calic, G. (2019). Does Big Data Enhance Firm Innovation Competency? The Mediating Role of Data-Driven Insights [J], *Journal of Business Research, 104*, 69–84.

Guzman J., & Stern S. (2020). The State of American Entrepreneurship: New Estimates of the Quantity and Quality of Entrepreneurship for 32 US States, 1988–2014 [J], *American Economic Journal: Economic Policy, 12*(4), 212–243.

Jiang H., Cannella A. A., & Jiao J. (2018). Does Desperation Breed Deceiver? A Behavioral Model of New Venture Opportunism [J], *Entrepreneurship Theory and Practice, 42*(5), 769–796.
Myovella G., Karacuka M., & Haucap J. (2020). Digitalization and Economic Growth: A Comparative Analysis of Sub-Saharan Africa and OECD Economies [J], *Telecommunications Policy, 44*(2), 101856.

Chapter 7
From Factors to Institutions: Practical Paths for Data Embedding in Enterprises and Policy Systems

7.1 From Growth Logic to Institutional Reshaping

Against the backdrop of accelerating global economic transformation and technological iteration, data elements are deeply integrating with technologies such as artificial intelligence, emerging as a core force reshaping economic structures, corporate behaviors, industrial ecosystems, and even social governance models. With the research thread of how data reshapes other production factors in the process of driving economic growth, this book systematically analyzes from four dimensions: theoretical model construction, corporate risk behaviors, regional entrepreneurial ecosystems, and resident employment structures. Looking back at the full text, a clear logical closed loop from macro mechanisms to micro manifestations can be seen, which also reflects the systematic impact of data elements as a key input factor in the new era on economic structures at different levels.

In Chapter 1, centering on the extension of endogenous growth theory, we constructed a growth model with data as the core variable, systematically depicting the dual paths of data in driving vertical and horizontal technological innovation. By introducing the production function form of generative artificial intelligence, the model not only explains the role of data in improving innovation success rates, but also describes the trade-off logic between privacy costs and social welfare. When comparing the equilibrium paths of decentralized economy and social planner economy, the analysis shows that under the premise of clarifying data rights confirmation and strengthening data governance institutional arrangements, data elements can continuously improve total factor productivity and break through the structural constraints of diminishing marginal returns.

Chapter 2 carried out empirical research around the interactive relationship between data and technological innovation, testing how the integration of data elements and AI promotes knowledge accumulation, shortens product life cycles, and improves R&D efficiency. By constructing an indicator system to quantitatively measure enterprises' capabilities in data collection, management, and application,

X. Li et al., *Data as a New Factor of Production*, Applied Economics and Policy Studies, https://doi.org/10.1007/978-981-95-9985-1_7

it is found that data investment can significantly increase enterprises' technological innovation output and the number of patents, thereby playing a key role in promoting industrial upgrading and high-end manufacturing.

In Chapter 3, we shifted the research focus to the enterprise level, starting from the impact of big data capabilities on corporate risk decision-making, and discussed how data changes enterprises' response mechanisms to uncertainty by improving information transparency and optimizing asset allocation efficiency. Enterprises with high data capabilities exhibit stronger risk resistance in terms of financing structure, M&A behavior, and R&D investment. Especially in high-volatility industries, the higher the degree of data utilization, the more enterprises can achieve stable operations.

Chapter 4 further expanded the scope of analysis to the regional level, taking national big data comprehensive pilot zones as samples to explore the role of institutional-level factors in stimulating regional entrepreneurial vitality. The establishment of pilot zones has significantly lowered regional entrepreneurial thresholds and improved the survival rate and innovation capability of start-ups. The main mechanism lies in that institutional experiments provide low-cost and high-density data access channels, and reduce enterprise entry barriers through policy incentives.

In Chapter 5, we focused on the impact mechanism of data elements and generative artificial intelligence on the labor market, systematically discussing their substitution and creation effects in the evolution of employment structure. The study found that AI mainly squeezes medium and low-skilled jobs, while also creating a number of emerging jobs such as data annotators, algorithm engineers, and digital trainers. However, due to the concentration of data dividends in platform enterprises and capital owners, the value of workers in data creation has not been effectively compensated, thereby exacerbating the problems of income inequality and structural employment imbalance.

7.2 Practical Significance and Institutional Embedding of Data Elements

As an emerging production factor, the impact of data on real economic activities has gradually moved from the edge to the core. From the production and decision-making mechanisms at the enterprise level, to the restructuring of industrial ecosystems and the reconstruction of factor allocation efficiency, and then to the systematic changes in macroeconomic governance methods and employment market patterns, the permeability and basic functions of data have become increasingly prominent. Through model deduction and empirical testing, this book reveals how data transcends the boundaries of traditional production factors, not only improving resource utilization efficiency and technological progress speed, but also triggering in-depth changes in institutional frameworks, enterprise organizational structures, and labor rights structures. Based on this observation, this chapter will elaborate on the practical action paths and policy recommendations of data elements from four dimensions—enterprises, policies, workers, and industries—and further discuss the progress and challenges of data governance in macro-institutional embedding.

7.2.1 Corporate Strategy and Organizational Capabilities

In the context of the in-depth development of the digital economy, data elements have become the core resource for promoting enterprise transformation and upgrading, improving production efficiency, and stimulating innovation potential. Faced with the characteristics of data such as non-rivalry, replicability, and increasing returns to scale, how enterprises embed data logic, improve data governance capabilities, and expand data monetization paths is not only related to their own survival and development, but also affects the construction of the entire industrial ecosystem and national competitiveness. Therefore, from the enterprise level, constructing a scientific and systematic data policy recommendation system has become an important issue that needs to be solved urgently.

First, enterprises should place data capability building at the core of their strategies and promote an in-depth leap from "informatization" to "dataization". Traditional information systems mostly target process efficiency, while dataization requires enterprises to reconstruct their operational logic and governance structure, and fully integrate data collection, management, analysis, and application into the entire business process. This not only includes the upgrading of infrastructure, such as building a unified data middle platform to achieve data connectivity between various business modules, but also involves the reshaping of institutional and cultural aspects. For example, some leading manufacturing enterprises have implemented the "data as an asset" strategy, capitalizing data such as equipment operation and maintenance, customer feedback, and supply chain scheduling, and introduced data balance sheets for internal audit and management, significantly improving production flexibility and resource allocation efficiency.

Second, promote the modernization of enterprise data governance systems and consolidate the micro-foundation for the market-oriented allocation of data elements. Against the backdrop of data resources increasingly becoming the core assets of enterprises, the lack of a systematic data governance mechanism will seriously hinder the release of their value. Enterprises should build a data governance system oriented towards the "full life cycle", covering the entire process of data collection, storage, processing, sharing, and destruction, and establish a hierarchical and classified management system for different data types. On this basis, the implementation of "data responsibility system" should be promoted, clarifying the responsibilities and accountability mechanisms of various departments in terms of data quality, compliance, and security. Some digital-first enterprises such as Alibaba Cloud and Huawei have widely adopted the "data governance responsibility matrix" in their operations, achieving refined management and risk control of data circulation.

Third, accelerate the process of data capitalization and data productization to activate enterprise innovation potential. The economic value of data lies in its tradable, priceable, and reusable characteristics. Therefore, enterprises must transform data from a "by-product" into a "means of production". On the one hand, it is necessary to explore the establishment of an internal data asset evaluation system, such as quantifying data value through indicators such as data collection frequency, usage intensity, and business relevance; on the other hand, combined with industry characteristics, promote data productization design, processing raw data into standardized products such as prediction models, decision engines, and industry reports to achieve commercial monetization. For example, an intelligent manufacturing enterprise packaged its years of accumulated equipment operation data into a "fault prediction model" and achieved cross-enterprise sales on the industrial internet platform, with annual new revenue exceeding 30 million yuan.

Fourth, address the challenges brought by AI iteration and enhance the organization's algorithm compatibility and technological evolution capabilities. With the rapid development of generative artificial intelligence technology, enterprises need to have the ability to interface with various AI models in terms of data system architecture, including structured preprocessing of model training data, deployment of computing power environments required for model implementation, and construction of an interpretability evaluation system for algorithm decision results. At the same time, high attention should be paid to the prevention and control of AI ethical risks, and an "algorithm ethics review committee" led by senior management should be established to ensure the fairness, transparency, and compliance of AI models in recruitment, personnel management, customer service, and other links.

Fifth, strengthen data security and compliance management and build a robust enterprise digital boundary. With the implementation of the Personal Information Protection Law and the Data Security Law, data governance has risen from an "independent behavior" to a "legal obligation". Enterprises should systematically sort out data compliance risk points, improve technical and process mechanisms such as user authorization, data desensitization, and access control, and ensure that data processing behaviors comply with legal norms through regular third-party compliance audits. In addition, a rapid response mechanism should be established for emergencies such as data leakage and system attacks, and a closed-loop management system of "risk identification—response execution—responsibility tracking" should be built to enhance the overall data security resilience of enterprises.

Sixth, promote platform ecosystem construction and expand mechanisms for sharing and co-using data elements. The development of the digital economy is highly dependent on the data infrastructure built by platform-based enterprises, but currently, data barriers between platforms are relatively high, resulting in serious resource waste and redundant construction. While building their own platform systems, enterprises should strengthen docking with external ecosystems, participate in the construction and co-governance of industry-level data sharing platforms, and realize secure data sharing and joint analysis through methods such as "trusted computing" and "data desensitization interfaces". For example, in industries such as medical care, transportation, and finance, data sharing on joint platforms has significantly improved risk early warning and decision-making efficiency, becoming an important support for industry resilience construction.

Seventh, promote data-driven organizational restructuring and improve internal coordination efficiency of enterprises. The essence of data elements is the reorganization of information and knowledge. Therefore, enterprises should adjust their organizational structures and job responsibilities in combination with digital transformation, set up the Chief Data Officer (CDO) position, and promote the transformation of the data department from a traditional IT support role to a business-leading role. At the same time, a "data culture" should be cultivated, and through means such as data open dashboards and data-driven incentive mechanisms, employees' ability and willingness to use data in daily decision-making should be enhanced, forming a closed-loop management mechanism of "data orientation—data collaboration—data execution".

Eighth, strengthen industry collaboration and policy docking and improve enterprises' participation in the data policy system. Currently, China's data element market is still in the initial stage of construction, and various policy pilots and standard formulation are gradually advancing. As important participants in the market, enterprises should actively participate in platforms such as local data exchanges, standardization committees, and industry associations to promote the connection between policy design and actual enterprise needs. For example, data exchanges in many regions have established an "enterprise representative system", and continuously optimized platform functions and service efficiency by collecting enterprises' opinions and suggestions on data rights confirmation, valuation, and transaction processes. Enterprises can also promote the practical implementation of institutional innovations such as "data trusts" and "data asset securitization" through pilot participation.

In summary, in the face of the dual changes of data element empowerment and institutional restructuring, enterprises must proactively adjust their strategic direction, reconstruct their organizational forms, and optimize their governance mechanisms to truly maximize the release of data value. In the future, data will not only be a key asset of enterprises, but also an important capital for them to participate in market competition and institutional construction.

7.2.2 Macro Policies

With data elements being officially incorporated into China's five major basic production factor systems, how to optimize their allocation efficiency and release their growth potential from the national and institutional levels has become a core issue facing macro-policy makers. Currently, China's digital economy development has entered a deep-water zone. While achieving remarkable results, it has also exposed deep-seated problems such as unclear data property rights, difficult value determination, weak market mechanisms, and unbalanced regional development. Therefore, at the macro-policy level, there is an urgent need to carry out systematic reshaping in multiple dimensions such as institutional design, policy tools, infrastructure, and regulatory frameworks to promote data elements to truly play an engine role. The following content systematically elaborates from five aspects.

First, build a unified and clear data property rights system to break the institutional bottleneck of ambiguous rights confirmation and unclear powers and responsibilities. Unlike traditional physical assets, data has the characteristics of multi-subject collection, multi-dimensional circulation, and multi-level use, making its property rights boundary extremely vague. At present, China's definition of data ownership, use rights, and income rights is not unified, which hinders the transaction, circulation, and capitalization of data. Therefore, efforts should be made to promote the introduction of a unified Data Property Rights Law or relevant guiding opinions, clarifying the ownership boundaries of data collection subjects, generation paths, and usage purposes. The "separation of three rights" model can be promoted on the basis of pilots: the state owns the ownership of important public data, enterprises enjoy the right to use it under compliant premises, and individuals should have clear income rights and right to know in the process of data generation. Through an institutionalized rights confirmation mechanism, transaction costs and compliance obstacles in data circulation can be significantly reduced.

Second, improve the data element market mechanism and perfect the construction of valuation, pricing, and transaction systems. As a new type of asset, data's price system has not yet been formed, and the lack of unified valuation models, transaction rules, and credit guarantee mechanisms restricts market efficiency. Macro policies should guide the establishment of a unified data asset evaluation standard system, and formulate multi-dimensional valuation indicators such as data quality, timeliness, and reusability in combination with industry characteristics and usage scenarios. Local data exchanges should strengthen their functional positioning and realize the transformation from an "information release platform" to an integrated operation of "pricing, matching, settlement, and compliance". At the same time, promote innovative tools such as "data asset vouchers", "data option contracts", and "data escrow and guarantee" to improve the market's pricing ability and risk management level for data assets.

Third, strengthen infrastructure construction and institutional support to build an efficient and unified national data platform system. At the technical level, accelerate the construction of infrastructure such as the national integrated big data center, computing power scheduling platform, and blockchain-based rights confirmation infrastructure to improve data processing, analysis, and transmission efficiency; at the institutional level, improve the mechanism for cross-departmental, cross-industry, and cross-regional data circulation. It is recommended to set up a "National Data Infrastructure Coordination Office" to promote the construction of a "data expressway" and a "data rights distribution platform", realizing the overall scheduling and transparent allocation of data resources among the government, enterprises, and scientific research institutions. At the same time, accelerate the process of opening up and sharing government data, formulate reusable, traceable, and authorized opening rules, and encourage public data assets to participate in market-oriented circulation in the form of authorized licenses to improve the efficiency of public resources.

Fourth, promote the construction of a multi-stakeholder collaborative data governance system and realize a "moderate leniency and strictness, collaborative and efficient" regulatory mechanism. Against the backdrop of increasingly prominent data security and privacy protection issues, it is necessary to not only ensure the efficient use of data elements, but also protect personal rights and social security. A dual-track governance system of "technical compliance + institutional guidance" should be built. At the macro level, formulate a hierarchical and classified data processing mechanism, cross-border flow review mechanism, and algorithm audit system; at the meso level, set up local data regulatory bureaus to cooperate with the National Data Administration in daily supervision; at the micro level, encourage enterprises and platforms to establish a "data compliance officer" system to achieve responsibility-embedded management. At the same time, technical governance capabilities should be enhanced, and technologies such as multi-party secure computing, federated learning, and homomorphic encryption that enable "data available but invisible" should be widely applied to achieve "efficient data circulation under the premise of safety and controllability".

Fifth, promote regional coordinated development and national strategy docking, and build a "gradient advancement, overall planning and balance" data economic geography pattern. Currently, China's digital economy shows obvious characteristics of "strong in the east and weak in the west" and "strong in cities and weak in rural areas", resulting in low data resource allocation efficiency and uneven distribution of digital dividends. Macro policies should further optimize the regional computing power resource layout based on national strategies such as "Eastern Data and Western Computing" and "Eastern Data and Western Cultivation", guide the eastern region to export redundant data resources and technical capabilities to the central and western regions, and promote the formation of a full-chain collaboration system of "data collection—processing—utilization". In this process, through institutional arrangements such as fiscal transfer payments, industrial guidance funds, and digital economy special zones, increase support for data infrastructure construction and talent introduction in the central and western regions to avoid the phenomenon of "digital enclaves". At the same time, support the western region to build data-intensive industrial clusters, such as intelligent manufacturing, smart agriculture, and green energy platforms, to achieve the deep integration of digital industries and local industries.

Sixth, build a global data governance system and enhance China's institutional voice in international rule-making. Cross-border data flow is the core channel for the integration of the global digital economy, but the current international data governance presents a pattern of "multi-headed governance and fragmented supervision". Standards such as the EU's GDPR, the US CLOUD Act, and Japan's "Trusted AI" system are different, leading to a sharp increase in the compliance costs of Chinese enterprises going overseas. Therefore, at the macro-policy level, we should actively promote the "institution-first" strategy, promote the construction of a China led cross-border data flow rule system centered on safety, controllability, mutual trust, and cooperation, and embed "China's data standards" in multilateral mechanisms such as RCEP, the "Belt and Road Initiative", and the Forum on China-Africa Cooperation. At the same time, encourage enterprises to establish compliant overseas service mechanisms, build an operating system of "data boundary identification—risk classification response—rule rapid adaptation", and help Chinese digital platforms and AI enterprises achieve global layout and risk control in parallel.

Seventh, formulate forward-looking strategic plans and performance evaluation mechanisms to guide the long-term optimization and upgrading of the data policy system. Current data policies are characterized by fragmentation, multi-department formulation, and emphasis on pilots over evaluation. It is necessary to build a systematic policy evaluation and feedback mechanism. It is recommended to establish a national-level "data governance performance indicator system", covering core indicators such as data rights confirmation efficiency, transaction activity, data opening rate, and number of security compliance incidents, and regularly release a "National Data Governance Blue Book" for systematic evaluation. At the same time, a "policy sandbox mechanism" should be established at the policy level to allow local governments or specific industries to explore new mechanisms for data circulation, use, and compliance within a certain scope, and stimulate institutional innovation through policy competition. In addition, it is necessary to strengthen the vertical linkage and horizontal coordination between policies, break "departmental barriers" and "industry standard", and form a systematic, collaborative, and forward-looking synergy of data policies.

In summary, macro-policy makers should start from top-level design and build a data element institutional system aiming at clear property rights, efficient markets, safe and controllable operations, regional balance, and global connectivity. As a core component of modern national governance capacity, data governance's institutional design will determine the direction of future growth models. Only through systematic institutional supply, collaborative policy implementation, and dynamic performance feedback can we truly promote the high-quality allocation of data elements in the economy and society, and release their lasting momentum as a new growth engine.

7.2.3 From the Practitioners' Perspective

Against the backdrop of data elements accelerating their integration into various economic activities, the occupational ecology and skill structure faced by workers are undergoing profound changes. From data collection, sorting, annotation, and governance to algorithm development, data operation, analysis and modeling, and product design, data labor has become a key link in the labor value chain in the new era. Data-intensive work scenarios dominated by platforms have also spawned a large number of "non-standard" employment positions, such as crowdsourced data workers, content reviewers, AI trainers, and algorithm labelers, whose work models, labor rights, and income structures are different from traditional formal employment. All these indicate that building a new practitioner support policy system matching the data era has become the key to promoting inclusive digital transformation.

Improve national data literacy and consolidate the foundation of labor adaptability: With the increasing integration of data in all walks of life, "understanding data, mastering tools, and being able to collaborate" is becoming a basic occupational ability. Currently, most workers lack systematic data literacy training, resulting in "technical barriers" in on-the-job transformation and re-employment. To this end, data literacy should be incorporated into the national education system, introduce courses such as "data logic" and "digital citizenship" at the basic education stage, set up modules such as "basic data analysis", "Python application", and "AI cognition and ethics" in vocational education and adult continuing education, and combine industrial development to promote local higher vocational colleges and industrial parks to jointly build "data skill centers" to achieve precise docking between data capabilities and actual job needs.

Build a multi-level data vocational training system and strengthen skill upgrading channels: The government should specially set up a "Special Plan for Data Vocational Capacity Improvement" under the framework of the "Skill China Initiative" and the "lifelong vocational training system", covering multiple levels such as primary data processing, AI annotation, platform operation, intermediate and advanced data modeling and engineering, and data security management. For low-educated laborers on the edge of the workforce, mixed online and offline training can be adopted to provide structured course packages, task-based learning sheets, and real-time evaluation mechanisms to lower learning thresholds. For college graduates, transferred engineers, and other groups, modular, project-based, and certificate-oriented advanced training systems should be provided, and their transformation momentum should be stimulated through methods such as "training instead of evaluation" and "competitions promoting training".

Clarify the legal status of data labor and improve the income and rights distribution mechanism: Currently, a large number of data workers participate in digital labor through platform crowdsourcing or outsourcing models, facing the common problems of "ambiguous identity, ambiguous rights and interests, and ambiguous payment". It is recommended to promote the introduction of the Regulations on the Administration of Platform-based Data Workers, clarifying the legal definition of data labor, the criteria for judging labor relations, and the income distribution mechanism. An income system with a two-tier structure of "algorithm performance + basic security" can be explored: on the one hand, the platform dynamically prices based on dimensions such as annotation quality and completion speed; on the other hand, introduce a minimum payment standard and risk subsidy system for data labor. At the same time, encourage the establishment of "data worker associations" or industry trade unions to strengthen their voice in contract negotiations, standard setting, and platform governance, and promote the formation of a labor rights protection mechanism supported by both "organization and platformization".

Promote the skill reproduction mechanism and build an internal circulation system for career development: Industrial changes driven by data elements require workers to continuously update their knowledge structure, making "skill reproduction" the key to achieving long-term employment stability and social equity. It is recommended to build a skill renewal mechanism based on the "occupational life cycle", matching different types of advanced course systems for workers of different ages, career stages, and industrial types. The government can provide "skill renewal savings accounts" and "skill renewal point cards" to encourage workers to take the initiative to learn according to job changes, industrial transfers, and personal interests, and link them with career promotion, salary growth, and social security contributions to promote the formation of an endogenous circulation mechanism between skills, income, and security.

Strengthen the right to participate in platform governance and build a new type of labor relations with "co-governance and shared management": The rapid development of the platform economy has promoted the decentralization of data labor organization forms, leading to a decline in the transparency of the labor process and an increase in platform dominance. To respond to workers' demands for participation in platform rules, it is necessary to promote the reform of platform governance structures: such as setting up a "Data Worker Representative Committee" to participate in decision-making mechanisms such as platform algorithm setting, price adjustment, and complaint adjudication; encouraging the construction of an "algorithm transparency rating system", with the government, industry organizations, and users jointly supervising the platform's data management and labor scheduling systems; supporting the development of third-party labor rights platforms to achieve external checks and balances and information symmetry for mainstream data platforms. Empowering workers through institutionalized channels is the fundamental way to achieve the sustainable development of the platform ecosystem.

Narrow the intergenerational and regional digital skill gaps and achieve inclusive transformation: In the process of data element development, inequalities in skill levels and digital access among different groups and regions may be further amplified. For issues such as youth unemployment, elderly job transfer, and rural hollowing out, policies should strengthen differentiated supply. For example, provide integrated "digital training + project incubation" support for young groups, develop "transferable digital tool application courses" for middle-aged and elderly people, and support their participation in "community data collaboration" projects; promote new service models such as "mobile data training vehicles" and "town data workshops" in the central and western regions, old industrial bases, and remote rural areas to ensure that the dividends of the data economy extend to the grassroots and achieve "technology empowerment + local transformation" growth.

Promote the institutionalization of diverse employment forms and support flexible employment and innovative labor: Faced with the new business forms and flexible employment trends driven by data, we should accept and support diverse employment forms at the institutional level. It is recommended to promote the establishment of a multi-track social security system based on "personal work accounts", allowing platform workers, freelancers, data creators, etc., to participate in insurance flexibly according to work frequency and income level; promote the establishment of a "labor point system", incorporating data such as project participation, customer ratings, and performance quality into credit and social security evaluation systems; encourage the development of a "data worker career file platform" to realize cross-platform and cross-project certification of their labor resumes, improving the career stability and identity recognition of flexible employees.

In summary, as the front-line force driving economic and social transformation driven by data elements, the capability improvement, rights protection, and structural support of practitioners will directly determine the inclusiveness and sustainability of digital development. Against the backdrop of rapid technological evolution and fragmented employment forms, policy makers need to change their thinking and upgrade from "traditional employment support" to "data labor system construction" to truly realize the all-round development of people and the coordinated progress of technology.

7.2.4 Deepening Mechanism Modeling and Interdisciplinary Integration

The comprehensive embedding of data elements has not only profoundly changed corporate operations, policy formulation, and labor forms, but also triggered systematic reshaping from macro to micro levels at the industry level. As a new type of basic production factor, the unique attributes of data—replicability, diminishing marginal cost, reusability, and dynamic iteration—endow it with great potential to reconstruct industry operation logic, reshape market structures, and promote collaborative innovation. The following systematically discusses the far-reaching impact of data elements on industry development from three levels: macro, meso, and micro.

At the macro level, the rise of data elements has spawned the digital economy as a new growth pole, promoting the transformation of traditional industries towards intelligence, servitization, and platformization. First, data has jumped from an "informatization accessory" to a "value center", forming a data-driven economic cycle system: collection—computation—training—feedback—reuse has become the key engine driving the improvement of total factor productivity. Second, data-intensive industries have become the core of emerging industries, such as artificial intelligence, digital healthcare, smart transportation, intelligent manufacturing, and financial technology, which have developed rapidly, driving the overall industrial structure to shift from "capital-intensive and labor-intensive" to "knowledge-intensive and data-intensive". In addition, data elements have also promoted the restructuring of regional industrial advantages, forming a coupling effect of "computing power density—data density—industrial agglomeration degree". The eastern coastal areas focus on the platform economy, while the central and western regions participate in the computing power division of labor through projects such as "Eastern Data and Western Computing", presenting a new pattern of regional economic division of labor.

At the industry level, data elements are breaking traditional industry boundaries and spawning cross border integration and platform-based collaboration mechanisms. Taking the transportation industry as an example, the development of autonomous driving systems has bundled automobile manufacturers with Internet companies, map service providers, and high-performance computing chip enterprises into a single entity, forming an integrated structure of "data ecosystem—algorithm ecosystem—operation ecosystem". In the medical industry, the introduction of electronic medical records, wearable devices, and individual health big data has prompted the migration of medical resources to a "platform + service" model, with traditional hospitals, pharmaceutical companies, medical insurance providers, and IT enterprises being re-embedded into a unified data architecture. In addition, data platforms have become new hubs for industry resource allocation, reshaping industry pricing mechanisms, credit structures, and competitive relationships by virtue of their control over supply and demand data. This platform-led resource coordination capability has broken the survival boundaries of small and medium-sized enterprises, and also triggered governance challenges such as rising industry concentration and increased risks of data monopoly.

At the micro-entity level, driven by data elements, the internal organizational forms and governance logic of enterprises are undergoing profound changes. First, the strategic focus of enterprises has shifted from "scale expansion" to "data-driven value re-creation", promoting the transformation of organizational structures from pyramid-shaped bureaucracy to "modularization + platformization", forming a flat collaboration model with the data department as the core node. Second, decision-making methods have evolved from experience-oriented to algorithm-oriented. More and more enterprises rely on data dashboards, prediction models, and real-time analysis systems for business judgment, with data visualization, algorithm transparency, and interpretability management becoming key governance priorities. At the same time, the gradual confirmation of data asset rights has also prompted enterprises to explore new mechanisms combining "data finance" and "data governance", such as building internal data balance sheets, establishing data asset management committees, and piloting internal data transaction systems, to gradually promote the institutional embedding of data.

Data elements have stimulated great potential for cross-entity collaborative innovation, and are spawning an industry innovation ecosystem characterized by "open platforms—multi-stakeholders—scenario co-creation". In this system, the government provides basic data and governance rules, enterprises contribute user data and business scenarios, universities and scientific research institutions provide algorithms and model optimization, and platform companies undertake technology implementation and resource coordination. Multiple entities achieve complementary advantages and value co-creation based on data sharing. For example, in the agricultural field, the integration of remote sensing data, meteorological data, and plot data provides sowing suggestions, pest and disease prediction, and supply and marketing financial services through agricultural algorithm platforms, realizing an integrated closed loop of "data middle platform + algorithm services + farmer terminals"; in the industrial field, the interconnection of equipment data is realized through industrial internet platforms, small and medium-sized enterprises share digital capabilities and achieve flexible manufacturing, greatly improving the overall response efficiency and resource utilization rate of the industrial chain.

Although data elements have injected great vitality into the industry, the systematic risks and governance challenges they bring cannot be ignored. First, frequent incidents of data abuse, algorithm discrimination, and privacy leakage have challenged the ethical and compliance bottom line of the industry; second, the increasing concentration of data platforms has triggered "data oligopolization", which may inhibit innovation and compress the living space of small and medium-sized enterprises; third, the lack of unified rules for cross-border data flow has restricted the global expansion of the industry. Therefore, at the industry governance level, it is necessary to improve institutional supply capacity: establish a hierarchical and classified industry data security management system, clarify the use boundaries and compliance requirements of different types of data; improve platform anti-monopoly rules to prevent the formation of exclusive competitive patterns by "data + algorithms + capital"; promote the alignment of industry standard formulation with international cooperation to form a dynamic balance mechanism among "governance—competition—innovation".

Looking to the future, data elements will continue to play a deep-seated leading role in industry evolution. With the development of technologies such as generative artificial intelligence, large models, edge computing, and 5G/6G, the methods of obtaining industry data will be more diversified, processing efficiency will be more efficient, and feedback paths will be more closed-loop. Industrial development will show a trend of "intelligence—autonomy—collaboration": smart factories will have the ability of autonomous learning and rapid adaptation, the service industry will optimize customer experience through real-time data feedback, and platform-based industries will form a more resilient supply chain structure through data integration. In addition, data elements will also promote the evolution of industry organizational forms towards a more networked and decentralized direction, spawning new cooperation models and value co-creation mechanisms.

In summary, data elements are promoting industry evolution from structural restructuring to institutional innovation, and their systematic impact runs through the upstream and downstream of the industrial chain, all nodes of the value chain, and all links of the institutional chain. In this process, policy makers, enterprise entities, and practitioners need to jointly address challenges and share opportunities to achieve the dual improvement of industrial upgrading and social welfare.

7.3 Deepening Mechanism Modeling and Interdisciplinary Integration

At the theoretical level, with the rising status of data elements, classic economic growth models, institutional economics, corporate behavior theories, and labor economics are all facing new paradigm challenges. Future research needs to build a new economic analysis framework adapted to the digital era from a higher dimension and deeper mechanism.

First, in the direction of growth models, there is an urgent need to build a multi-margin growth path model based on data elements. Existing models mostly assume that the marginal effect of data is constant or increasing, but in reality, the marginal value of data is greatly affected by institutional constraints, usage capabilities, data quality, and algorithm feedback, showing phased and nonlinear characteristics. Therefore, it is necessary to introduce endogenous variables such as "data quality function", "data governance constraint function", and "platform concentration function" into the model to more realistically describe how data affects long-term growth trajectories in the institutional environment. At the same time, how to quantify the synergistic effect between data and AI and build an endogenous chain of "data—AI—growth" will also become the focus of future modeling.

Second, the institutional attributes of data require theoretical models to pay more attention to the dynamic evolution of property rights structures and transaction mechanisms. At present, institutional economics research on the property rights structure of data elements is still at an abstract level. Future research should focus on the design of game structures under the decoupling of data ownership and income rights, such as how to form a stable property rights coordination mechanism among platforms, users, and regulators, how to design a sharing mechanism for "quasi-public goods" type data resources, and how to achieve the maximization of data use efficiency and the minimization of abuse risks through incentive contracts.

Third, research in the field of labor economics needs to break through the dual framework of "employment quantity—wage level" and shift to a ternary structure model of "data creation—data distribution—algorithm scheduling". In the employment environment dominated by data capital, workers are not only providers of working hours in the traditional sense, but also providers of behavioral data, preference data, and feedback data. This new type of labor form has not been formally included in statistical calibers, nor is there a theoretical system to explain it. Future theoretical research should attempt to establish a data labor pricing mechanism using a "behavioral data—labor value" function model, and explore the manifestations of data labor participation rights in various institutional arrangements, such as collective bargaining, platform autonomy, and algorithm negotiation.

Finally, global data governance research will also become a new frontier of economic theory. Faced with the increasingly complex contradictions between cross-border data flow, sovereign data requirements, and corporate compliance obligations, a multilateral data governance model that balances national interests and global efficiency should be built. Theoretically, starting from institutional games, an interactive model including data sovereignty preference function, compliance cost function, and digital diplomacy benefit function can be designed to explain the behavioral logic of various countries in data governance negotiations, and provide game strategy support for China in the reconstruction of global data rules.

In summary, data elements are reshaping the fundamental mechanisms of economic operation. They are not only a new growth driver, but also a new institutional challenge and a new governance opportunity. Only by continuously deepening research at both theoretical and practical levels and establishing a set of systematic theoretical tools and institutional systems matching the digital economy can we truly release the era dividends of data and promote China's economy to achieve a strategic leap from high-speed growth to high-quality development.

7.4 Research Prospects

Currently, as a key factor driving the growth of the digital economy, data has increasingly become the focus of economic theory and practice. At the theoretical level, although certain explorations and accumulations have been made, overall, the research on data elements is still in a stage that urgently needs major breakthroughs. Traditional economic growth models often regard data as an exogenous variable, failing to fully reveal its endogenous role and complex characteristics as a production factor in the growth mechanism, which limits the theoretical explanatory power for complex phenomena in the digital economy era. Future research should focus on the unique attributes of data elements and the practical needs of the digital economy, systematically build a more scientific and comprehensive theoretical framework to support the theoretical guidance and policy design for the high-quality development of the digital economy.

First, at the level of macroeconomic modeling, existing mainstream models mostly follow the framework of neoclassical growth theory, regarding data as an exogenous driving factor of technological progress, ignoring the inherent attributes of data such as non-rivalry, reusability, and cumulativeness. This exogenous perspective is difficult to capture the dynamic feedback effect of data in promoting technological innovation and economic growth. In fact, the value of data lies not only in single use, but also in its continuous promotion of artificial intelligence algorithms and innovation systems after continuous accumulation. Through continuous reuse and in-depth mining, data has shaped the path dependence of technological evolution and become a core variable affecting long-term growth trajectories. Therefore, building a macroeconomic model that can internalize data, especially coupling the data accumulation process with the technological progress mechanism, is an inevitable direction of theoretical development. Drawing on the data sharing model proposed by Jones and Tonetti (2020), future research should integrate the non-rival capital characteristics of data on the basis of the neoclassical growth framework, introduce indicators such as multi-sector data reuse coefficients, platform dominance, and the degree of dependence on artificial intelligence training, and finely depict the nonlinear contribution of data to total factor productivity (TFP). In addition, the model should reveal the interdependent relationship between data and computing power, regard them as dual production factors in the digital economy, and discuss the bottleneck effect of the two at different stages and its constraints on economic growth potential. The design of such models should also fully consider the phased leap characteristics of data, that is, after the data volume and quality reach a critical point, algorithm performance and innovation capabilities will experience explosive growth, thereby driving the overall economy into an accelerated growth track.

To ensure the practical relevance and policy guidance value of the theory, a simulation module for data governance policies should also be embedded in the macro model. By simulating scenarios such as the improvement of the efficiency of different data rights confirmation mechanisms and the enhancement of data interoperability between platforms, evaluate their impact on long-term economic growth rates and technology diffusion. For example, if the efficiency of data rights confirmation is increased by 50% and the interoperability between platforms is enhanced by 20%, simulation results show that the long-term economic growth rate can be increased by 0.7 to 1.2 percentage points. This not only highlights the importance of data governance system design, but also provides a quantitative basis for policy makers to make scientific decisions in promoting the rational allocation and efficient utilization of data resources. At the same time, further incorporating knowledge spillover effects into the model to build a dynamic growth path of "data—algorithm—knowledge reinvestment" can reveal how the data-driven digital economy achieves sustained and stable accelerated growth, enriching the connotation of existing growth theories.

Second, as an important foundation for data elements to play a role, the institutional environment also faces major theoretical challenges. China's data governance system has a unique political and economic structure and historical path dependence, making it infeasible to simply copy the private property rights-oriented data governance model of Europe and the United States. China's data governance system reflects the dynamic balance among national sovereignty, corporate usufruct, and personal privacy rights. This ternary structure plays a coordinating role in safeguarding national security, promoting industrial innovation, and protecting personal rights and interests. At the national sovereignty level, it emphasizes the centralized management and control of strategic data to ensure national security and public interests; corporate usufruct endows platform enterprises with space for data innovation to stimulate the vitality of the digital economy; the protection of personal privacy rights, although limited by the overall institutional framework, is gradually incorporated into the legal and policy system to strengthen the protection of personal data rights and interests. The core of institutional innovation lies in how to seek a reasonable institutional balance among these three, promote the efficient circulation and utilization of data resources, and at the same time prevent risks and improper use.

Future research should focus more on institutional adaptability, exploring how institutional arrangements at different regional and hierarchical levels can promote the optimal allocation and value realization of data elements. For example, Zhejiang Province's "digital government + market mechanism" model, through data rights confirmation and transaction pilots, strengthens data interconnection between the government and enterprises, and improves governance efficiency and market vitality on the basis of respecting data sovereignty, becoming a model of institutional innovation. At the same time, Guizhou Province's data policy sandbox mechanism provides pre-regulatory experiments for innovative data products, effectively reducing innovation resistance and ensuring the healthy development of the digital economy. Systematically sorting out the institutional logic behind these practical cases, such as the determination of the open level of government data platforms, the institutionalization of data responsibility chains, and the inclusion of data utilization efficiency in local performance evaluations, will provide rich empirical materials for theoretical construction. Furthermore, theoretical research should deeply explore how to design regionally differentiated data governance structures to solve the problem of unbalanced data resources between developed and underdeveloped regions, and promote the balanced flow of data elements and the maximization of shared value; how to transform the public value of data into social wealth shared by all through institutional embedding, breaking the limitations of private interests; how to build a soft governance system oriented towards the international community, promote the promotion of the "China data governance plan" in multilateral cooperation platforms such as RCEP and the "Belt and Road Initiative", and enhance China's voice in global digital governance. These issues require in-depth interdisciplinary research in political science, public policy, and information governance to lay a solid foundation for the innovative development of the data governance theory with Chinese characteristics.

Third, the issue of distribution mechanisms of data elements in the digital economy has become increasingly prominent, becoming the focus of theoretical and policy attention. By virtue of their control over massive user data and in-depth analysis capabilities, platform enterprises have formed a substantial "algorithm monopoly". On the one hand, this has improved market efficiency and promoted precise matching and service optimization; on the other hand, it has exacerbated the disadvantaged position of workers, leading to a marginal decline in their labor remuneration. In fact, the control right of data determines the value distribution right. Platforms' comprehensive control over workers' behavioral data places them in a dominant position in income distribution, resulting in a general decline of 3% to 5% in the proportion of workers' wages, and even more than 7% in individual industries. This reality challenges the traditional labor economics' understanding of labor value and income distribution, prompting the academic community and policy makers to pay attention to the protection of "data labor" rights and interests and income distribution issues.

Therefore, it is imperative to build a research system of distribution mechanisms that integrates ethical and economic dimensions. First, the contribution rights of data producers, especially workers, in the data value chain should be clarified. For workers such as food delivery riders, ride-hailing drivers, and content creators who take behavioral data as the core means of production, their "data contribution rights" must be established to ensure their profit sharing in algorithm training and personalized recommendation systems. This can be achieved by establishing a data labeling system to finely record and measure workers' data contributions, thereby setting up a special "data incentive fund" at a reasonable ratio (such as 15%-20%) to realize the fair distribution of data dividends. Second, designing operable redistribution mechanisms is an important path to narrow the welfare gap caused by data monopoly. For example, a "platform excess data profit regulation tax" can be used as an innovative tax tool, using 5% of the profits of leading platforms to set up national special funds such as the "digital skill retraining fund", "vulnerable group data security fund", and "community data service co-construction fund" to support workers' skill improvement and the protection of digital rights and interests of vulnerable groups.

Preliminary calculations show that this tax mechanism is expected to raise more than 80 billion yuan of fiscal funds annually, becoming an important financial support for digital equity policies. Third, a data ethics evaluation tool should be established, such as the "Data Well-being Index", covering an indicator system including "digital income sense of gain", "data right to know realization rate", and "platform data use transparency", to quantify the contribution of platform enterprises to social equity, and become an important reference for government regulation, policy evaluation, and public investment, promoting the implementation of corporate social responsibility and ethical norms.

The high complexity and cross-border characteristics of the data economy have made traditional economic theories face the boundary of explanatory power, which urgently requires interdisciplinary integration and innovation. Future research should promote the in-depth integration of data economics with ethics, institutional economics, computational social science, network science, and other fields to jointly build a multi-dimensional and systematic theoretical system. At the theoretical level, we can try to combine evolutionary game theory with platform economic models to analyze the incentive structure of platforms for data workers and its dynamic evolution; at the methodological level, use modern technical means such as large-scale micro-data, natural experiments, and machine learning to carry out policy effect identification and mechanism verification research; at the discourse system level, shift from simply emphasizing "factor value" to focusing on "social well-being", and establish a theoretical bridge between data-driven growth and inclusive development to achieve effective connection between theory and practical needs. Such interdisciplinary integration not only enriches theoretical connotation, but also enhances the scientificity and pertinence of policy formulation.

In addition, a global perspective is indispensable. China, the United States, and Europe have significant differences in data systems, ethical constraints, and market governance, forming different institutional paths and governance models respectively. On the basis of fully learning from international advanced experience, China should combine its own national conditions to propose a "Chinese theory" with international adaptability and strategic competitiveness, actively participate in the formulation of global data governance rules, and enhance national soft power and voice. This will not only help China occupy a favorable position in the international digital economic pattern, but also provide diversified institutional choices and theoretical contributions to global digital economic governance.

In summary, research related to data elements is in a critical transition period from empirical induction to theoretical reconstruction. Whether it is the innovation of macroeconomic growth models, the systematic construction of institutional environments, or the ethical reshaping of distribution mechanisms, we must jump out of the traditional single-disciplinary framework and move towards a more systematic, collaborative, and multi-dimensional knowledge construction system. Only in this way can data economic theory truly respond to the complex practical needs of the economy and society in the digital era, provide solid theoretical support and policy guidance for the high-quality development of China's and even the global digital economy, and promote the realization of more equitable and sustainable economic and social progress.

7.5 Application Prospects

With the deep integration of data elements and artificial intelligence technology, the application prospects of the digital economy are showing revolutionary breakthroughs. As the core force driving a new round of technological changes, data intelligence is setting off a paradigm shift in many key fields such as manufacturing, healthcare, and urban governance, further promoting the reshaping of social relations of production and governance models. In the future, these applications will not only significantly improve economic efficiency and productivity, but also become a key driving force for achieving social fairness, justice, and sustainable development. Based on current typical cases and development trends, this chapter deeply analyzes the breakthrough applications of data intelligence in three major fields, and discusses the technical paths, institutional challenges, and future development directions behind them.

As an important pillar of the national economy, manufacturing is the forefront of data intelligence applications. Represented by the technological integration of "digital twin + artificial intelligence", manufacturing is ushering in a profound transformation of production methods. Digital twin technology achieves accurate simulation and prediction of equipment status and process flows by establishing a real-time mapping between physical equipment and digital models. When artificial intelligence algorithms are involved, manufacturing systems can not only achieve intelligent monitoring, but also proactively predict equipment failures and performance degradation based on big data analysis. Taking Sany Heavy Industry's AI prediction of stamping die wear as an example, through deep learning of equipment operation data and historical wear data, it has successfully achieved wear early warning and maintenance optimization, significantly extending equipment life and reducing downtime risks. It is expected that such technologies will be promoted and applied in 70% of discrete manufacturing industries within the next 3 to 5 years, driving the average equipment failure rate down by 40%, and at the same time achieving a 18% reduction in energy consumption through precise control and optimization of process flows. This transformation not only reduces manufacturing costs, but also improves the flexibility and response speed of production systems, laying the foundation for manufacturing to move towards intelligence and greening.

More profoundly, the industrial chain collaboration model driven by data intelligence is undergoing revolutionary changes. Information silos and data barriers between enterprises in traditional manufacturing have restricted the overall efficiency and innovation capability of the supply chain. Haier's COSMOPlat platform has built an open and shared industrial ecosystem by integrating equipment data from more than 3,000 enterprises, providing process optimization solutions and risk early warnings to participating enterprises based on massive equipment operation data and process parameters, promoting collaborative efficiency improvement in all links of the supply chain. This "data-driven industrial chain collaboration" model is expected to improve the overall efficiency of the supply chain by 22%, and at the same time, drive the digital transformation costs of small and medium-sized enterprises down by 35% due to the scale effect of shared resources and technologies. This not only enhances the resilience and innovation capability of the industrial chain, but also makes the manufacturing ecosystem more open, transparent, and collaborative, promoting the profound leap of traditional manufacturing to digital manufacturing and intelligent manufacturing.

The healthcare field is also experiencing a wave of data intelligence popularization. Traditional medical diagnosis relies on the experience of professional physicians and limited examination methods, with problems such as low diagnosis efficiency and uneven accuracy. Represented by SenseTime's AI vision solutions, its lung CT nodule detection technology has been widely used in more than 1,000 hospitals, with a detection accuracy rate of up to 98.6%, significantly bringing the diagnostic level of primary hospitals closer to that of tertiary hospitals. In the next 5 years, such data intelligence-based diagnostic technologies are expected to cover 80% of medical imaging diagnosis scenarios, greatly improving the popularization rate and quality of medical services. At the same time, more revolutionary "predictive medicine" is emerging. By integrating multi-dimensional information such as genomics data, wearable device data, and environmental exposure data, AI systems can predict the risk of major diseases such as chronic diseases 3 to 5 years in advance, realizing early intervention and precision treatment. Relevant research predicts that the popularization of predictive medicine will reduce the incidence of major diseases by 15% and medical expenditures by 8%. However, the realization of this vision depends on breaking medical data silos and improving the cross-institutional data sharing rate. Currently, the domestic cross-institutional medical data sharing rate is only about 30%. If it is increased to 70% in the future, the accuracy rate of AI diagnosis can be further improved by 12 to 15 percentage points. This requires the medical industry to establish a unified data standard and secure sharing mechanism, balancing the relationship between data privacy protection and data open utilization, to maximize the value release of medical data resources.

As an important scenario for the integration of the digital economy and social governance, urban governance is also undergoing a qualitative change towards "real-time intelligent response". The construction of smart cities represented by Shanghai's "City Brain" has achieved remarkable results. By integrating multi-source data such as transportation, environmental sanitation, and public security, it has improved urban operation efficiency and reduced the traffic congestion index by 18%. In the future, with the extensive deployment of 5G communication technology and edge computing, urban governance will achieve minute-level or even second-level response capabilities. For example, the automated processing rate of scenarios such as trash bin overflow warning and manhole cover anomaly monitoring is expected to reach 90%, reducing urban management costs by 25%. More forward-looking is the construction of "digital twin cities". Through full-factor and multi-dimensional data modeling, digital twin technology can reflect the operating status of various urban systems in real time, realizing intelligent regulation such as building energy consumption optimization, traffic flow control, and environmental quality monitoring. Taking the Beijing Sub-center as a pilot area, it has achieved a 20% optimization of building energy consumption. It is expected that within the next 10 years, digital twin technology can be promoted in 50% of cities, improving the overall urban operation efficiency by 18% to 22%. This will provide a new solution to the urbanization challenges of population density and resource constraints, promoting the transformation of urban governance from passive management to active regulation.

At the same time, the rapid development of generative artificial intelligence has brought unprecedented ethical challenges. Taking GPT series models as an example, their text generation capability has reached a similarity of more than 90%. The widespread generation of such highly realistic content has made audio and video produced by deepfake technology indistinguishable from real ones, posing a severe test to information authenticity. It is expected that by 2025, the cost of identifying and verifying false information will increase by 40%. To address this challenge, the industry urgently needs to develop an information traceability mechanism combining "digital watermarking" and blockchain technology to achieve non-tamperability and traceability of information sources, improving the efficiency of information credibility verification by 50%. In addition, the problem of algorithm bias has become increasingly prominent. For example, recruitment AI systems may have an implicit discrimination of 7% to 10% against female job seekers, seriously damaging the right to fair employment. In this regard, it is imperative to establish an "algorithm audit" system, requiring the transparency of AI system decision-making processes to reach more than 80% to ensure the fairness and interpretability of algorithms, thereby safeguarding social fairness and justice. This is not only a technical challenge, but also a core ethical issue in the construction of digital civilization, which requires the joint efforts of law, technology, and society to solve.

The global governance system for cross-border data flow also urgently needs to be reconstructed. Currently, China's data output has reached 8.1 ZB, making it a global data power, but it faces multiple rule games in cross-border flow. The EU's GDPR requires data export to pass the "adequacy assessment", and the US CLOUD Act forces enterprises to provide access to overseas data, leading to the fragmentation of international data governance and increasing the compliance costs of Chinese enterprises by as much as 120 billion yuan annually. Faced with this challenge, in the next five years, establishing a multilateral governance rule combining "data sovereignty + secure flow" has become an inevitable choice. Taking the "negative list for cross-border data flow" model under the RCEP framework as an example, as the number of participating countries increases from the current 15 to 25, the efficiency of regional data element allocation is expected to increase by 15%, driving the growth of digital trade volume by 28%. This will not only help promote regional digital economic integration, but also provide a Chinese solution for global data governance, enhancing China's influence in the formulation of international digital economic rules.

Overall, the deep integration of data elements and artificial intelligence is driving human society into a new stage of "digital civilization". The prominent characteristics of this stage are not only the improvement of production efficiency and economic scale, but more importantly, the profound changes in social relations of production and governance models. The traditional linear and closed production system is transforming into an open, collaborative, and intelligent one; while the governance model is shifting from post-event management to real-time response and forward-looking regulation. In this process, theoretical innovation, technological application, and ethical norms need to be advanced simultaneously to ensure that technological progress ultimately serves the all-round development of people and social fairness and justice. Future research should focus on building a theoretical framework adapted to digital civilization, promoting cross-field technological integration and innovation, strengthening data ethics governance, and promoting digital technology to become a core driving force for social progress and harmony. This is not only the mission of academic research, but also the responsibility of the industry and policy makers, and the ultimate goal of achieving high-quality development of the digital economy and building a better society.

7.6 Research Directions and Prospects

With the deep integration of data factors and artificial intelligence technologies, the digital economy is profoundly transforming global economic, social, and governance models. This revolution not only brings enormous economic benefits but also triggers numerous new theoretical and practical challenges. Based on systematic theoretical modeling, empirical research, and policy analysis, this paper thoroughly explores the multiple impacts of data factors on boosting economic growth, restructuring corporate behaviors, stimulating regional entrepreneurial vitality, and reshaping employment structures. However, current research is still in the exploratory stage. The unique attributes of data factors and the complexity of the digital economy mean that there remains vast room for future research. The following is an outlook on potential future research directions:

Although this paper has incorporated the economic properties of data factors—such as non-rivalry, increasing returns to scale, and privacy sensitivity—into the construction of endogenous growth models, existing models still have significant scope for further refinement and expansion. First, in the construction of macro-growth models, the dynamic accumulation process of data factors and their long-term impact on technological progress have not been fully characterized. The accumulation of data not only affects current production efficiency but also exerts a profound influence on future innovation and technology diffusion through knowledge spillovers, algorithm optimization, and other channels. Therefore, future research needs to build more sophisticated dynamic models that integrate the accumulation, utilization, and updating processes of data into the production function, exploring the heterogeneous effects of data factors on economic growth across different development stages.

Second, the property rights structure and transaction mechanisms of data factors are key determinants of their allocation efficiency. The current data property rights system is still imperfect, with many ambiguities in defining the ownership, use rights, and income rights of data. This not only hinders the market circulation of data factors but also may lead to problems such as data abuse and privacy breaches. Future research needs to conduct in-depth theoretical exploration of the optimal design of data property rights, using game theory models to analyze the trade-offs among data producers, users, and regulators under different property rights systems, thereby providing theoretical support for institutional innovation in the data factor market.

Third, as data factors become increasingly prominent in the economic system, their challenges to traditional economic theories have become more pronounced. For example, the non-excludability and positive externality of data factors require a re-examination of the resource allocation efficiency theory in traditional neoclassical economics. Future research can explore new mechanisms for resource allocation in the context of data factors, investigating how to achieve the optimal allocation of data factors through policy tools and market mechanisms, and improving the utilization efficiency and social welfare of data factors.

The economic effects of data factors are not limited to areas such as economic growth and technological innovation, but also extend to social, legal, and ethical dimensions. Therefore, future research needs to strengthen interdisciplinary integration and innovation, exploring the impacts of data factors from multiple perspectives. For instance, in the legal field, issues such as the definition of data property rights, the legality of data transactions, and the protection of data privacy require joint research by legal scholars and economists to propose solutions that balance economic efficiency and legal fairness. In the sociological field, the impact of the popularization of data factors on social structures, group behaviors, and social equity also needs in-depth investigation. For example, the data divide may further widen the digital gap between different social groups, affecting social equality and stability. Future research can use methods such as social network analysis and field surveys to study how data factors influence social relations and social governance models.

In the field of ethics, the application of data factors and the development of artificial intelligence have raised a series of ethical issues, such as algorithmic discrimination, data bias, and the moral responsibility of artificial intelligence. These issues not only affect individual rights and interests but also may impact social values and moral norms. Future research needs to establish a theoretical framework for data ethics, exploring how to balance economic benefits and ethical values in the utilization of data factors, and ensuring that the development of data factors conforms to the basic ethical principles of humanity.

This paper has discussed the impacts of data factors at both the enterprise and individual levels, but there are still many aspects of the behavioral patterns and decision-making mechanisms of microeconomic agents that deserve further study. For example, how do enterprises adjust their production strategies, innovation models, and market competition behaviors driven by data factors? Will the improvement of data capabilities lead to changes in the market power of enterprises, thereby affecting market structures and consumer welfare? These questions require the use of microeconomic analysis methods, combined with enterprise case studies and field investigations, to thoroughly explore the impact of data factors on corporate strategies and market competition patterns.

For residents, the popularization of data factors has transformed the supply–demand relationship in the labor market and individuals' career choices. Future research can focus on the rise of data labor and its impact on the traditional labor market, investigating how to improve workers' digital skills through the reform of education and training systems, and promoting workers' re-employment and career transformation. At the same time, the development of data factors has also brought about new forms of employment, such as the gig economy and the sharing economy. Future research needs to conduct in-depth analysis of the characteristics, development trends, and social welfare impacts of these emerging employment forms, providing a scientific basis for policy formulation.

With the development of the global digital economy, different countries and regions have shown diverse characteristics in the utilization and governance of data factors. Future research can adopt international comparative analysis to explore the experiences and lessons of different countries in the construction of data factor markets, data governance systems, and digital economy industrial development, providing references for China's participation in global digital economic competition. For example, the United States leads the world in data technology innovation and industrial development, but its data privacy protection system is relatively weak; the European Union emphasizes data ethics and privacy protection, regulating data use through a strict legal framework, which may, to a certain extent, inhibit the market vitality of data factors. China has unique advantages in the scale of data factors and application scenarios, but needs to further improve its data property rights system and data security governance. Through international comparative research, we can better understand the impact of different institutional arrangements on the development of data factors, providing insights for China to formulate more targeted policies.

At the same time, the cross-border flow of data factors is an important feature of the globalization of the digital economy. Future research needs to focus on the rule-making and international coordination mechanisms for cross-border data flows, exploring how to promote the cross-border circulation of data factors while safeguarding data sovereignty and national security, and enhancing the coordinated development level of the global digital economy. As a major data country, China should actively participate in the formulation of global data governance rules, propose a "China Plan" that aligns with its national conditions, and enhance its voice in global digital economic governance.

The development of data factors poses new challenges to the traditional macro-policy framework. How to adjust and optimize macro-policies to adapt to the data-factor-driven economic growth model is an important direction for future research. For example, the non-rivalry and increasing returns to scale of data factors may lead to market failure and resource misallocation, requiring government intervention through appropriate policy tools. Future research can explore the innovation of macroeconomic policy tools in the context of data factors, such as data fiscal policies and data monetary policies, investigating how to promote the rational allocation and efficient utilization of data factors through policy guidance.

At the same time, the development of data factors also places higher requirements on the government's governance capacity. Governments need to establish more effective data governance systems, strengthen the supervision of the data factor market, and prevent data risks and privacy breaches. Future research can use methods such as case studies and policy evaluations to analyze the experiences and shortcomings of different local governments in data factor governance, and put forward policy recommendations for optimizing data governance mechanisms. In addition, the development of data factors may also impact social equity and balanced regional development, requiring the adjustment of macro-policies to promote the inclusiveness and balance of data factors, narrow the digital divide, and achieve sustainable economic and social development.

The development of data factors not only has a profound impact on current economic growth and social structures but also raises new issues for future development paths and sustainability. Future research needs to focus on the long-term impacts of data factors, exploring their effects on the environment, resources, and social stability. For example, the rapid development of data factors may lead to increased energy consumption and environmental pollution, requiring technological innovation and policy guidance to achieve the green development of data factors. At the same time, the popularization of data factors may also exacerbate social differentiation and the wealth gap, requiring social policies and institutional arrangements to promote the fair distribution of data factors and common prosperity.

Within the framework of sustainable development, future research can explore the coordinated development mechanisms of data factors with society, the economy, and the environment, investigating how to achieve the rational use of resources and social equity and justice in the data-factor-driven economic growth. By constructing a comprehensive evaluation index system, we can assess the impacts of data factors across multiple dimensions, providing a scientific basis for policy formulation. In addition, the sustainable development of data factors also needs to focus on technological progress and social adaptability, studying how to improve the overall data literacy of society through education, training, and policy guidance, and promoting the healthy and orderly development of data factors.

Although this paper has verified the impacts of data factors on enterprise risks, regional entrepreneurship, and resident employment through empirical research, the mechanism of action and causal relationship of data factors still need further clarification. The exploration of micro-mechanisms can help us better understand how data factors affect economic behaviors and social structures through specific channels. Future research can adopt methods such as natural experiments, quasi-natural experiments, and event studies to conduct in-depth analysis of the micro-mechanisms of data factors in different scenarios. For example, by studying the success rate of corporate data investment projects, the impact of data-driven decision-making on performance, and the role of data factors in the enterprise life cycle, we can reveal the specific impact paths of data factors at the enterprise level.

In terms of empirical research, future studies need to expand data sources and sample scope to improve the representativeness and reliability of research. At the same time, combined with big data analysis technologies, we can use massive micro-data to conduct more detailed stratified analysis and heterogeneity research, exploring the differentiated impacts of data factors across different industries, regions, and groups. Through rich empirical research, we can provide a more solid basis for the testing of theoretical models and policy formulation.

The development of data factors depends on technological progress and also exerts a profound impact on social structures and governance models. Future research needs to focus on the coordinated development of technology and society, exploring how to promote the rational utilization of data factors and sustainable social development through technological innovation. For example, emerging technologies such as artificial intelligence, blockchain, and cloud computing provide new means for the storage, management, and analysis of data factors, but the application of these technologies may also bring new risks and challenges. Future research can use technology assessment and policy analysis to explore how to optimize technology applications, promote the efficient utilization of data factors, and at the same time prevent technological risks and protect social rights and interests.

At the same time, the development of data factors also puts forward new requirements for social organizational forms and governance models. Future research needs to focus on the impact of data factors on social organizations, social governance, and social welfare, exploring how to achieve the coordinated development of technology and society through institutional innovation and policy adjustment. For example, studying the impact of data factors on government governance capacity, corporate social responsibility, and citizen participation, and putting forward policy recommendations to promote collaborative social governance.

As the core driving force of the digital economy, the development of data factors not only has a profound impact on economic growth, corporate behaviors, regional entrepreneurship, and resident employment but also poses new challenges to social structures, governance models, and ethical values. Future research needs to conduct in-depth exploration in multiple aspects such as theoretical models, interdisciplinary integration, micro-mechanisms, international comparisons, macro-policies, and sustainable development, providing a scientific basis and policy recommendations for promoting the rational utilization of data factors and sustainable social development. Through continuous theoretical innovation and empirical research, we can expect to build a more complete theoretical system of the digital economy, contributing to the high-quality development of China's and even the global digital economy.

Bibliography

Acemoglu, D., & Robinson, J. A. (2015). *Why nations fail: The origins of power*. Profile Books.

Admati, A. R., & Pfleiderer, P. (1990). Direct and indirect sale of information. *Econometrica, 58*(4), 901–928.

Akçura, M. T., & Srinivasan, K. (2005). Research note: Customer intimacy and cross-selling strategy. *Management Science, 51*(6), 1007–1012.

Bertrand, M., & Schoar, A. (2003). Managing with style: The effect of managers on firm policies. *Quarterly Journal of Economics, 118*(4), 1169–1208.

Bhagat, S., & Welch, I. (1995). Corporate research & development investments: International comparisons. *Journal of Accounting and Economics, 19*(2–3), 443–470.

Braganza, A., Brooks, L., Nepelski, D., Ali, M., & Moro, R. (2017). Resource management in big data initiatives: Processes and dynamic capabilities. *Journal of Business Research, 70*, 328–337. https://doi.org/10.1016/j.jbusres.2016.08.006

Brandt, M. W., & Wang, K. Q. (2010). The idiosyncratic volatility puzzle: Time trend or speculative episodes? *Review of Financial Studies, 23*(2), 863–899.

Brown, P., & Zheng, H. (2020). Firm-specific risk and equity market development. *Journal of Financial Economics, 84*(2), 358–388.

Bruce, H. L., Bruce, M. A., McLaren, R., & O'Callaghan, J. (2020). Resource integration, value creation and value destruction in collective consumption contexts. *Journal of Business Research, 103*, 173–185.

Cai, Y. Z., & Chen, N. (2019). Artificial intelligence, high-quality growth and high-quality employment in the context of the new technological revolution. *Journal of Quantitative & Technical Economics, 5*, 3–22.

Chaivisuttangkun, S., Sun, P., & Jiraporn, P. (2021). The effect of co-opted directors on firm risk during a stressful time: Evidence from the financial crisis. *Finance Research Letters, 39*, Article 101664. https://doi.org/10.1016/j.frl.2020.101664

Chari, M. D. R., Ou, C., & Rao, R. (2014). Determinants of the share of equity sought in cross-border acquisitions by US firms. *Journal of International Business Studies, 40*(8), 1277–1297.

Cheng, H., Chen, W. J., & Li, T. (2018). Robots in China: current situation, future and impact—Evidence from China's manufacturing industry. *Economic Research Journal, 8*, 119–134.

Choy, E., Gul, F., & Yao, J. (2009). Does freezing a defined benefit pension plan affect firm risk? *Journal of Accounting and Economics, 47*(1–2), 1–21.

Colak, G., Durnev, A., & Qian, Y. (2017). Political uncertainty and IPO activity: Evidence from U.S. gubernatorial elections. *Journal of Financial and Quantitative Analysis, 52*(6), 2523–2564.

Cui, L., Sun, P., & Xiao, Z. (2016). Evolution of MNE parent–subsidiary distance: The role of cultural distance and parent strategic orientation. *International Business Review, 27*(1), 207–217.

Du, J., & Li, C. (2019). The road to Industry 4.0: Predicting the driving forces of China's artificial intelligence economy. *International Journal of Production Economics, 204*, 426–442.

Dubey, R., Gunasekaran, A., Childe, S. J., & Wamba, S. F. (2020). Big data analytics and organizational culture as complements to swift trust and collaborative performance in the humanitarian supply chain. *International Journal of Production Economics, 210*, Article 120412.

Erevelles, S., Fukawa, N., & Swayne, L. (2016). Big data consumer analytics and the transformation of marketing. *Journal of Business Research, 69*(2), 897–904.

Fang, L., Huang, S., & Karpoff, J. (2016). Capitalizing on capitalism: The benefits of corporate political connections. *Journal of Financial and Quantitative Analysis, 51*(3), 887–913.

Fee, C. E., Hadlock, C. J., & Pierce, J. R. (2013). Managers with and without style: Evidence using exogenous variation. *Review of Financial Studies, 26*(3), 567–601.

Feng, S., Ling, C., & Yao, Q. (2020). Do political connections affect the transparency of corporate disclosures? Evidence from whistleblowing reports. *Journal of Banking & Finance, 118*, Article 105874.

Ferracuti, N., & Aragão, L. (2019). Big data analytics, governance, and the risk management function. *International Journal of Disclosure and Governance, 16*(1), 1–11.

García-Meca, E., Mateo-Martínez, J., & Servera, M. (2021). Big data: New insights on CEOs' social capital, firm performance, and risk. *Journal of Financial Stability, 56*, Article 100949.
Gong, D., Zhou, Z., Kochhar, I., & Luo, J. (2020). When do firms' overseas R&D investments enhance innovation performance? A study of ownership in cross-border acquisitions. *R&D Management, 50*(1), 135–148.
Gong, Y., Tang, Y., & Li, D. (2019). Information technology and financial development: City-level evidence from China. *Pacific-Basin Finance Journal, 54*, Article 101213.
Gupta, A., Li, H., & Zhu, H. (2018). A cloud platform for real-time IoT applications. *Service Oriented Computing and Applications, 12*(3), 279–291.
Habib, A., Masud, M., Kim, D. H., & Naidu, V. (2020). Big data analytics, management accounting and firm performance: A sociotechnical perspective. *Accounting & Finance, 60*(3), 2455–2484.
He, J., & Tian, X. (2013). The dark side of analyst coverage: The case of innovation. *Journal of Financial Economics, 109*(3), 856–878.
Huang, Z., & Li, J. (2019). Revolutionizing entrepreneurship: The role of big data in financing entrepreneurial ventures. *International Review of Economics & Finance, 64*, 111–123.
Ittner, C. D., & Larcker, D. F. (2001). Assessing empirical research in managerial accounting: A value-based management perspective. *Journal of Accounting & Economics, 32*(1–3), 349–410.
Jensen, M. C. (1986). Agency costs of free cash flow, corporate finance, and takeovers. *American Economic Review, 76*(2), 323–329.
Ji, P., & Guo, L. (2022). Big data analytics for risk management in the Chinese banking industry. *Journal of Risk and Financial Management, 15*(6), 251.
Jiménez, G., Ongena, S., Peydró, J.-L., & Saurina, J. (2014). Hazardous times for monetary policy: What do twenty-three million bank loans say about the effects of monetary policy on credit risk? *Econometrica, 82*(2), 463–505.
Jones, C. I., & Tonetti, C. (2020). Nonrivalry and the Economics of Data. *American Economic Review 110.*
Khan, M. T., Liang, L. W., & Shahzad, A. (2020). Big data analytics capabilities and firm performance: The mediating role of competitive advantage. *Journal of Management Analytics, 7*(2), 216–232.
Kim, H., Kim, J. W., & Sohn, H. (2018). Social media and firm value: The role of communication channels. *Journal of Internet Electronic Commerce Research, 18*(2), 73–87.
Kou, G., Xu, Y., Peng, Y., Shen, F., Chen, Y., & Chang, K. (2021). Big data analytics in fintech: Leveraging machine learning and statistical models for risk management. *European Journal of Operational Research, 293*(3), 1068–1079.
Peng, M. W., Sun, S. L., & Markóczy, L. (2015). Human capital and CEO compensation during institutional transitions. *Journal of Management Studies, 52*(1), 117–147.
Sun, T., Yuan, Z., Li, C., Zhang, K., & Xu, J. (2022). The value of personal data in internet commerce: A high-stake field experiment on data regulation policy. *Management Science*. Advance online publication.

MIX
Papier aus verantwortungsvollen Quellen
Paper from responsible sources
FSC® C105338

If you have any concerns about our products,
you can contact us on
ProductSafety@springernature.com

In case Publisher is established outside the EU,
the EU authorized representative is:
Springer Nature Customer Service Center GmbH
Europaplatz 3, 69115 Heidelberg, Germany

Printed by Libri Plureos GmbH
in Hamburg, Germany